DAVE BRANON Editor, *Sports Spectrum*
JOE PELLEGRINO

MOODY PRESS
CHICAGO

PHOTO CREDITS

Cover: Boston Red Sox vs. California Angels at Anaheim Stadium; © David Madison 1990.
Page 217: Kevin Seitzer, by Milwaukee Bewers Major League Baseball Club, used by permission; page 247: Bill Wegman, © *Milwaukee Journal* 1987, used by permission.

All other player photographs courtesy of the Atlanta Braves, Boston Red Sox, California Angels, Detroit Tigers, Los Angeles Dodgers, Minnesota Twins, New York Mets, New York Yankees, Seattle Mariners, and Toronto Blue Jays Major League Baseball clubs.

ISBN: 0-8024-7672-4

3 5 7 9 10 8 6 4 2

Printed in the United States of America

To my wife, Sue Branon, and our children, Lisa, Julie, Melissa, and Steven, who supported me as I wrote about the sport I enjoy, players I respect, and a Savior they know I love.

To my wife, Bethanne Pellegrino, and our children, Joey and Jennifer, a family who is always there to pick me up when I despair. To my parents, John and Gloria Pellegrino, who sacrificed all so their children would not fall.

And most important, I dedicate this book to the Lord, who has entered my heart and made me new!

Contents

Part 3: Extra Innings

Acknowledgments

Like a successful baseball team, many people must work together for a book such as *Safe at Home* to have the winning edge. Two people have contributed greatly to this book. One is my wife, Sue, who never let me quit believing that something like this could happen. The other is Joe Pellegrino, my long-distance friend whose idea this book was—and who worked diligently and persistently until he had talked with all 20 of the men featured in "On the Field."

In addition, Andy Scheer of *Moody* magazine and John Long of Moody Press helped to steer us in the right direction. Another invaluable person in this project was Dave Swanson of Baseball Chapel. His excitement about this book and his willingness to encourage the players to talk with Joe got us through some doubtful times.

Then there are the people who prayed: our friends John and Gail Lillis; my wife's parents, Ralph and Lenore Tuttle; and my parents, John and Kathleen Branon.

Finally we appreciate the players who were willing to give their time during the off-season, during spring training, or during the season so Joe could interview them.

Books, magazines, newspapers, and various other sports communications tools helped us know the players and the game they play. The gold mine of information we dug from includes *The Baseball Encyclopedia*; *Closer Walk*, a newsletter by our good friend Watson Spoelstra; *The Greatest Game Ever Played*, by Jerry Izenberg; *The 1992 Information Please Sports Almanac*; *The Sporting News Baseball Register*; *The Sporting News Baseball Guide*; and Sports Spectrum radio. Some interview material came from articles or chapters in the following publications: *Sports Illustrated*, *Sports Spectrum*, and *Sharing the Victory* magazines; *The Sporting News*; *Tuned to Baseball*, by Ernie Harwell; and *Out of the Blue*, by Orel Hershiser.

Foreword

So much has changed about baseball since the days I played second base for the New York Yankees. When I retired in 1966, only one indoor stadium existed and no one had heard of long-term contracts worth millions of dollars. The first Super Bowl had yet to be played, so the World Series was the premier sporting event in the land. And there were no divisional playoffs in baseball. A team had to finish first in the league to get to the Series.

But the change that I am most excited about in baseball has been the increased interest in spiritual things among so many of today's players. When we began Baseball Chapel, our dream was to help the players see that what goes on inside of them is as important as what happens on the field. We wanted to give them an oasis from the many distractions and activities that keep their lives so busy that they never have time to stop and reflect on what God means to them.

Now Baseball Chapel, through the active leadership of Dave Swanson, makes it possible for players in every city in the majors to take a few minutes to gather together to reflect on the gospel of Jesus Christ and the teachings of the Bible. Through the chaplains and visiting speakers, many major and minor league players are coming to faith in Christ, and those who already know Him are being strengthened in those often informal clubhouse meetings.

An exciting result of Baseball Chapel is spreading the impact beyond the locker room. A network of Christian spokesmen is being raised up among the ranks of Major League Baseball players, athletes who are willing to stand up and be counted for God and who are willing to let sports fans across North America know how much Jesus Christ means to them.

That eagerness to take the message of God's love beyond the confines of the clubhouse and disseminate it to the people in the stands is what is behind a book like this. Only because people such as Brett Butler, Joe Carter, Tim Burke, Frank Tanana, and Ernie Harwell believe in the vital message of the gospel and are willing to tell others about it are we able to compile such an important collection of stories that take us beyond baseball.

Baseball keeps changing—sometimes for better, sometimes for worse—and so do the people who play, manage, announce, and organize the game. But the people behind Baseball Chapel and the Christian baseball players who are a part of it know that there is only one person who never changes and who always has our best interests at heart. He is Jesus Christ, the reason for Baseball Chapel, the reason I find life so enjoyable and fruitful, the reason for this book, and the only hope any of us ever has of eternal life.

If you're a baseball fan, the on-the-field stories in *Safe at Home* will entertain and thrill you, and the ballplayers' off-field testimonies should challenge you. And I pray that God's rich blessings will be yours as you trust Him with your life.

BOBBY RICHARDSON
President, Baseball Chapel

Bobby Richardson played in more than 1,400 games for the New York Yankees between 1955 and 1966. As a Yankee, he participated in more than 30 straight World Series games, and he holds the record for most runs batted in during a World Series. The second baseman was named to the American League All-Star team seven times and was a five-time Gold Glove winner.

Introduction

Many baseball moments stay in my mind as welcome reminders of games gone by, but perhaps the ones that stand out most vividly are certain World Series memories of heart-stopping drama.

Maybe you too remember scenes such as Kirk Gibson hopping around the bases, pumping his arms like steam train pistons after his improbable two-strike blast off Dennis Eckersley that propelled the Dodgers to victory in the 1988 Series. I recall as yesterday Carlton Fisk's first-baseline body English that seemed to help wrap his game-winning home run around the foul pole in game 6 of the 1975 classic. Fisk used his arms and hands, seemingly pushing that fly ball fair as it headed to the stands in the bottom of the twelfth inning, and the Red Sox beat the Reds in a battle of the ages.

And there's Jack Morris's gutty pitching performance in the 1991 World Series, as he put together the longest stint on the mound ever in a Series' seventh game—10 innings. His complete game shutout gave the Twins a thrilling 1-0 victory and the Series' crown.

But if you have either a long memory or a father who regales you with baseball stories, one image probably stands tall above the others—Bill Mazeroski's 1960 blast into history. The Pirate second baseman imprinted his number 9 in our baseball memory books forever with the first, and still only, bottom-of-the-ninth home run ever to win the seventh game of the World Series. More than 30 years later, the sight of his jubilant dance around third and the ecstatic welcome-home party that greeted him at home plate remains etched in the minds of all who have seen this spectacular moment in the history of the Fall Classic.

The thought of that game and that Series, though, brings to my mind the accomplishments of the other second baseman in the 1960 October showdown. His name has not been stored in our memory banks with the same flair as has Bill Mazeroski's, yet he could easily have been remembered as the conquering hero of this confrontation between the Pirates and the Yankees.

In fact, you could say he had a better Series than Mazeroski. He had 11 hits to 8 for the Maz. He knocked in 12 runs in the Series to the Pirates' second baseman's 5; indeed, he had one more RBI than that in game 3. Four of those came on a grand slam home run. And the Yank had the better batting average for the Series, .367 to Mazeroski's .320. In the end, even after the Pirates were through celebrating their Forbes Field triumph, it was the Yankees' second baseman who took home the 1960 World Series Most Valuable Player Award.

His name is Bobby Richardson, a 5-foot 9-inch sparkplug of a player who chose this conspicuous October occasion to outshine such stars as Roberto Clemente, National League MVP Dick Groat, American League MVP Roger Maris, Mickey Mantle, Yogi Berra, and Whitey Ford.

Although I vaguely recall that Series and Bobby Richardson's marvelous contributions to it, I more vividly remember him for something of even greater importance than his on-the-field display of power, athleticism, and skill.

Bobby Richardson is important to me because he was the first athlete I knew about who was willing to let people know that he was a Christian. He was not ashamed to tell people that he believed in Jesus Christ. As one story goes, he even witnessed to Jose Pagan of the San Francisco Giants at second base during the 1962 World Series.

As a youngster from southern Ohio who thought the new year began in April and ended in October, I was thrilled to find out that a real live major league baseball player knew the same Jesus Christ that I knew. Bobby Richardson didn't have to hit .367 against the Pirates for me to think he was special. I already knew it.

He was so special that I could forgive him for not playing for the Cincinnati Reds. I could overlook the fact that in the 1961 World Series he batted .391 against my beloved Jim O'Toole and Bob Purkey and Joey Jay. I was not angry with him for helping the hated Yanks wipe out my all-time favorite players Frank Robinson and Vada Pinson and their Crosley Field teammates in five games in a quick Series that was mercifully over by October 9.

Bobby Richardson was a lone ranger in his day, or so it seemed to me. Rarely did we hear of other baseball people who were willing to let the fans and the world at large know that they were Christians.

Today, it's a whole new ball game. What Bobby Richardson started—and then continued with his work with Baseball Chapel —continues into the 1990s. Now we see recognition of Christian baseball players from such diverse sources as the *Pittsburgh Press*, which ran a series of articles on born-again athletes, to *M Inc.* magazine, which splashed four L.A. Dodger Christians across its cover and then let them tell their stories of faith.

We've seen Brett Butler stand tall for his faith as the secular media drilled him with skeptical questions. We've watched Howard Johnson's wife at the 1991 All-Star game tell CBS's Pat O'Brien that everything is in the Lord's hands—even the birth of their obviously imminent child. We've seen Harold Reynolds put his faith into practice by starting a foundation to help kids. We've heard Frank Tanana hold nothing back in giving God the glory for his accomplishments. But it's not just the players on the field who are setting a spiritual tone in baseball. In the broadcast booth, in the coach's box, and even in the front office are men who live by faith. We've picked two of the best-known of these off-the-field men of class to feature with the players: Sal Bando, general manager of the Milwaukee Brewers; and Ernie Harwell, Hall of Fame play-by-play voice of the Dodgers, Giants, Orioles, and Tigers through the years. Both men have earned widespread respect for their contributions to the game as well as for their clear testimony for Christ. They too know how to be *Safe at Home*, whether home is the ballpark, the family house, or the ultimate home: heaven.

Like a founding father proudly surveying the results of his work, Richardson can look in the clubhouse of perhaps every team in baseball and see men who are willing and eager to tell whoever will listen about their relationship with their Savior Jesus Christ. And he can see every team in both leagues open up their facilities to Baseball Chapel to bring in the spiritual dimension. Teams have as many as 18 guys out for chapel. "If it's Sunday, this must be chapel" could easily be the theme in baseball as players unashamedly attend these clubhouse praise and Bible study services. Attended by players who are noted for their faith as well as by players who are just searching for life's true meaning, these pre-game services go far beyond a prayer for success.

So now you can take your pick among Christians in baseball. The type of youthful excitement I had in following Bobby Richardson because of my admiration for his faith can be multiplied for you many times over as you read about the men of baseball in this era who not only stand out on the diamond but also stand up for Jesus.

The 29 baseball people whose stories appear in the following pages will give you a compelling cross-section of what is happening in the lives of Christians in baseball today. Of course, not every player who is a believer in Jesus appears in this book. Perhaps even your favorite Christian player isn't mentioned. There are several reasons for this. In some cases other obligations prevented players from being interviewed. Other players felt their story had already been told and were hesitant to garner more coverage.

And, of course, we have limited our coverage to keep the book from becoming overly long. In fact, one reason we kept the profiles shorter in Extra Innings was to cover as many players as possible in this book.

Whether it's Kevin Brown of Texas starting an All-Star game or Kevin Seitzer of Milwaukee making a great comeback, more and more Major League Baseball players excel on the field while maintaining a vibrant testimony for Jesus Christ. You will enjoy reading how many major leaguers have discovered that a strong relationship with Jesus Christ can help them be *Safe at Home.* And we hope their stories will help you make sure you have a faith that will sustain you through the successes and losses of this earthly life and prepare you for eternal life with God.

Part One
ON THE FIELD

Jesse Barfield
A Save by the Relief Pitcher

VITAL STATISTICS

Born October 29, 1959, in Joliet, Illinois
6 feet 1, 201 pounds
Current Team:* New York Yankees
Position: Right Field

Current Team refers to team during 1992 season.

CAREER HIGHLIGHTS

- Led American League outfielders in double plays in 1985 and 1986
- Selected to American League All-Star team once
- Led American League in home runs in 1986 with 40
- Has led American League outfielders in assists 4 times

WARMING UP

The Blue Jays and the White Sox were involved in a tight contest. Late in the game, Roy Lee Jackson was called on to pitch for the Blue Jays. He came in and gave up the winning hit, and Toronto lost.

"This was the moment I had been waiting for," Jesse Barfield says, recalling the glee he felt, knowing that no pitcher could react properly to what Jackson had just gone through. "Here was my chance to see Mr. Roy Lee Jackson expose himself for who he really was. I knew he would take out his frustration on someone or something, cursing and kicking. But much to my surprise he came into the locker room, sat in his chair, and took off his spikes. He laid—he didn't throw—down his glove in his locker, took off his uniform, went into the shower, put on his street clothes, and walked out."

Jesse Barfield

It was 1981, and Jesse Barfield had just been called up from the minor leagues. He had flown alone to Chicago and had met the rest of his new teammates, the Toronto Blue Jays, at Comiskey Park where the Jays were to play the White Sox.

It had to be a time of nostalgia for the 21-year-old kid from nearby Joliet. Less than a decade earlier Jesse and his 12-year-old buddies had sat in the outfield seats at Comiskey Park, watching their beloved White Sox in action.

Incredible memories flooded back. Perhaps he remembered those excursions north from Joliet to visit the stadium and sit in the outfield seats to watch guys like Pat Kelly and Dick Allen and Carlos May take opposing pitchers downtown. Maybe he remembered his vow to his buddies that "I'm going to be out there someday." And he may even have recalled that they didn't believe him.

But it's the latter part of 1981 now, and he has made it. Here comes the new kid, Jesse Barfield, just out of Knoxville in the Southern League. He walks into the ballpark with his Walkman® on, listening to the Motown sounds of the Confunction. Cool dude that he is, the rookie sidles up to one of the players, relief pitcher Roy Lee Jackson, and tells him, "Check out this new cut I'm listening to."

Jackson looks the new guy over and asks, "What kind of music is that?"

"Confunction," says Barfield, proudly.

Roy Lee Jackson looks at Jesse with a straight face and says, "I don't listen to that kind of music."

Barfield recalls his shock: "Right about then I was thinking, 'Well, you're black! What do you mean you don't listen to this kind of music?'"

But before Barfield can say anything, Jackson surprises him with this announcement: "I listen to Christian music."

Not one of those guys! Barfield thinks. *Let me get away from him.*

From that point on, Barfield kept a very close eye on the Jays' relief pitcher. Perhaps he was intrigued. Perhaps he just wanted to be around to see a righteous man fall. Whatever the reason, Barfield remembers, "I began to watch Roy to see if what he said was in line with what he did."

He got his first glimpse of the kind of person Jackson really was that night. The Jays and the White Sox were involved in a tight contest. Late in the game, Roy was called on to pitch. He came in and gave up the winning hit. The relief pitcher had failed, and Toronto lost.

"This was the moment I had been waiting for," Barfield says, recalling the glee he felt, knowing that no pitcher could react properly to what Jackson had just gone through. "Here was my chance to see Mr. Roy Lee Jackson expose himself for who he really was. I knew he would take out his frustration on someone or something, cursing and kicking. But much to my surprise he came into the locker room, sat in his chair, and took off his spikes. He laid—he didn't throw—down his glove in his locker, took off his uniform, went into the shower, put on his street clothes, and walked out."

No cursing. No kicking. All Barfield saw was a guy who had finished his job and was going home. Disappointed yet under control.

It started Jesse thinking. "Man, if that was me, I would be kicking and cursing and in a downright nasty mood because that is the way Jesse Barfield handles things of that nature."

The next day manager Bobby Mattick stuck Roy Lee into another tight situation, but this time he shut down the Sox, and the Blue Jays came out on top. Now Barfield is really watching Jackson. He had already discovered that he had his temper in check, but what would he do now? Perhaps he'll be so excited about the game that he'll go out and party with the guys. Barfield was sure he would do something un-Christian.

Jesse was wrong again. Jackson came into the locker room, sat in his chair, took off his spikes, laid his glove in his locker, took off his uniform, went into the showers, dried off, put on his street clothes, and walked out. Barfield noticed that a pattern seemed to be developing: This guy doesn't get nasty when he loses, and he doesn't go crazy when he wins.

Jesse Barfield decided that this type of consistency was not normal, and it was something that he personally admired.

But besides the consistency, there were other things that made Barfield take notice of this strange reliever. "I realized that to make his point he never once quoted Scripture, never once rammed the Bible down my throat, and most important, never preached. He simply showed me, through the way he walked with the Lord, how I too could find an inner peace. That's what I needed and what I wanted."

Roy would always make it a point to invite Barfield to a Bible study that included many other players, but Jesse would always turn him down with some lame excuse. He would say things like "Well, Roy, I'd like to but my cousin is coming in from Transylvania today, and I have to pick him up at the airport." Jesse would lie like a dog, and Roy would simply respond, "No problem, man. I'll be praying for you."

It took a long time for Roy Lee Jackson's message to sink in, but finally Jesse reached a point "where I took a good look at myself and realized I had no joy in my life, and I needed to do something."

Finally, in 1982, Jesse accepted Roy's invitation and attended a Bible study at his home with some of the other players including Alvin Woods and Lloyd Moseby. Barfield's girlfriend Marla (now his wife) also went to the Bible study.

"I'll never forget the tape we listened to that night," Jesse recalls. "It was called 'Eternal Destiny.' That tape opened my eyes to many things, one being myself and what I was all about. I realized that I didn't like what I had become."

After the tape was over, Roy asked Jesse if he wanted to give his life to Jesus Christ. When Barfield said that he would like Roy to explain further what that meant, the reliever read Scriptures, showing him that the only way to God was through Jesus Christ. To reach God, Barfield was told, a person had to be born again spiritually. "Sure enough, we did it," Barfield says with a smile. "That was the beginning of a great new life for me."

Part of that new life for Jesse Barfield was learning to respond in a new way to difficulties. "Sometimes in my situation," he confides, "I get into a battle for playing time with other outfielders. Even though I am never happy about that, the Bible says, 'When angry, sin not.' Therefore, I just go about my business with a smile on my face, and I know that things will work out, just like Roy taught me. If some other players or writers or anyone else locks his eyes on me at a troubled time like that, maybe, just maybe, I might be to someone else what Roy Lee Jackson was and still is to me—the man who saved me by leading me to Jesus."

Jesse Barfield also uses what he first learned from Roy to reach out in love and concern to people off the field as well. Once while in Seattle between games with the Mariners, Barfield took some time to drop off packages at a local post office. Walking down the street, he hesitated when a lady approached him and asked directly, "Got a minute?" She promptly explained that down the street a film was about to start, a film about Jesus Christ.

"Well, it's certainly a subject I'm interested in," Barfield said. "Tell you what. As soon as I mail my packages, I will be over to see it."

"I kept my word and showed up to see the video," Barfield recalls. "Some of what I saw seemed to be all right, but there were other things I could not agree with. When the woman asked me about it, I told her just that, and further explained that I really didn't enjoy it."

As they were talking, a salesman entered the building with a suitcase full of No Smoking signs. He had signs in more than 20 languages, and asked if anyone was interested in making a purchase. Though he found no interest, the woman who showed the video about Jesus invited him to stay and watch it.

"Sorry, Ma'am. I just don't have time. I got to sell the signs."

Into Barfield's mind came a thought that grew in urgency: *I've got to get out of here and introduce this man to the real Jesus Christ.*

"Look, I'm leaving anyway, why don't you have lunch with me before you go to your next place," the ballplayer asked the salesman.

"No thanks, I really don't have time," the man repeated.

"Man, if you're selling No Smoking signs for a living, you've got time to hear what I have to say," Barfield said with unaccustomed boldness.

"So now the guy has two invitations—one to see a video and one to have lunch with me," Barfield recalls. "He chose the video. He went into the room where the woman was showing the tape. When he did, I felt it in my heart to go into that room and take him out. So that's what I did. I told the man to come have lunch with me so we could talk."

The woman who had asked Barfield to come view the film became very angry. "Just a minute. We do things a certain way around here . . . You have no right to take away this man here—"

"I had apparently violated their ways of doing things," Barfield says. "She certainly wasn't teaching the Spirit of God. But I knew that already anyway. Eventually, I discovered that the group was part of the cult known as Moonies.

"As the man with the signs and I left, I discovered that his name was Ronnie. We headed for a restaurant at my hotel for lunch. We talked for more than an hour and a half. By the time I had to leave to get ready for our game that night, Ronnie had come to know Christ as his Savior.

"What a great experience that was for me! As we talked, Ronnie told me that he remembered some of the things his mom told him about Jesus and that meeting me had confirmed that he had to get right with Jesus Christ and with God. He cried as he talked about it.

"The next year when I returned to Seattle, we spent some time together and I found out that he had a good job. The following year he had a better job, and it seems that every year I go back he is moving up."

Jesse emphasizes that his time with Ronnie "is not a one-way relationship. One time we arrived in Seattle and I was feeling particularly blue. Guess who called me? That's right, my buddy Ronnie. I was so fired up to see how great he was doing and how he was reaching out to help others through a ministry he was a part of that I forgot about my woes and just rejoiced in Jesus' works through Ronnie."

Jesse wouldn't give up on Ronnie—just as Roy Lee Jackson never gave up on Jesse. He stretched his arm out as far as it could go, and Ronnie finally grabbed it. Roy Lee Jackson to Jesse Barfield to Ronnie. Now that's a combination that beats the old double-play combination of Tinkers to Evers to Chance any day.

It was another kind of combination that Jesse Barfield used in his playing days at Toronto to help establish one of the best outfield trios in the game. It is not known what Jesse's old buddies from Joliet thought of his rise to stardom with the Blue Jays in the '80s, but we know what some of the best experts in baseball thought of him. *Baseball's Ultimate Biographical Reference* rated Jesse Barfield as the player with the "best outfield arm of the '80s."

With George Bell and Lloyd Moseby holding down left field and center and with Barfield in right, the Blue Jays had one-third of an All-Star team in the outfield. In 1986, for instance, these three amigos pounded out 92 home runs and knocked in 302 runs. Jesse Barfield led the way with a league-leading 40 round-trippers and 108 runs batted in.

This phenomenal outfield of Bell, Moseby, and Barfield was one of the primary reasons the Blue Jays went from a team with average attendance to the top draw in both leagues. As Barfield says of his first years in Toronto, "It was an opera-like setting. When you made a big play, the fans would just clap with a pittypat." But by the time Barfield left the Canadian city in a trade in 1989, he says, "The fans knew the game, and it was great!"

The outfield broke apart in 1989, with Barfield going to a no-man's land of baseball danger, the New York Yankees. A team that had dominated baseball for decades now was one of the weakest teams in the game. And while Barfield was in the outfield, in the front office was George Steinbrenner—he of the famed nasty temper and the inability to treat people right.

Yet Jesse Barfield holds an opposing view of the man. Despite the appearance toward the end of 1989 that Steinbrenner had mistreated Barfield in contract negotiations, Barfield remained loyal to his boss. After previous contract extension talks had broken off with Barfield left high and dry, the two men met together. At that meeting, Steinbrenner paid Barfield some high compliments, telling him he was the kind of leader he wanted in the clubhouse and that he had the qualities the Yankees were looking for.

A three-year agreement was signed, and Jesse Barfield went away from the meeting saying, "I left there thinking he was great. In my eyes, he's OK." Barfield responded to his new contract by hitting 65 home runs for the Yankees in the next three seasons as the men in the pinstripes began to edge toward respectability.

It's been a long road for Jesse Barfield from those boyhood days in the right field seats at Comiskey Park to right field in Yankee Stadium. But along the way he has learned from a relief pitcher how to have peace with God, from a sign salesman how to share that peace, and from a baseball trade how to survive despite bad circumstances. And he continues to be, as Roy Lee Jackson was for him, a man who helps people change for the better.

Q & A WITH JESSE BARFIELD

Q: *How do you handle things when you go into a slump?*
Jesse: The baseball is the size of a golf ball during a slump. I've learned not to think about the circumstances or to listen to all the bad reports. I can remember going 0 for 27 once. It happens so

fast. I'd go 0 for 4. Then it was 0 for 8. And 0 for 12. Pretty soon I'm not concentrating. I have learned that God will help me concentrate. My advice is press on. Look ahead, not back—in baseball and in the Christian life.

Q: *What was it like going from a winning team in Toronto to the Yankees, who were struggling?*
Jesse: I prayed and said, "Lord, I feel like I'm alone here. This team is in last place, and we don't have a lot of Christians here." I discovered that He needed me to be there. I learned that you can't just be comfortable in your own little world. You have to help as many people as you can.

Q: *Who was your favorite baseball player as you were growing up?*
Jesse: Ernie Banks, Hall of Fame player for the Cubs.

Q: *How do you deal with all the things that some other players do after a game that you think are not right?*
Jesse: They know I don't drink, but they don't criticize me. If they ask me why, I answer, "My body is not only my job, but it is also the temple of the Holy Spirit."

MAJOR LEAGUE CAREER PATH

June 7, 1977:   Selected by Blue Jays in the 9th round of free-agent draft
April 30, 1989: Traded to Yankees for pitcher Al Leiter

THE BARFIELD FILE

Year	Team	G	AB	R	H	2B	3B	HR	RBI	Avg.
1977	Utica	70	234	37	53	9	3	5	35	.226
1978	Dunedin	133	441	40	91	12	3	2	34	.206
1979	Kinston	136	477	66	126	24	5	8	71	.264
1980	Knoxville	124	433	63	104	12	8	14	65	.240
1981	Knoxville	141	524	83	137	24	13	16	70	.261
1981	Blue Jays	25	95	7	22	3	2	2	9	.232
1982	Blue Jays	139	394	54	97	13	2	18	58	.246
1983	Blue Jays	128	388	58	98	13	3	27	68	.253
1984	Blue Jays	110	320	51	91	14	1	14	49	.284
1985	Blue Jays	155	539	94	156	34	9	27	84	.289
1986	Blue Jays	158	589	107	170	35	2	40	108	.289
1987	Blue Jays	159	590	89	155	25	3	28	84	.263
1988	Blue Jays	137	468	62	114	21	5	18	56	.244
1989	Blue Jays/Yankees	150	521	79	122	23	1	23	67	.234
1990	Yankees	153	476	69	117	21	2	25	78	.246
1991	Yankees	84	284	37	64	12	0	17	48	.225
1992	Yankees	30	95	8	13	2	0	2	7	.137
Major League Career (12 years)		1428	4759	715	1219	216	30	241	716	.256

Sid Bream
You Can Go Home Again

VITAL STATISTICS

Born August 3, 1960, in Carlisle, Pennsylvania
6 feet 4, 175 pounds
Current Team: Atlanta Braves
Position: First Base
Attended Liberty University, Lynchburg, Virginia

CAREER HIGHLIGHTS

- Holds National League record for assists by a first baseman in one season (166) in 1986
- Finished third in National League in doubles in 1986 (37)
- Collected 3 hits, including 2 doubles, in 1991 World Series
- Winner of the 1990 Hutch Award, given to the professional baseball player who overcomes a physical adversity and best exemplifies the spirit of former major league manager Fred Hutchinson

WARMING UP

Sid Bream was thrilled with the fan response as he returned to Three Rivers Stadium on May 10, 1991. "When I went back to Pittsburgh as an Atlanta Brave, the people in Pittsburgh gave me a standing ovation for five minutes. Then I went out and—with my knees knocking and my eyes watering—hit a home run to center field. After that, they gave me another standing ovation for another five minutes. I would have to say that was my best experience in the game of baseball."

Sid Bream

Barry Bonds couldn't believe it. He had just seen his friend and former teammate Bobby Bonilla receive a less-than-gracious welcome back to Three Rivers Stadium in June of 1992, and he was stunned. "It was terrible the way they treated Bobby," Bonds told reporters after the Pirates' fans greeted the Mets' Bonilla with a chorus of boos when he returned to Pittsburgh for his first game there after signing with New York in the off-season. "When Sid Bream came back here after he went to Atlanta, they gave him a standing ovation," Bonds continued.

In Pittsburgh, Bobby Bonilla had reached superstar status, while Sid Bream had become a very good player whose several injuries had held back his performance. Most observers would give Bonilla the edge on the field. So why the different reaction?

It's a difficult question to answer, for fans can be fickle with whom they favor and whom they deride. But one thing is clear about Sid Bream—without Hall of Fame stats in Pittsburgh, he had become appreciated for who he was as a person as much as for what he did as a player. The native Pennsylvanian found out that if you earn the respect of people and refuse to alienate them, you can go home again to the cheers of the crowd.

Bream was thrilled with the fan response as he returned to Three Rivers Stadium on May 10, 1991. "When I went back to

Pittsburgh as an Atlanta Brave, the people in Pittsburgh gave me a standing ovation for five minutes. Then I went out and—with my knees knocking and my eyes watering—hit a home run to center field. After that, they gave me another standing ovation for another five minutes. I would have to say that was my best experience in the game of baseball."

Maybe part of the difference that Barry Bonds noticed in the two homecomings was this: While Bonilla reportedly seemed to be eager to get out of the Steel City, Bream was not looking for a ticket out of town.

As it turns out, this greatest thrill—complete with the standing ovations and the returning-hero home run—came only after what Bream experienced what he considers one of the worst things that has happened to him, being allowed by Pittsburgh to sign with Atlanta as a free agent. "Pittsburgh was saying to me, for the first time in five years, that Sid Bream was their first priority. But when they came down to talking about how things were going, we found out how much loyalty was there. We had all our hopes and dreams of staying in Pittsburgh, and they never materialized. So we went to Atlanta."

Yet the timing was perfect. Because of that move, Bream now has the memory of two World Series safely stashed away. How could he have known that his leaving the team with the second-best record in baseball and signing with the team with the worst record in the majors would mean that 10 months later he would be playing in the Fall Classic? And that in 1992 he would be in the Series again?

Of course no one on earth could know that. But Sid Bream knows Someone who did understand what this new situation would hold for him. He credits God with guiding him to the home of the Braves.

"Now that it's over with," he says of that whole process of switching teams through free agency, "we understand what was happening. God knew what was going on, as He always does. He used our going to Atlanta to set up a lot of neat things as far as Bible studies and chapels, and we've started to work with a lot of people."

Sid Bream feels that he went to Atlanta for more than just baseball and the next two World Series. He was there not only to help the Braves win, but also to help meet the needs of a new group of people in Atlanta. He is confident that his position in baseball is a gift that he can use to keep on giving to others. "God gave me an opportunity to play up here in the major leagues. I think the reason I am here is because of what God has done for me. He has told us that some will be preachers and some will be teachers, and He said, 'Sid, you're going to be a baseball player.' And I truly believe that God had plans for me to be here, and that's why I'm here."

Because he sensed a clear leading for him to move on from Pittsburgh to Atlanta, he feels that he has a spiritual responsibility with his team. "I've had the opportunity to sit down with several of the Atlanta Braves' players and have them drill me with questions and be able to talk with them," he says about his commitment to challenge his teammates spiritually.

Of course not all of the players are as interested in Bream's eternal message as he is. When he talks to his teammates, he feels that "there is definitely an amount of respect there for me." But he knows that despite that respect, what he says is not universally accepted. "There are certain individuals," he explains, "who will make a comedy act out of it. But for the most part, every one of those guys on our team respects where I'm coming from, and I think it's only because of the life that I lead. I try to be straightforward, and I think they respect that."

Bream admits, however, that a few players in the game make it tough for him and others who are committed to living as Christians and testifying about Jesus Christ. "I know that there are a lot of players in this game who are Christians, but that's as far as they've gone. Some of the guys in baseball I do talk to about Jesus say, 'Why should I change? Look at this guy. He says he's a Christian, but he does the same things I do.'

"That is something that hurts me. Not that every Christian is going to do everything right right off the bat. There is a learning stage. But I think in the game of baseball, and outside of baseball as well, people who become saved sometimes don't go any further. They don't really realize the relationship can be there with Jesus Christ, and the responsibility they have."

Perhaps one of the reasons the people in Pittsburgh let Sid Bream come home again was because they knew that he was an honest, straightforward man who was as good as his word. That is the kind of person who leaves behind enough good will to smooth his reentry.

Sid Bream grew up only 200 miles from Pittsburgh's Three Rivers Stadium, in Carlisle, Pennsylvania. There he found help in becoming a man even an opponent could cheer for. His family weren't athletes; they were musicians, and the Breams had their own team as Sid was growing up, playing and singing music. "We had a Christian singing group that would go around singing on Sunday night and at other times during the week.

"My mom and dad are tremendous Christians. We were at church every Sunday morning. Any possible time we were supposed to be at our church, we were at church." And that constant exposure to the message of the gospel paid off with Bream just after he became a teenager. "I was saved on August 25, 1973, at my church. We had a revival going at our church that week, and I gave my life to the Lord.

"For my family, it was a burden that was lifted," he says of that decision many years ago. "They didn't have to worry about Sid Bream not going to heaven. It's the same type of a feeling that I have for my two children right now. I want to make sure that I see them accept Jesus Christ into their life. I want that confidence to know that I'm going to see my children in heaven."

The Bream household of today—his wife, Michelle, and two boys, Michael and Tyler—is another place where Sid Bream can go home again. But not as often as he would like. "The family is very important to me. My two boys are at the age right now when daddy is very important to them at home. And being away from them at least 81 days out of the year puts the damper on daddy's feelings because I don't get to see them grow up a lot. That hurts. The thing that helps us so much is that we are so close. I know that when I am gone, my wife is pumping "daddy" into them all the time and not letting them get down on daddy by any means. We share the Lord with them, and I think those are the things that help us out."

Sid Bream's road to the major leagues has been like that of many players today: the youth leagues, high school ball—both junior varsity and varsity—American Legion, and finally college.

But for Bream, the college path was a bit different from most. While many players opt for a powerful baseball school with designs on an NCAA national championship (an Arizona State, for instance), Bream chose a small NAIA school that was more known for its Bible training than for its baseball trophies. Sid Bream, however, leaves no doubt that this decision was a good one—if for no other reason than because of his baseball coach.

The school was Liberty University in Lynchburg, Virginia, and the coach was Al Worthington, a former pitcher with the New York Giants, the Red Sox, the White Sox, the Reds, and the Twins. In 1968 Worthington led the American League in saves with 18, and in 1965 he played with the Twins in the World Series. During his 14-year career, he won 75 games and racked up 110 saves.

His influence continues today through his impact on Sid Bream. "I give a lot of credit to Al Worthington," Bream declares. "He not only taught me a whole lot about the game of baseball, but he taught me about character and Jesus Christ, and he really involved the whole spectrum of what to expect."

Bream describes his hitting experiences in professional baseball as a trip on a roller coaster, and Worthington has helped him hang on for the ride. After hitting consistently over .300 in the minor leagues, Bream's first trip to the majors as a member of the Los Angeles Dodgers ended on the bottom of the roller coaster hill with a .118 mark. Back to Albuquerque went the young first baseman, where he posted huge numbers: 20 home runs, 90 RBI, a .343 average. Then back to L.A., where he hit a measly .184 at the end of 1984. To begin the next year Bream hit .230 while playing for the Dodgers and his new team, the Pirates. In between, he visited Albuquerque again and hit .370.

That is expected, though, of new players in the game as they get acclimated to big league pitching. But Bream's roller coaster ride resumed during two frustrating years, 1987 and 1988. "I would start off hot and then get in a slump. Then I would get hot and go into a slump again. I was really beginning to question the Lord, and saying, 'Why are you doing this to me? I'm trying to do everything to serve you and the ones who are cursing your name are doing well, and here I am struggling all the time." Bream decided to talk with Worthington.

"If God wanted you to hit .190, could you do it?"

"I'm better than that," Bream answered.

"I'm not talking about that. If God wanted you to hit .190, could you do it?"

"No, I don't think I could," Bream replied.

"Sid, you've got to understand that you were a Christian before you were a baseball player. Until you are willing to give everything you have over to the Lord, He's not going to allow you to do well. Baseball for the most part is where He's going to use things in your life to draw yourself closer to Him."

Bream eventually learned that when he endured trials and tribulations, many times those trials "are designed to get me back on the right track."

That conversation, and later ones with his former mentor, have helped keep Sid Bream on track. And as he looks back on those years, he feels they were beneficial. They helped especially during the 1989 season, which was practically wiped out by knee surgery. That summer he had three operations, two of them to clean out cartilage, and one a replacement of the anterior cruciate ligament.

"I think that those times in 1987 and 1988 allowed me to go through that 1989 experience a lot easier. It allowed me to say, 'Lord, I'm going to do my best to get me back to where I need to be, but if you have something better for me, I know that's what it's supposed to be like.' So because I went through the experience of asking questions in 1987 and 1988, I'm able to trust in the Lord and know that whatever He has for me is better than what I have now."

Bream bounced back from that surgical summer of '89 with a solid performance for the Pirates in 1990. After starting slowly with a .221 average after 34 games, Bream caught fire. Between May 25 and June 17, he hit .421. In July he pounded out 5 home runs and had 18 RBI. And in August he hit .333. He finished that comeback effort with 15 home runs, and the Pirates made good use of them. They were 15-0 in games in which Bream homered.

He wasn't done after 162 games. In the playoffs against the eventual World Champion Cincinnati Reds, Bream hit .500 (4 for 8) with a home run and 3 RBI while fielding a flawless first base.

That's the kind of season the Pirates fans remembered from their first baseman after he went south, and it is also the kind of courageous performance that earned him one of baseball's major awards after the season. For his efforts in overcoming those three operations and helping his team win the division, Bream received the 1990 Hutch Award.

Sid Bream boarded the roller coaster again in 1991 as a new member of the Braves. He was hitting .288 with 9 home runs and 34 RBI after the first 60 games. He was at the top of his game. But the car started hurtling downhill on June 18 when he suffered a new knee injury while the Braves were in Philadelphia. It was time for surgery number four. This time the doctors removed a bone chip and repaired torn cartilage. Sandwiched around his time on the disabled list that summer, he pounded out two grand slam home runs. It was another up and down year.

You can sense the frustration in Bream's voice when he talks of his on-again, off-again success in the majors. "When I first started playing the game of baseball, I just wanted to be consistent, and I have been consistent. Over my years, except for when I've gotten hurt, my home runs and my RBI and my average have basically been pretty much straight on."

And if he can keep those knees healthy, he has some goals in mind. "I think that there is more there for me. I think a 20-home-run season should be very easy for me. In 1991 I started off on that road, and then I got hurt. In 1992 I started to hit the ball good, and then I got a hamstring pull and that kind of set me back."

More important to Bream than goals is consistency, though he "would love to have an 80-RBI season" as well as 20 home runs each year. Whether those things ever come to reality for Bream or whether he ever reaches the on-the-field consistency he desires are unknown. But one thing is sure. He doesn't have to worry about establishing consistency in his life. He has done that in his Christian faith, which he nurtures and cherishes day after day. He has done that with his family, who knows that he cares for them very much. And he has done that in the communities he has lived in, working through churches, the Salvation Army, and other civic organizations to make a genuine impact on his hometown.

Because of his strong testimony in all of those areas, he can rest assured that no matter what hindrances he faces in reaching his baseball goals, he has already reached his goals for how he wants people to remember him. Sid Bream wants to be remembered by those who know him or know about him as "a person who cared—a person who is loyal to the game of baseball. I don't want people to think by any means that Sid Bream was an egomaniac or an individual who strived to be the highest paid ballplayer or to think of money. I want people to remember me as someone who cared for the fans and respected them because I knew that they were part of our lives. Without them we would be nothing."

No wonder the fans in Pittsburgh rose to their feet when Sid Bream strolled to the plate wearing a shirt that had Atlanta written across the front. People like him can always go home again.

Q & A WITH SID BREAM

Q: *Who is the toughest pitcher you've ever faced?*
Sid: The toughest pitcher that I faced is no longer in the game of baseball . . . Dave Dravecky. Dravecky gave me fits as a hitter. He was a tremendous competitor, and his life and his example as a ballplayer is an example to look at, not only in the baseball world, but also in the business world. He was a competitor, but he also maintained Jesus Christ first in his life. That's someone I respect very much.

Q: *Should baseball players be looked upon as role models?*
Sid: We are definitely role models. I don't think there are very many individuals who want to be put into that role, but we are role models. . . . What I want people to see in me is someone who is at peace with himself. I don't want them to see someone who is lost or lonely. I'm playing for Jesus Christ, and I shouldn't have to worry about what goes on in my life. I know that He is there, and He's going to stick closer than a brother. I want them to see a peace in me that no matter what goes on in the game of baseball, I'm going to be able to handle it.

Q: *Do you have any thoughts about how the players in the game today should view the money side of things?*
Sid: There is definitely a lot of money in baseball and in all athletics. It's a two-sided coin. I don't want baseball to get to the point where they are robbing everything they can from the ownership, but I also don't want the ownership to sit there and think they have all the rights to make all the money in the game of baseball. I hope the players are wise enough that if [the game and their jobs were threatened], they wouldn't say "We want a salary increase." Instead, they will say, "We'll decrease our salaries to keep the game alive.""

Q: *What kind of a player should a Christian be?*
Sid: I don't think that because we are Christians we should be slack in our competitiveness. I think God wants us to be the very best. I think He wants every business person, housewife, fireman, employee, whatever, to be the best at what we do. I don't want people to say of me, "He's a Christian, he's not going to give it his best." I want to show people that Christians are champions.

Q: *What challenge do you have for someone who refuses to understand what makes a Christian who he or she is.*
Sid: I'll challenge any non-Christian to live the Christian life and see how it goes. They talk about the person who won't take drugs as being the chicken. I challenge anybody to live the Christian life, because it's not a bed of roses.

MAJOR LEAGUE CAREER PATH

June 8, 1981:   Selected by the Dodgers in 2d round of free-agent draft
September 9, 1985: Traded with Cecil Espy and R. J. Reynolds to the Pirates for Bill Madlock
November 5, 1990: Granted free agency
December 5, 1990: Signed with the Braves

THE BREAM FILE

Year	Team	G	AB	R	H	2B	3B	HR	RBI	Avg.
1981	Vero Beach	70	260	35	85	12	5	1	47	.327
1982	Vero Beach	63	226	41	70	13	5	4	43	.310
1982	San Antonio	70	259	43	83	18	0	8	50	.320
1982	Albuquerque	3	8	3	3	1	0	1	2	.375
1983	Albuquerque	138	485	115	149	23	4	32	118	.307
1983	Dodgers	15	11	0	2	0	0	0	2	.118
1984	Albuquerque	114	429	82	147	25	4	20	90	.343
1984	Dodgers	27	49	2	9	3	0	0	6	.184
1985	Dodgers/Pirates	50	148	18	34	7	0	6	21	.230
1985	Albuquerque	85	297	51	110	25	3	17	57	.370
1986	Pirates	154	522	73	140	37	5	16	77	.268
1987	Pirates	149	516	64	142	25	3	13	65	.275
1988	Pirates	148	462	50	122	37	0	10	65	.264
1989	Pirates	19	36	3	8	3	0	0	4	.222
1990	Pirates	147	389	39	105	23	2	15	67	.270
1991	Braves	91	265	32	67	12	0	11	45	.253
1992	Braves	125	372	30	97	24	1	10	61	.261
Major League Career (10 years)		**925**	**2770**	**311**	**726**	**171**	**11**	**81**	**413**	**.262**

Tim Burke
Baseballs and Babies

VITAL STATISTICS

Born February 19, 1959, in Omaha, Nebraska
6 feet 3, 205 pounds
Current Team: New York Yankees
Position: Relief Pitcher (right-handed)
Attended University of Nebraska

CAREER HIGHLIGHTS

- Set National League record for most rookie appearances in 1985 with 78
- Selected to one National League All-Star team
- Maintained an earned run average of less than 3.00 in five of his first six seasons

WARMING UP

When you look back over the past 10 years of Tim Burke's life, you see things that might not seem so important in the realm of athletics. Babies. Trades. Open-heart surgery. International flights. Bible studies. All-Star games.

It is a strange intermingling of events for most people, but for the Burkes, it is becoming standard as they mix the lives of their children with their lives as baseball people. An international baseball star—having played for teams in both the U.S. and Canada—has an international family—having children from southeast Asia and Central America.

Tim Burke

It's an odd combination. Baseballs and babies, that is.

You don't hear the two mentioned together very often. They have nothing in common, you think. But don't tell pitcher Tim Burke that. When you talk about him, you have to talk about babies as much as you do about a sharp curveball. Two of the most important baseball events in the life of Tim and his wife, Christine, are intertwined with two very important baby events.

To understand those two incidents we must first peek in on Tim and Christine as children growing up in Omaha. The story starts as 12-year-old Christine Atkinson stares unabashedly at the mentally impaired child who is being ushered through an Omaha department store. Clearly touched, she looks up at her mom and comments, "I bet it would be hard to have a child like that."

Wisely, her mother doesn't ignore the remark or criticize it. She just looks at her soon-to-be-teenager and reminds her, "You know, honey, when it's your child, it wouldn't be hard at all."

As with most things moms and dads tell their children, no one knows which comment—which thought—will later be something they need to depend upon. For Christine, this will become one of those memorable moments that later gives her strength and hope.

In another part of Omaha lives a young man who is probably not very interested in memorable moments and impaired children. He's having too much fun playing baseball.

"I was a baseball fanatic," he says now about his growing up days. "I just loved baseball." Tim Burke loved baseball as early as age eight as a little leaguer. With his strong arm, he became a pitcher halfway through his first year. "I could throw harder than anybody else. I was real wild. On days I was throwing strikes I was better than everybody, but on days I wasn't throwing strikes, that didn't set me apart. I was still just walking guys. So I was more known for my hitting and for playing shortstop and first base."

But no matter what position he played, he was happy.

And he apparently loved it for all the right reasons. He wasn't dreaming and scheming of big bucks in the big leagues or of being a famous flame-throwing righty in the World Series. He just loved to play. As a kid, he "never thought of playing college ball or pro ball. I was just having fun doing what I was doing."

But along about his senior year at Roncala High School in Omaha, Tim started getting letters from people who thought he might have a future in the game. Maybe it was time to think about life after high school. Eventually, the call of the professionals made Tim Burke get serious about baseball. Drafted by the Pirates in 1980, this boy who just wanted to have fun was suddenly under the pressure of having to perform well or say good-bye.

"When I went to being a pro ballplayer, baseball went from just being a game to being a business. I realized that if I didn't do what the team wanted, they would just ship me out. They would send me home to get a real job."

Baseball wasn't the only serious matter in Tim Burke's life at this point. There was also Christine Atkinson—that girl in the Omaha department store of years before.

"We both lived in Omaha, but one day in October of 1980, we were both visiting friends in Lincoln and we happened to meet —in a bar." A non-Christian, Tim had put in one summer in the minors (although he didn't pitch because of an injury), and was headed back to the Carolina League the next year to play at Alexandria, Virginia. He and Christine dated during the next two off-seasons after they met, and they made plans to be married after the 1982 season.

But when Tim went to Buffalo that spring to continue his drive to the major leagues, he was very lonely, so lonely that he called Christine and asked if she would move up their wedding. She consented, and the two Nebraskans were married on May 5, 1982. Buffalo was their honeymoon home.

Tim and Christine Burke almost did not make it out of Buffalo still married to each other. And to Tim, it was no mystery why.

"She was packed up and ready to go home and get a divorce after two weeks of being married to me. She realized what a mess I was," he says now in reflection, realizing that he was rather hard to get along with at the time.

The pressure of trying to be successful in baseball made Tim tense at home. In fact, he says regretfully, "The responsibility of having a wife [was something] I couldn't handle and I didn't want."

But that wasn't all. "My drinking problem was worse," he says ruefully. In college, drinking was a sport to Tim, who was famous for being able to drink more than anyone else. "I thought that was kind of fun," he recalls. But the fun disappeared with the pressure of pro ball. He had to perform or else.

"Baseball had become my god. That was what was most important in my life. And so all of a sudden I realized that I had to perform, because if I don't, my god will be destroyed, and I won't have it any more.

"To handle the pressure, I just started drinking even more. I went from being a big drinker to being a problem drinker. I had a drinking problem after I got into pro ball to handle the stress. It just got worse and worse."

To add to the pressure, Burke's pitching went bad during those early honeymoon days in Buffalo. "I just couldn't get anybody out," he says bluntly. "I was pitching terribly and my drinking was at its worst."

No wonder Christine's bags were packed and she was ready to go after a fortnight of being hitched to a baseball star.

Just when they needed help the most, a few of Tim's teammates stepped forward with a solution that the Burkes neither sought nor really desired—an invitation to a Bible study. Though the Burkes could have laughed them off, "We really didn't have anywhere else to turn," Tim recalls.

"I figured I was pretty good, and I figured that was good enough to get me to heaven. But with everything going wrong, we figured, what have we got to lose?

"So, we went to that Bible study in late May, and that's when I found out for the first time in my life—that was the biggest shock in my life—I realized I was not a Christian. I realized that it was a matter of having a relationship with Jesus Christ. Instead of having baseball being number 1 in my life, I had to put Jesus Christ first. I realized that I had to confess my sins and ask Him to forgive me. At that first Bible study, we really understood where we were [spiritually]."

But understanding that truth and doing something about it are two entirely separate things, and the Burkes weren't ready for the big step from one to the other. Tim estimates he spent three months "just fighting with the Lord. We didn't want to give up running our own lives. I didn't want to give up my life, and she didn't want to give up hers."

As the season wore on, however, the truth just wouldn't go away. "Finally I was so convicted by the Holy Spirit," Burke explains. "All the fun stuff I used to do, He took the fun out of it. I would still do it, but it wasn't any fun, 'cause all of a sudden I knew that I was doing something the Lord didn't want me to do. I knew I was not a Christian, and I wouldn't go to heaven if I died right then and there."

The Burkes concluded they "just couldn't go on any longer. We were just so convicted that we both decided at the same time—the morning of August 25, 1982—to turn our lives over to the Lord and [ask Him to] forgive us and change us and make Him number 1."

Some things in their relationship improved immediately, but others took time. The first things to go were Tim's drinking problem and his bad language. "I knew that I meant business with Him," Burke says about his salvation, "and when that happened, it showed that the Lord meant business with me."

Little by little, their newfound faith brought Tim and Christine closer together. "It was a gradual change," he explains. "I was able to see her in a different light. With Christ in me, I could see her with true, loving eyes, and I could see her with a love I hadn't had before. It took me a while to realize, but that was Christ in me loving her."

A rescued marriage, a conquered drinking problem, the confidence of being right with God. Life looked good again for Tim and Christine Burke.

And to top it off, the baseball part of life also improved during the next three years, as he posted winning records while pitching for minor league clubs with the Yankees and eventually the Expos.

By 1985 he won the tenth spot on the Expos' pitching staff, and by season's end he was becoming one of the premier relievers in baseball. In that first year with the Expos, he set a National League record for most games pitched by a rookie, appearing in a league-leading 78 games while compiling a 2.39 ERA and carving out a 9-4 won-lost record.

More records fell in his sophomore year. In the 202d game since he joined the Expos, Burke appeared in his 100th game. It was the fastest any pitcher in major league history had reached the century mark. And in 1987, he was perfect. Well, maybe not in every way, but his record was. He finished the year with a 7-0 mark and an ERA of 1.19. The future was bright indeed.

But there were clouds at home. Oh, the marriage was intact. The relationship that had such a rocky start was sailing along quite smoothly. But there was bad news.

The Burkes were not able to have any children of their own.

Christine Burke describes her feelings. "I was devastated. I felt like all the lights went out and my world was completely dark." The bright future of a star athlete and his wife was dimmed by something out of their control. The stats meant nothing. The relative wealth was unimportant, empty. The most important thing in life was to somehow open the curtains of sorrow that the Burkes felt closing in around them.

The answer began to come to them within a few months. At first the talk about adopting a child was tentative, for Tim was not at all sure this was something he was interested in. "I think it's a nice idea for other people," Tim told Christine, "but I don't know if I can love someone else's child."

Perhaps Christine's mother's words came back to her when she heard that—those words that assured her so many years ago that she could love even a child with impairments if it was "your own child," as her mother had said.

One thing is sure. Something had to be done to change Tim's mind, and Christine knew what to do. "Christine was kind of praying behind my back for a few months," Tim explains now, laughing at the recollection. "All of a sudden, like out of nowhere, the Lord completely changed my heart. I can change my mind. I've done that quite a few times, but only the Lord can change your heart like that, so I knew it was the Lord."

Christine knew her prayers had been answered when the man who wasn't interested in adoption turned to her while they were in the car one day and said, "I woke up this morning with a strong desire to adopt a little Korean girl."

With that statement, the door of opportunity swung open for the Burkes. First came Stephanie, who had been born prematurely. She arrived in the Burke household on December 8, 1987, by way of Des Moines. When the woman who brought Stephanie from Korea handed her to her mom and dad, they did what most new parents do. They looked at her and cried. The lights had come back on for Christine and Tim Burke.

The next child, though, did not come as quietly and as peacefully into their lives as Stephanie had. Burke baby number 2 became a national event—thanks in part to his daddy's ability to throw baseballs past hitters in late innings.

Dodger manager Tommy Lasorda had noticed the success of the Expos' ace reliever during the first part of the 1989 baseball season, and he picked Burke to pitch for the National League in the All-Star game in Anaheim. Six months earlier, the Burkes had arranged with their adoption agency to adopt a little boy from an orphanage in Guatemala.

"We wanted to adopt a special needs child who had already been born," Tim explains. And as they were leafing through their adoption agency's book and saw the picture of this little guy with some thyroid problems, they knew he was the one God had for them. So, during those preseason days of '89, as they compared Tim's baseball schedule with when he would be available, they concluded that the All-Star break in July would be perfect.

But when July 6 rolled around, Tommy Lasorda intervened unexpectedly and chose Burke to pitch in the All-Star game five days later.

As excited as the Burkes were about Tim's selection to the All-Star team—he calls it "a thrill beyond thrills"—it had created an unusual situation for Christine and him. Instead of flying together to Guatemala to pick up their son, the Burkes went two different directions—he to Anaheim to pick up six of the best hitters in the American League and she to Guatemala to pick up one of the best gifts they had ever received.

Despite missing Christine and wondering about his second child, Tim was thrilled when he entered the game. "I had grown up watching the All-Star game every year. . . . And then all of a sudden I'm there. Then I get into the game and I look around and see Ozzie Smith playing behind me at shortstop and all these other guys—and facing all these other stars on the other team. But being a peer with them in the same game was a great thrill. And being able to pitch two scoreless innings was a lot of fun."

The whole nation got wrapped up in the event after the TV network announcer revealed the Burkes' plans. Doubly excited about his coveted All-Star appearance and his firstborn son, Dad Burke fired those scoreless innings, dashed to the airport, and by 6:00 A.M. the next day was in Guatemala City.

Named Ryan after Tim's good friend Ryan Walter, a player in the National Hockey League, the youngest Burke was not impressed initially that his dad was an All-Star pitcher. In fact, he didn't have much to do with either Mom or Dad at first. "He was scared to death of me," Christine recalls. And Tim claims, "Ryan didn't want anything to do with me."

But, of course, that has all changed. And so has the family situation. There's also Nicole Burke, the third baby in Tim and Christine's growing family. Nicole, the second Korean-born Burke, was hospitalized early for a heart problem. As Christine and Tim waited at the hospital for some tests to be run for open-heart surgery she was to have the next day, he received a phone call. "I knew something was unusual that the Expos would be calling me at the hospital. Sure enough, they were telling me that I was traded to the New York Mets." Nicole's surgery was a success, and soon Daddy and family were packing for New York.

That a team with championship aspirations like the New York Mets would want to add Tim Burke to their bullpen is no surprise. He had followed his strong rookie season at Montreal with several seasons of stellar performances and low ERAs, proving his value as a big-game pitcher. There's a good reason for that success, and Burke calls it his "mental toughness."

"When I go out there, I really believe that I'm going to get that hitter out. And I don't give up. I think that's a trait that is really necessary. When a pitcher goes out there without confidence, he's basically defeated already. So I've got a lot of confidence."

But apparently not a lot of cockiness. In an age of prima donna baseball players who have often earned such labels as the "Boors of Summer" as *Philadelphia Inquirer* writer Glen Macnow called them, Burke is a breed apart. He doesn't even take personal credit for his confidence and courage in the face of late-inning pressure.

Speaking of the source of his confidence, he explains, "I think it stems from when I became a Christian. I know that the Lord has given me this ability, and I've got to do the best I can with it. That's what He expects of me. So the confidence stems from that because I know that as long as I do my best, things will take care of themselves. I'm going to be in the game as long as I'm good enough, and so I do the best with what the Lord has given me. Until it's not good enough, then I'll just keep going out there and having fun and playing hard."

That refreshing attitude carries over into other areas of Tim Burke's life as well. In real life, as in baseball, he does his best for reasons that could restore a lot of people's confidence in today's athlete as role model. "I try not to get wrapped up in everything that is going on around me, because a lot of it is out of my control. I just try to live my life on a basis that is consistent with Scripture.

"I hope that what little influence I can have will be good. It would be great to influence people for the Lord, but I also know that I can't change a lot about the world and the direction it is going. But I do know that because I'm a big league baseball player, there's an awful lot of people watching me each and every day."

One of the ways Tim Burke works hard to be a positive role model is in the care and concern he has for his family. But he also knows that without the help of Someone very important to him, he would not have this family to love and cherish. That's why he says, "My relationship with the Lord is definitely the most important thing, because that kind of carries over into all aspects of my life. If I'm not right with the Lord, then things aren't going to go right in my relationship with Christine or my kids. I'm just not going to be happy or peaceful. And if I'm not peaceful, that messes up everything. After that, it's my relationship with Christine, and then to my children that is most important."

And, as if to underline his love for his wife and family, he reveals that although pitching to Will Clark and Darryl Strawberry might be a challenge, "I think the toughest job is being the wife of a baseball player. She's got to be mom and dad for a week or two while I'm gone.

"The kids really miss me a lot, and so when I'm gone, it really messes the kids up. They sense that instability when I'm gone. In 1991, toward the end of the year, I got my first chance to talk to them on the phone, and Stephanie told me she wanted me to come home right now! There was nothing I could do. I was out on the road playing ball, and she really needs me at home. So do the others. It is really difficult."

But oh, the rewards! After the 1992 season, the Burkes began the process for adopting a fourth child, a boy from Vietnam.

"It's been really neat. Adopting these kids has really taught me a lot about the Lord and His love for us. I just look at these children and I don't see them as Korean or Guatemalan, I just see them as my kids.

"Christine and I love our family so much. We have fun together. We go out to parks. We read books. We have a good time wherever we are. We just like being together. It's my favorite thing to do."

There's an added dimension that Tim has discovered in his short career as a father. "The love I have for them is nothing compared to the love the Lord has for me—and for everybody. So I think that's pretty exciting. Once I realized how much I love my children and realized that that didn't hold a candle to the love the Lord has for me, I was amazed."

When you look back over the past 10 years of Tim Burke's life, you see things that might not seem so important in the realm of athletics. Babies. Trades. Open-heart surgery. International flights. Bible studies. All-Star games. It is a strange intermingling of events for most people, but for the Burkes it is becoming standard as they mix the lives of their children with their lives as baseball people. An international baseball star—having played for teams in both the U.S. and Canada—has an international family.

It seems fitting that Tim Burke once said to his wife, "I want a child from every country," only to have her calmly correct him with, "Every continent, honey."

Q & A WITH TIM BURKE

Q: *How do you share your faith with others?*
Tim: I share my faith whenever the opportunity comes up. I'm not an evangelist, I'm a ballplayer, but when the opportunity comes up I'll talk about the Lord. I need to be sensitive to other people. I have fun talking to groups about the Lord. It is exciting, because I know the power of the Lord and what He has done in my life. I'm like anybody else in this world. I'm just a normal person who had a lot of problems and still has problems, but now I've got the Lord to help me through them. I know I'm going to heaven. A lot of people can't say that, and I'd just like to be used however the Lord wants to use me.

Q: *Do most players share your belief that major leaguers should be good role models?*
Tim: For the most part, players are thoughtful enough to try to conduct themselves properly. Sure there are exceptions, but there are exceptions in every walk of life. There are a lot of good role

models in baseball. You just don't hear about them. You just hear about the bad ones.

Q: *What was one of the funniest incidents in your career?*
Tim: During my rookie year when I was pitching in Montreal, we were playing San Francisco, and there weren't very many people in the stands. Fortunately, the game wasn't being broadcast back to San Francisco. I was warming up to go into the game. Right before I went out, my zipper broke. You know, our pants are tight in baseball. So I just had to run out on the field with an open zipper. I went through the whole inning pitching, but every time I wasn't in my windup that glove was right there. I made a quick inning out of it. Maybe that's the key. Maybe I should go out there with a broken zipper.

Q: *What is it like pitching to the big guys like Will Clark and Darryl Strawberry?*
Tim: I'm probably a little more careful to them. They're going to hit your mistakes more often than the average player. So I think it makes me a little more careful.

It also makes it more fun. It's fun to face them. I feel confident that I'm going to get them out, but I don't get them out all the time. It's not intimidating, because it's what I do for a living. You don't think about it when you're out there. You might think about it afterward. But it's fun to face the best in the game. It's a great challenge. When you get them out, it feels really good. But when they get you, it's another humbling experience in the game of baseball.

Q: *What do you think about the escalating salaries in sports?*
Tim: I think that for whatever reason, the players are made out to be the bad guys because we are making so much money. . . . But nobody is going to sit there and turn down money. Baseball is a very successful business. These people [the owners] are very successful in business, so they're not throwing around money that they don't have. It's just the way the game is. . . .

I do have a problem with a Christian athlete renegotiating [his contract]. I think that when a player enters into an agreement with a team, he should stick to the contract. The Bible calls on us to stick to our contracts. You play for what you agree to play for. You're getting paid to play the best you can; that's what the contract calls for. All of a sudden, you go out there and have a great year. Your market value goes up. So you renegotiate. I have a problem with that. You don't see any players negotiating when they have a bad year and their market value goes down.

Q: *What is the worst thing that ever happened to you?*
Tim: What has happened, whether good, bad, or indifferent, it serves a purpose. Especially the hard times. It really strengthens me. I can learn a lot from difficult situations.

The most difficult of all circumstances was when Christine and I went through Nicole's open-heart surgery. I got traded the day before the surgery. Just the stress of the surgery, and then I had to leave right after the surgery and be away from my family for one month. Nicole had a really tough time recovering from that surgery. She had a lot of ups and downs.

That was the most difficult time in my life, yet I learned a lot; I grew a lot as a person. I learned to really trust the Lord a lot more. Those are priceless things.

Q: *What is your favorite Bible verse?*
Tim: 1 Peter 5:7: "Cast all your anxieties on Him, for He cares for you."

MAJOR LEAGUE CAREER PATH

June 3, 1980:	Selected by the Pittsburgh Pirates in 2d round of free-agent draft
December 22, 1982:	Traded with John Holland, Jose Rivera, and Don Aubin to Yankees for Lee Mazilli
December 19, 1983:	Traded to Expos for Pat Rooney
July 15, 1991:	Traded to Mets for Ron Darling and Mike Thomas
June 9, 1992:	Traded to Yankees for Lee Guetterman

Year	Team	G	IP	W	L	H	SO	BB	ERA
1981	Alexandria	23	149	8	10	139	111	48	3.44
1982	Buffalo	25	144	7	10	162	93	57	5.19
1983	Columbus	4	12	1	0	15	6	8	6.75
1983	Nashville	20	129	12	4	124	64	37	3.21
1984	Indianpolis	35	180	11	8	192	108	61	3.49
1985	Expos	78	120	9	4	86	87	44	2.39
1986	Expos	68	101	9	7	103	82	46	2.93
1987	Expos	55	91	7	0	64	58	17	1.19
1988	Expos	61	82	3	5	84	42	25	3.40
1989	Expos	68	85	9	3	68	54	22	2.55
1990	Expos	58	75	3	3	71	47	21	2.52
1991	Expos/Mets	72	102	6	7	96	59	26	3.36
1992	Mets/Yankees	23	27	2	2	26	8	15	3.25
Major League Career (8 years)		**483**	**683**	**48**	**31**	**598**	**437**	**216**	**2.70**

Brett Butler
Big Return on a Small Investment

VITAL STATISTICS

Born June 15, 1957, in Los Angeles, California
5 feet 10, 160 pounds
Current Team: Los Angeles Dodgers
Position: Center Field
Attended Arizona State University
Graduated from Southeastern Oklahoma State University (B.S. in
    education)

CAREER HIGHLIGHTS

- Led National League in triples in 1983 with 13; was fourth in 1992 with 11; led American League in 1986 with 14
- Named to National League All-Star team one time
- Led American League outfielders in fielding percentage in 1985 with a .998 mark
- Led National League in runs scored in 1988 (109) and 1991 (112)
- Tied for National League lead in hits in 1990 (192)

WARMING UP

Brett Butler's arrival at the baseball mountaintop was not the joyous experience he had always envisioned. The Braves were receiving the first returns on their small investment, but Butler found that his athletic prowess did not guarantee personal satisfaction and happiness.

"After all the excitement was over," Butler recalls, "I went back to my room, and do you know what I did? I cried. To tell you the truth, I felt terribly empty inside."

Brett Butler

A dollar a run. Although they didn't know it at the time, that's the investment cost the Atlanta Braves put up in 1979 to sign Brett Butler. The return on their major league investment has made the All-Star outfielder one of the best bargains in draft history.

Braves' scout Bobby Mavis did a favor for a college coach friend that spring of 1979, agreeing to draft Butler in the 23d round and pay him $1,000 to sign on as a minor leaguer. With more than 1,000 runs scored in his major league career, Butler has made the investment look pretty solid. Imagine how many strikeouts Yankee pitcher Brien Taylor ($1.5 million signing bonus) will have to rack up to match that kind of return!

But Brett Butler was no superstar phenom who came roaring out of high school ready to take on the best pitching in the National League. He was, he says, "a lot less than average" player. "I think the reason why," he explains, "was because I was so little." His lack of size haunted him all the way through his amateur career.

When the family moved to Illinois when Brett was a teenager, Butler played on the Libertyville High School team, but still didn't give anybody the impression that he would one day be playing down the road at Chicago's Wrigley Field. "I sat on the bench as a junior and kept score. Then I played sparingly as a senior."

Yet there was something that kept driving Brett Butler along. It was something his dad told him. "Son," his dad had said, "if you don't believe in yourself, no one else will." For a small kid who loved baseball and wanted a chance to grow into it, those words gave him hope. With his dad's encouragement in mind and his own determination intact, Butler set off to Arizona State after high school, believing that it was "the best school in the nation to play ball."

He was one of 200 walk-ons who showed up on the baseball field in Tempe to try out for a spot on the Sun Devils' team. The problem was, there were only eight uniforms to be given out. Brett Butler finally got one—for the junior varsity team. He drew scant attention from the ASU coaching staff. After Butler was firmly entrenched in the majors, his college coach Jim Brock heard that this Brett Butler fellow was claiming that he went to Arizona State. His response was, "He never went to this school. If he did, I would have known he was here." Only when former Sun Devil player Chris Bando told him, "Hey, Coach, he was here a full year," did Brock believe it.

Perhaps the reason Brock forgot was because Butler didn't hang around for a second year at ASU. After his year of J.V. ball, he changed directions. He joined a semipro traveling team in Zion, Illinois, a small town near the Wisconsin border. Eventually someone in the league said he could get Butler a baseball scholarship to Southeastern Oklahoma State.

Butler responded by asking "Where?!" Born in Los Angeles and reared in Chicago, "I was a city boy, and he was wanting me to go down to Podunk, USA." Actually the school is in Durant, Oklahoma, but it is nothing like the City of Angels or the Windy City.

"I went down there believing that God directed me, and I was there for three years." Just as NBA star Dennis Rodman would find out a few years later, Southeastern Oklahoma State was just the ticket. While there, Butler came into his own. He was a two-time All-American, and he earned a 23d round draft pick from the Braves.

The S. E. Oklahoma State coach had known Braves' scout Bob Mavis for years and told him about Brett. "Bobby, this is one of the best players I've ever had," the coach said. "Would you just draft him for me?" Despite the All-American status, there was still some hesitation, for as Butler says, "I was still little then."

Yet he put some big stats on the boards as a pro. In his first four years of minor league play, Butler hit .316, .369, .298, and .366. But he was still playing Single A ball, and he needed to do something to show the Braves that their tiny investment in this rather small player would pay off big-time.

The chance to prove himself came in the Instructional League at the end of the 1980 season. He was hitting .400, and Braves manager Bobby Cox, owner Ted Turner, and Hank Aaron came calling. When Butler stroked 12 hits in four days, Cox invited him to the big league camp. Butler stayed through spring training, only to be the last player cut.

This time, though, they sent him to Atlanta's Triple A team, where he hit .335 and was named the league's MVP. That was enough to convince the Braves, and he joined the team after the strike of 1981. The next season he was sent down to the minors for a couple of months and then returned to the big leagues to stay.

So how did this "less than average" player make it big? His father's counsel, of course, spurred him to work hard and face the future with determination. But according to Butler, there's more. "First and foremost it was only by the grace of God that He could take a kid who couldn't start on his high school team and put him in the big leagues for all these years."

Butler remembers as a bench-warming high schooler coming face-to-face for the first time with the need for God in his life. He attended a conference of the Fellowship of Christian Athletes (FCA), coming to Fort Collins, Colorado, mainly "for the sports. I felt like I was brought up in a Christian home, so I thought I would fit in. Somebody asked me in one of the meetings, 'If you were to die tonight, would you go to heaven?' I wanted that assurance. So I got down on my knees by myself and asked Christ to come into my life."

That decision was real, and it has guided his life since, but his faith has not always directed his baseball career. He remembers, for instance, his reaction after his first game as a Braves' starter. Coming off his MVP year at Richmond, the man with the name that seemed perfect for the only deep South team in baseball was greeted in Atlanta with great expectations. On August 20, 1981, Brett Butler strode to the plate, wanting to be sure those expectations would not be gone with the wind.

The new kid came through in that first game by scoring a run and later knocking in the winning run. The investment had paid off. "There I was after the game surrounded by a throng of reporters all wanting to talk to me. I had made it to the top." Somehow, though, Brett Butler's arrival at the baseball mountaintop was not the joyous experience he had always envisioned. The Braves were receiving the first returns on their small investment, but Butler found that his athletic prowess did not guarantee personal satisfaction and happiness.

"After all the excitement was over," Butler recalls of that first game, "I went back to my room, and do you know what I did? I cried. To tell you the truth, I felt terribly empty inside. I thought baseball would make me happy. It didn't fulfill my deepest needs."

As he contemplated what had sidetracked his success express, Butler decided that it wasn't his destination that was wrong. It was that he had turned to the wrong guide for his journey.

"Years before, I had come to know God personally," he explains, referring to that FCA meeting in 1973. "But instead of following Him, I made baseball my god."

That revelation back in 1981 led to a resolution that has made the travels of Brett Butler take a little different course in the years that followed. He understood, as he says, that "baseball couldn't give my life ultimate meaning. Over the years, I've realized that only God can truly make life worth living."

He needed that hope in a special way two years later. After his best year with the Braves in 1983, in which he hit .281, scored 84 runs, and accumulated 154 hits, he was shuffled off to Cleveland. He looked forward to playing in Municipal Stadium, as the Indians were one of his favorite teams growing up. But Butler disliked how he had left the Braves. He was actually traded on August 28. On that late August day the Braves and Indians completed a deal that sent Len Barker to Atlanta. Butler was one of three players to be named later. So the remainder of the season he played for the Braves, unaware he was bound for Cleveland. On October 21 the deal was complete; Butler the Brave became Butler the Indian.

"It was hard. Atlanta was the first team I played on, and I had fallen in love with the city and the fans. I knew it was kind of a cover-up, because I knew if they told Brett Butler that he was traded, he would still go out there and play hard. Like I said, I think things happen to us for a reason. And now I see it as a blessing. It gave me a chance to establish myself as a player to go into Cleveland."

During the off-season, Butler was preparing for the move to Cleveland, when another change rocked him. One January night he talked with his father about the trade.

"You know, I never thought I'd see the day when you'd be playing in a Cleveland uniform," his dad joked. Sadly, Mr. Butler didn't.

"He died the next day of a heart attack. He was only 49 years old. He had been to the doctor that morning, and he said he was in perfect health, but he died that night. That was hard, and only by my faith in knowing that he was saved and that he was in heaven was I able to cope with that."

Years earlier in college, Brett had had a nightmare that his father had died. So when he returned home from school, he confronted his dad with a crucial question.

"Hey, Dad, I've got to ask you a question. If you were to die tonight would you go to heaven?" It was the same question Brett was asked the night he became a Christian.

His dad quoted Revelation 3:20: "Behold, I stand at the door, and knock; if any man hear my voice, and open the door, I will come in to him, and will sup with him, and he with me.' Then he added, "Son, I've done that, so don't worry about it. If I die, I'll be all right."

The sudden, devastating loss of his dad—a man who had so much to do with his continuing to pursue baseball as a career despite the odds—could have sidetracked Butler. Here he was going to a new team in a new league—and his mentor was gone. But Butler had the comfort of knowing that his father was better off now, so he was able to play through this setback.

He did more than just cope with the tragedy. He excelled in Cleveland. He put together a string of four excellent seasons. He helped the Indians gain a level of respect for the first time in years. And he averaged 166 hits, 26 doubles, and 11 triples a year while batting .288.

But in the middle of it all, Brett realized he was falling into the same trap that had snared him in 1981 when he became a starter for Atlanta. Now the winter of 1986, he had just won an arbitration case. As he played raquetball before the start of his third season with the Indians, the ball flew into his face, shattering his glasses and cutting his right eye. He was in the hospital for five days. In the hospital bed, with both eyes patched, he saw clearly.

"What was revealed to me there was that I loved baseball so much that I was making baseball my god instead of God. This was more or less a spanking. I had been giving God the game with a closed fist. It was revealed to me that night that I had to give God the game. So with an open hand I said, 'Lord, if you want me to do something else, I'll do it. If you want me to play the game, You can do it, because You made me.'

"The doctors gave me a 70 percent chance of getting my sight back in my right eye. Before the injury, the vision in my right eye was 20/20 with astigmatism. Three weeks before I went to spring training with the Indians, they did tests and the vision in my right eye was 20/15 and the astigmatism was gone. The doctors said it was kind of a quirk the way the ball hit my eye, and I said, 'Sure it was.'" Brett Butler knew a miracle when he saw it, especially now that he could see even better.

A few years later in his career, Butler witnessed another miracle, one that electrified the nation, reminding spectators of another dimension to a simple game—the dimension of faith.

Now a member of the San Francisco Giants, Butler and his teammates were chasing the 1989 National League pennant. Among the leaders was a pitcher who had been sidelined all season but was about to inspire and lead his team.

Dave Dravecky had suffered through a shoulder injury, the discovery of cancer, and surgery on his pitching arm, followed by a painful rehabilitation process. On August 10 Dravecky took the mound in a major league game for the first time in more than one year, ready to beat cancer. Dravecky warmed up in the bullpen with dozens of photographers trained on his every pitch. And when he came out of the dugout to take on the Cincinnati Reds, the crowd of 34,810 roared as they watched his incredible comeback. The scoreboard lit up with a huge WELCOME BACK DAVE sign; the atmosphere at Candlestick Park was electric.

Butler calls the day "one of my greatest thrills." He wasn't the hero, but a friend of his was, for Dravecky shut down the Reds on two hits through eight innings. And when Steve Bedrosian retired the Cincinnati batters in the ninth to preserve the Giants' win, Dravecky's astounding return to baseball was complete. And Brett Butler was there to wrap an arm around his brother in the Lord and share in the joy.

"Here's a man who they said would never pitch again," Butler marvels. "And he said, 'If God wants me to pitch, I'll pitch.' " And pitch he did.

The next week, in Montreal, Dravecky pitched again. But Dravecky's arm suddenly snapped as he whipped a pitch toward home plate. "The next week was one of my biggest hardships," Butler declares. The emotional ride for the Giants wasn't over, though, for Roger Craig's team also made it into the World Series that year. That, of course, was a huge thrill for Butler and all his teammates, but even that was tempered by events they couldn't control. "The earthquake put that in perspective," he says of the tremor that jolted Candlestick Park before game 3.

Perspective is something Butler tries to maintain in all areas of life, not just in baseball. There are many interests that vie for the attention of professional athletes, and he knows he has to be careful not to let the wrong ones influence him. "You have to put God first," he says. "If you try to please the people around you, you're in trouble. So try to live according to the things that would make God happy. That's first and foremost."

He knows that one of the things that makes God happy is letting others know about his faith. "I share my faith when the Spirit moves me to share my faith, and that's every day. You're to live by example and let your yes be yes and your no be no. Live as you talk," he explains. "The guys know my faith. But I'm not a judge. I'm one to be an encourager. I am a pawn for the kingdom of God, and what I try to do is encourage and give direction when asked, and try to live my life in a way so that they see it in me.

Maybe they'll come to me and ask, 'What's different?' or, "How can you help me with this problem?'"

One time that scenario unfolded for Butler and a photographer. "When I was a rookie in Atlanta, a photographer and I talked on the field, and we were kind of sharing some stuff. I explained the gospel to him. Maybe eight years later, the guy came up to me at the ballpark and said, 'You were influential in my life. I just wanted to let you know that I accepted Christ.' This was after a number of years when the seed was planted." Another small investment, with the characteristic big result.

Perhaps the biggest investment Brett Butler makes is in his family. And to make sure that investment matures properly and yields successful dividends, he and his wife, Eveline, base it on the same foundation he bases his life on. "To me, our faith is the cornerstone of our family," he says. "When my wife and I were married, we decided it takes three, not just two, to make a marriage work. And God is the third.

"We have four beautiful children. On January 5, 1992, our two oldest children asked Jesus Christ into their lives. We've tried to give them the gospel and let them make the decisions and try to live our lives accordingly. It's been the most important thing in life for Eveline and me. We are trying to instill that to our children."

When Butler joined the Dodgers in 1991, his job brought taunts to his two oldest, Abbi and Stephanie. The Butlers live in Georgia, so the girls' friends are Braves fans. "They were all pulling for the Braves and my kids, you know, their daddy plays for the Dodgers. There was a lot of bad-mouthing and making the children feel bad. When they come home and tell you, you just try to deal with it the best you can and let them know that we have to live as God wants us to. I told them, 'If those people bad-mouth you, you've still got to be nice and try to avoid the people who are really mean.' It does get to the family."

The life of a major leaguer takes a toll on his family. "It takes a special woman to be married to a ballplayer, to raise four kids. For us the answer is to have a loving family that stays together, encouraging each other. The most important thing in my life, other than my relationship with God, is my family and my friends. Baseball comes third."

For a guy who likes to come in first, that's quite a statement, for Brett Butler is one baseball star who didn't grow up knowing that he was the best player in town. He had to work and claw his way up each step of the ladder. He had to overcome a small stature. He had to prove and reprove himself. And he had to battle his way through the war that is minor league baseball without the benefit of being a high draft pick or a huge investment on the part of his team.

But one thing will always be true of Brett Butler. He is a man with a big heart, a bigger faith, and one of the biggest returns on a small investment any baseball team ever made.

Q & A WITH BRETT BUTLER

Q: *How do you want people to remember you?*
Brett: I want to be a positive influence for the kingdom of God. And when I leave this game, obviously the game has been good to me, and hopefully Brett Butler will have been good for the game. I want people to remember me as someone who gave 100 percent every day.

Q: *What would have happened to Brett Butler if he had not played major league baseball?*
Brett: I kind of wanted to act, so I might have ended up being an actor. Or I might have become a high school coach.

Q: *Who is the toughest pitcher you ever faced?*
Brett: John Candelaria. He hit me the first two times I faced him. From that point on I thought, "Get that guy out of here."

Q: *Do you have any responsibility to people who watch you?*
Brett: I think everybody is a role model, and you're either going to be a positive or a negative one. Being a Christian, I have to be a positive role model for the kingdom of God. Because of the pedestal we are put on, to whom much is given, much is required. It's my responsibility to be a positive role model for kids.

Q: *What about all the money baseball players get? How do you respond to that?*

Brett: Everything you have is from God. As the Scriptures tell us, you can't serve two masters. Brett Butler couldn't start on his high school team, and now he's in the big leagues, only by the grace of God. So, it's His money. He's just lent it to me, and it's my responsibility to do the right thing with it, and that's what I try to do.

Major League Career Path

June 5, 1979:   Selected by the Braves in 23d round
October 21, 1983:   Traded with Brook Jacoby and Rick Behenna
                      to the Indians for Len Barker
December 1, 1987:   Signed as a free agent with the Giants
December 14, 1990:   Signed as a free agent with the Dodgers

THE BUTLER FILE

Year	Team	G	AB	R	H	2B	3B	HR	RBI	Avg.
1979	Greenwood	35	117	26	37	2	4	1	11	.316
1979	Bradenton	30	111	36	41	7	5	3	20	.369
1980	Anderson	70	255	73	76	12	6	1	26	.298
1980	Durham	66	224	47	82	15	6	2	39	.366
1981	Richmond	125	466	93	156	19	4	3	36	.335
1981	Braves	40	126	17	32	2	3	0	4	.254
1982	Braves	89	240	35	52	2	0	0	7	.217
1982	Richmond	41	157	22	57	8	3	1	22	.363
1983	Braves	151	549	84	154	21	13	5	37	.281
1984	Indians	159	602	108	162	25	9	3	49	.269
1985	Indians	152	591	106	184	28	14	5	50	.311
1986	Indians	161	587	92	163	17	14	4	51	.278
1987	Indians	137	522	91	154	25	8	9	41	.295
1988	Giants	157	568	109	163	27	9	6	43	.287
1989	Giants	154	594	100	168	22	4	4	36	.283
1990	Giants	160	622	108	192	20	9	3	44	.309
1991	Dodgers	161	615	112	182	13	5	2	38	.296
1992	Dodgers	157	553	86	171	14	11	3	39	.309
Major League Career (12 years)		**1678**	**6169**	**1048**	**1777**	**216**	**99**	**44**	**439**	**.288**

Gary Carter
Still a Pretty Good Quarterback

VITAL STATISTICS

Born April 8, 1954, in Culver City, California
6 feet 2, 210 pounds
Current Team: Montreal Expos
Position: Catcher

CAREER HIGHLIGHTS

- Holds major league record for fewest passed balls in a season, 1978 (1)
- Holds National League records for most games, putouts, and chances accepted by a catcher lifetime
- Hit three home runs in one game on April 20, 1977, and on September 3, 1985
- Led National League in RBI in 1984 (106)
- In 1992 became only the third player to catch in more than 2,000 games (Bob Boone and Carlton Fisk were the first two)
- Named to All-Star team 11 times

WARMING UP

We may have watched Gary Carter quarterback the UCLA Bruins to their 1976 victory over the Ohio State Buckeyes in the Rose Bowl game. And we may have seen Gary Carter become a first-round draft pick in the NFL that year, as was the New York Jets' Richard Todd from Sugar Bowl champion Alabama. If not for that injury.

Now, as an All-Star catcher, Carter is still leading—still quarterbacking. He has achieved all his goals and is not afraid to harbor thoughts of baseball immortality. "I guess the ultimate now is to one day make it to the Hall of Fame."

Gary Carter

If it wasn't for an injury, Gary Carter may have never become one of the best catchers in baseball history. We may never have seen him blast two home runs in the 1981 All-Star game and be named the game's Most Valuable Player. We may have never seen him receive the award again in 1984, making him only the second player to do that (Steve Garvey was the first). We may never have seen him bang out two home runs and bat .276 as he helped the New York Mets win the 1986 World Series over the stunned Boston Red Sox.

Instead, we may have watched Gary Carter quarterback the UCLA Bruins to their 1976 victory over the Ohio State Buckeyes in the Rose Bowl game. And we may have seen Gary Carter become a first-round draft pick in the NFL that year, as was the New York Jets' Richard Todd from Sugar Bowl champion Alabama.

If not for that injury.

It was the fall of 1971, Gary Carter's senior year at Sunny Hills High School in Fullerton, California. Carter had already put together a high school career that would make any athlete jealous. He was captain of the baseball, basketball, and football teams his junior year, an honor he would also hold during his senior year. He had been named an All-American football player in his sophomore and junior years. Coach Pepper Rodgers of UCLA had inked

Carter's name to a letter of intent, and the high school phenom was looking forward to running the wishbone formation in front of 100,000 people at the Rose Bowl. The world of football was a wide open door for Gary Carter.

"Then I tore the ligaments in my right knee," Carter explains about the injury that would dash his Bruin dreams and send his future in a different direction. He missed his entire senior season on the gridiron and had to turn to his first love in sports—baseball—to fulfill his longtime goal of playing professional sports.

And although he would never again stand behind the center, take the snap, and lead his team as it marched downfield, he became the baseball equivalent of a quarterback as he directed pitchers and led teams such as the Expos, Mets, Giants, and Dodgers from his position behind the plate.

The knee injury that took UCLA out of the picture wasn't the greatest adversity that visited Gary Carter in his young life. As a 12-year-old Little Leaguer, he lost his mother, Inge, to luekemia.

When James and Inge Carter found out that she had just a few months to live, they did all they could to keep their children's lives normal. Despite her tremendous pain and the full knowledge that she was soon to die, Inge, age 37, mounted a courageous effort to let life go on. Even when she would go to the hospital for transfusions, Gary and his brother were not aware of the pain she was enduring.

On the day she checked into the hospital for the last time, the boys had no idea the end was so near. "Hurry back, I love you," Gary told his mom, not knowing those were his last words to her. His mother, "the warmest, most loving person in the world," died while he was playing baseball.

James Carter then devoted his life to his boys—getting up early to make their lunches and send them off to school, then coming right home from work to care for them. His dedication did not go unnoticed, and in 1985 he was named Father of the Year at the Little League World Series.

Inge Carter's death left an emptiness that Gary filled in the best way he knew how: through sports. "Sports became my outlet after she had passed. She died in 1966, and I spent about six straight years on just sports, sports, sports."

It wasn't a new interest for young Gary Carter, but it was a positive outlet for the energies of someone who had suffered such a loss and had legitimate questions about why God would take a person as good as his mother.

"I had a burning desire way back when, even in Little League," he recalls. "I wanted to be a professional athlete. I didn't know what it was going to be, but baseball was my big sport growing up." He made his way up through the usual ranks as a shortstop but ironically turned to catching, which could have been the roughest position for someone whose football career would end with a knee injury.

Though he missed his mother, his dad was there as a coach and teacher—not as an overbearing dad, but as a caring, enthusiastic father. And at age 18, bad knee and all, Gary Carter signed with the Montreal Expos. Instead of going through two-a-day workouts for Pepper Rodgers in Los Angeles, he began working out for Gene Mauch in West Palm Beach.

Going to spring training with players such as Tim Foli, Ken Singleton, Ron Hunt, and Bob Bailey was exciting, but equally exciting and life-changing was what he learned from his roommate, John Boccabella, another catcher. Boccabella introduced him to Jesus Christ. Carter had told Boccabella about losing his mom.

"He was the one who said that I should ask Christ into my life. I was looking for that peace that comes from knowing Him. So, on March 22, 1973, I asked Christ into my life."

Having settled the question of his relationship with God, Carter continued to shine in his quest to make it to the majors. Although he didn't make the big club that spring, by the time he was 20 years old, he was in Montreal, and by the next summer he had found a regular spot in the Expos' lineup, playing 92 games in the outfield and 66 behind the plate.

Equipped with an enthusiasm that is contagious and with those leadership qualities that all good quarterbacks possess, Carter was just the person the Expos needed as they tried to revive a team that had sunk to the bottom by 1976. Montreal won only 55 games that year.

In 1977, they added 20 more victories as Carter took over the duties as full-time catcher and the Expos picked up Tony Perez,

Warren Cromartie, Andre Dawson, Dave Cash, and a rather successful manager named Dick Williams. Carter blasted his way into stardom that year by hitting .284 with 31 home runs and 84 runs batted in.

With Carter behind the plate, the Expos kept improving until they finally reached the National League playoffs in 1981 against the Dodgers. On a cold day in late October, the Expos lost the chance to play in the World Series when Rick Monday's two-out home run in the ninth inning sent Carter and his teammates home empty-handed. Carter hit a remarkable .438 in the playoffs.

The Expos could do no better than third in the next three seasons, and in 1984 the Montreal organization, uneasy with the contract they had given their seven-time All-Star catcher, shipped Carter and his leadership skills off to the New York Mets.

In 1986 the Mets went wild, winning 108 games during the regular season, whipping the Houston Astros in the championship series, and edging past the Boston Red Sox 4 games to 3 in the World Series. As usual, leading the charge was Mr. Gung-Ho himself, Gary Carter. During the season he had pounded out 24 home runs and knocked in a team-leading 105 runs while guiding a pitching staff of Dwight Gooden, Ron Darling, Bob Ojeda, and Sid Fernandez. Perhaps it felt a little like being a quarterback directing a backfield of O. J. Simpson, Walter Payton, Jim Brown, and Barry Sanders all at once. And as usual, Gary Carter made the All-Star team.

One pivotal point of those playoffs with the Astros came in game 5. The Astros and Mets had staged hand to hand combat through 11 innings and the score was tied at 2-2, as was the series. Gary Carter was struggling. He was 1 for 17 in the series, and the pressure in the bottom of the 12th inning was intense. The Mets had put Wally Backman on second and Keith Hernandez on first, and now Carter strode to the plate.

Carter faced Astro pitcher Charlie Kerfeld, the adrenaline flowing. In a previous at-bat in the series, Carter had hit a ball back through the pitcher's mound and Kerfeld had snagged it. While Carter was legging his way toward first, Kerfeld had made a motion with the ball—as if he was waving it in Carter's face. Whether he did or didn't isn't absolutely clear, but Carter felt Kerfeld had tried to show him up.

And now they stood 60 feet 6 inches apart. Just as a good script would call for, the count went to 3 balls and 2 strikes. Carter fouled off the next two pitches.

Kerfeld fired pitch eight toward home and Carter drilled it back where it came from—but this time Kerfeld couldn't reach it. The ball bounded into the outfield as Backman motored around third and slid home with the winning run.

In the next game the Mets and the Astros tangled for 16 innings in Houston in what some people think was the one of the best baseball games ever played. When Jesse Orosco faced Kevin Bass in the bottom of the 16th inning with a one-run lead, Gary Carter told Orosco to throw all sliders. Carter's advice finally did the Astros in. On the sixth one, coming with the count full, Bass swung and missed. The Mets were in the World Series.

Gary Carter came alive at the plate in the showdown with the men from Fenway. He hit 2 home runs, knocked in 9 runs, and hit .276 as the Mets defeated the Red Sox. And he kept alive a fielding string that has followed him throughout his career. In 30 post-season games and 10 All-Star games, he has never made an error. High performance under pressure. The sign of a great quarterback, no matter what the sport.

In a career that has spanned three decades, Carter has also had his share of disappointments. One is the treatment he feels he received by the notoriously difficult New York press. "It hurts," he says, "hearing the negative things that come out in the papers." The 1989 season was especially hard because Carter suffered a knee injury and could not perform as he had before. So, unlike the situation in Montreal, when it was time to depart New York, Carter was relieved to be leaving town.

"When the Mets let me go at the end of the 1989 season," he explains, "I was in a situation where I tried to find a team that I could settle in upon again and kind of call home."

But that hasn't been easy. First, he signed with the Giants. "I felt I had a good year in San Francisco, and two days before the end of the season they told me they were not going to offer me a contract." Throughout the winter, he searched for a new place to hang signs and help the pitching staff.

"In 1991 I had to go to the Dodgers' spring training as a non-roster invitee and make the club. I ended up making the club, but I went through a kind of difficult season with the Dodgers."

Then for 1992, it was back to where it all started: Montreal. He felt that he had "found a home again with a team I played for for 10 years." For Carter, the shuffling from New York to San Francisco to Los Angeles and back to Montreal had been unsettling. As a player for 15 years and an All-Star for 11, he called the recent shuffle "the most difficult thing in my career." Yet he says the moves gave him a greater appreciation for the game.

He showed his appreciation to the faithful Montreal fans as the '92 season ended. In his final at bat in Montreal's Olympic Stadium, he smacked a game-winning RBI double. With one stroke, he broke up Cub pitcher Mike Morgan's one-hitter and shutout, and Montreal went on to win 1-0. Carter stood on second, raised his arms in victory, and exulted like the curly haired kid he's embodied the past 19 years. Morgan stepped off the mound and watched as the fans thundered a loud and long ovation. Three days earlier, Gary Carter had announced he was retiring at season's end.

"He's a first-class man, a fine catcher, with a nice wife and family," Morgan later told reporters. "He deserves his moment." For five minutes the fans continued their heartfelt standing ovation.

The game is not all there is for Gary Carter, though. Mike Morgan knew of his family, whom Gary calls "very loving and supportive. My wife, Sandy, is all of those qualities. She is a very strong Christian woman, and she has been tremendous. She is just as much a part of my successes as I have been, in the sense of what God has blessed me with. When you have a marriage, it takes the other person just as much to be involved, and she is definitely that."

A major part of Sandy's role as Gary Carter's wife, of course, has to do with keeping things going during the long stretches when he is away from the home, in Florida. "She tries to keep the family together. She comes up in July and spends a couple of weeks. She usually brings the family together in the early part of May and does a lot of traveling. She tries to take things in her hands to try to take care of things down in Florida."

Having to balance the always tough demands on any family with the extra burden of fame doesn't seem to have caused too much of a problem for the Carters' three children, daughters

Christy and Kimmy, and son D. J. Oh, there's the little matter of one of the kids—who will remain anonymous—who "feels that she can use that [fame] to her advantage." But for the most part, Carter feels, the added pressure of Dad's popularity is nothing to get all upset about.

"They do get a lot of kids that request my autograph," Carter mentions as one side effect of their situation, "and they bring that home. They are proud of their dad, but they don't get so caught up that they feel that I'm different from everyone else. I still think they look at me as just being Dad."

Another problem that can surface for major league dads is that they spend long stretches of time on the road with nothing much to do. For dads and husbands with less spiritual maturity than Gary Carter, this can be an invitation to trouble.

"It is very difficult at times," Carter says of the life of a major leaguer off the field. "There are a lot of temptations, and a lot of dangers. You just have to keep your focus on Christ and try and get into His Word as often as you can. When you keep turning to Him, He always seems to have the answers." Carter has enjoyed attending Bible studies with other players, and especially enjoyed the Christian camaraderie among the San Francisco ballplayers.

He has declared his Christian faith before churches and the general public. He has also spoken to youth in detention halls and at prisons, as well as at athletic conferences.

"I've had the opportunity on many occasions to share my testimony, and the wonderful thing about it is that you hear back—either at a conference or a banquet or through somebody writing to you through the mail—that they came to know Christ."

Another cause Carter has supported is the National Leukemia Society. In honor of his mother, and to try to help arrest this disease, he has served as the society's national sports chairperson in the past.

Still leading—still quarterbacking. It just seems natural for Gary Carter to apply to off-the-field activities the same drive that he has put into baseball for so long. Carter is not afraid to harbor thoughts of baseball immortality, as he remarks, "I've pretty much achieved all the goals or milestones that I ever thought I would achieve. And I guess the ultimate now is to hopefully one day make it to the Hall of Fame."

Whether Cooperstown opens its doors to Carter or not, he believes that he has at least earned the reputation of being "a conscientious, hard-nosed-type ballplayer who always went out on the field and gave 110 percent." It's an attitude that comes naturally from a player who feels that his secret to success "really is no secret. God has blessed me with the ability to play the wonderful game of baseball, and I just think it takes some hard work and dedication. I don't think it's really any secret. It's a matter of applying yourself and utilizing the skills and abilities that the Lord has blessed me with."

At a time when an NFL quarterback his age would have been retired for 10 seasons, Gary Carter is just now facing that inevitable change that comes to all pro athletes—even Nolan Ryan. The glory years are behind him as a player, but with a supportive family and a strong faith, the best just may still be ahead.

Q & A WITH GARY CARTER

Q: *If you could change one thing about baseball, what would it be?*
Gary: If I had the opportunity of changing anything, I think it should be the umpiring. If there was a change to evaluate their performances, I think their level should be based on their performance, almost like players. If they start going downhill and if their performance level is not good, they should be able to be sent to the minor leagues, just like a ballplayer is sent down. I think if anything, the umpires of today are protected by the union, so that cannot be done. It should be a situation where umpires would work just as hard on their performance level as players have to.

Q: *What do you think would have happened to Gary Carter if you had not played professional sports?*
Gary: I probably would have been a coach of some nature. I would have worked with youth. I don't know in what capacity, but I would have wanted to stay in athletics in one way or another.

Q: *Pro athletes are often viewed as role models. What do you think about that label?*

Gary: I feel a role model is very important. It gives the kids an opportunity to follow someone and look up to him and maybe direct themselves in the same capacity for the future for their lives, and I think it is important to take that responsibility because the kids of today are going to be the superstars of the future.

Q: *The money athletes make is very well known. What do you think of the salaries that players are making today?*
Gary: I think that's something that is in all of sports of today. I think that if you're an athlete, whether you're a Christian or a non-Christian, you've got to realize that your career is a short-lived one and you've got to make the most of it.

I think in today's market, where TV is so prominent, the biggest thing that has to be done is that you have to build some security for your family. And the kind of salary that you would be paid would be based on the principle of what other players may be making. That's how you set up what you think would be fair in regard to how much you should make.

If you're a Ryne Sandberg, who's earning $7 million a year, well, you're going to be spotlighted. It's a matter that you may not have a life, and what happens is that you end up giving up the privacy of your own life, and that's the toughest thing to have happen. . . . The biggest thing that you end up losing as a high-profile type superstar is your privacy. It's something that I've given up in my career.

MAJOR LEAGUE CAREER PATH

June 6, 1972:	Selected by Expos in 3d round of free-agent draft
December 10, 1984:	Traded to Mets for Hubie Brooks, Mike Fitzgerald, Herm Winningham, and Floyd Youmans
November 14, 1989:	Released
January 19, 1990:	Signed by Giants
November 5, 1990:	Granted free agency by Giants
Spring, 1991:	Signed by Dodgers
November 15, 1991:	Acquired by Expos from Dodgers through waiver claim

THE GARY CARTER FILE

Year	Team	G	AB	R	H	2B	3B	HR	RBI	Avg.
1972	Cocoa	18	71	6	17	3	0	2	9	.239
1972	West Palm Beach	20	50	9	16	2	2	0	5	.320
1973	Quebec City	130	439	65	111	16	1	15	68	.253
1973	Peninsula	8	25	2	7	2	0	0	1	.280
1974	Memphis	135	441	62	118	14	7	23	83	.268
1974	Expos	9	27	5	11	0	1	1	6	.407
1975	Expos	144	503	58	136	20	1	17	68	.270
1976	Expos	91	311	31	68	8	1	6	38	.219
1977	Expos	154	522	86	148	29	2	31	84	.284
1978	Expos	157	533	76	136	27	1	20	72	.255
1979	Expos	141	505	74	143	26	5	22	75	.283
1980	Expos	154	549	76	145	25	5	29	101	.264
1981	Expos	100	374	48	94	20	2	16	68	.251
1982	Expos	154	557	91	163	32	1	29	97	.293
1983	Expos	145	541	63	146	37	3	17	79	.270
1984	Expos	159	596	75	175	32	1	27	106	.294
1985	Mets	149	555	83	156	17	1	32	100	.281
1986	Mets	132	490	81	125	14	2	24	105	.255
1987	Mets	139	523	55	123	18	2	20	83	.235
1988	Mets	130	455	39	110	16	2	11	46	.242
1989	Mets	50	153	14	28	8	0	2	15	.183
1989	Tidewater	5	16	2	3	0	0	1	3	.188
1990	Giants	92	244	24	62	10	0	9	27	.254
1991	Dodgers	101	248	22	61	14	0	6	26	.246
1992	Expos	95	285	24	62	18	1	5	29	.218
Major League Career (19 years)		**2296**	**7971**	**1025**	**2092**	**371**	**31**	**324**	**1225**	**.262**

Joe Carter
Is That All There Is?

VITAL STATISTICS

Born on March 7, 1960, in Oklahoma City, Oklahoma
6 feet 3, 225 pounds
Current Team: Toronto Blue Jays
Position: Right Field
Attended Witchita State University in 1978 on a baseball scholarship

CAREER HIGHLIGHTS

- College Baseball Player of the Year in 1981
- Hit three home runs in one game on four different occasions (tied American League record)
- Named to All-Star team two times
- Knocked in more than 100 runs in four consecutive seasons, with 119 RBIs in 1992 (second highest in American League)

WARMING UP

As a sophomore quarterback Joe Carter led his high school team to the state finals in football. Although his basketball team was not picked to go anywhere, they surprised everyone by winning the coveted state championship. In one school year, the youngster who had dreamed of winning a state title was a two-time finalist.

But the gnawing emptiness he had felt after winning in football had begun inside. "Suddenly that old feeling hit again. A week after the tournament, the joy of winning the state championship was gone—just like before. I decided right then that there's got to be more to life than this." The thought was there, but nothing substantial was done to fill this void.

The question returned to his mind, *Is that all there is?*

Joe Carter

The only place Joe Carter wanted to go was to the state championship. He didn't like it when his parents insisted that he also go to church.

He grew up in a dedicated church-going family in Oklahoma City, and his parents pretty much decided that when Sunday morning rolled around, Joe Carter would be in church. It wasn't enough that his mom was on the steward board and that his dad was a deacon. Dad Carter also drove the church bus. Whether Joe wanted to go or not, the Carter family always had a way to get to church. And with a family that included 11 brothers and sisters, the Carters needed the bus just to get their clan to the house of the Lord.

"Some things in life you do because someone makes you do them—you have no understanding of why you are doing them," he says now, looking back on those days in the '60s and '70s. "Going to church was like that for me. It was like I had to go, and I did it mainly for Mom and Dad."

But his heart wasn't in it. His heart was in sports.

"My parents were trying to raise me right by making me go to church," he admits, "but I would rather have spent my Sundays at home watching the Dallas Cowboys play football. When I got a little older, that's exactly what I did. I put everything I had into sports, and that included Sundays."

It wasn't that he didn't hear the messages and the lessons that came from the pastor and his teachers before he gave up church for football, it was just that he never let them sink in. "I knew all about God and about His Son, Jesus Christ. But it wasn't in my heart."

Four things rated tops with Joe Carter. And despite his parents' sincere attempts, going to church was not one of them. Joe's Top Four Things To Do were play football, play basketball, play baseball, and run track.

"Nearly 24 hours a day sports, sports, sports was all I ever talked about," Joe explains, perhaps a little amazed when he recalls his one-track mind. "I can remember when I was growing up that the ultimate goal was to win a state championship in high school."

As a teen, Carter left the church thing behind and put his dreams in front of him, taking his exceptional talents to Millwood High School. There he began the pursuit of his goal to win the state championships in football and basketball.

It wasn't long before Carter was within striking distance of his dream. As a sophomore quarterback, Carter led his team to the state finals. It all sounds like pretty heady stuff for a 15-year-old, but instead of basking in the glory of such an achievement at a young age, Carter's reaction was a combination of sorrow and ambition. "Talk about disappointment!" he says, describing his teenage feelings after losing in the championship game. "It made me strive that much harder for something I wanted to achieve."

But Joe Carter didn't have to wait till next year. Although his basketball team was not picked to go anywhere, they surprised everyone by winning the coveted state championship. In one school year, the youngster who had dreamed of winning a state title was a two-time finalist.

He may have been young, but he was mature enough to begin putting things together about sports and life. He began to notice the reactions of people, and he was somewhat confused by what he saw. "When we lost in football, people talked about it for a long time. But when we won the state championship in basketball, it seemed like after a week it was forgotten.

"We had spent all this time trying to achieve something—you can't get any higher than winning the state championship—but after you win it, it's gone. It's like you never did it. All it is is a memory. It doesn't last." The kid who didn't want to sit in church and learn about eternal things was starting to see the relative insignificance of temporal things—things like trophies and championships and awards.

Yet this philosophizing was not about to kill his drive for more championships. When he was a junior, his basketball team lost in the state finals. In his senior year, Millwood High won its second state title in three years. Carter led the way for his team, scoring 11 points in the last two minutes of the game to spark a come-from-behind victory. Joe Carter was bowing out of his high school career in style.

"I was on cloud nine," he recalls.

But then the gnawing began inside. "Suddenly that old feeling hit again. A week after the tournament, the joy of winning the state championship was gone—just like before. I decided right then that there's got to be more to life than this." The thought was there, but nothing substantial was done to fill this void.

The question returned to his mind, *Is that all there is?*

Wichita State University was the next stop in Joe Carter's search for the holy grail of sports—more championships. Here Carter cut his sports involvement in half, concentrating on baseball and football.

In his second year as a Shocker, Carter met someone who had more of a single focus. It was Kevin Scott, his roommate and a member of the Shocker football team. Kevin didn't just play major college football; he was a football junkie. "All he talked about was football," Carter says, still marveling at the recollection. "I mean, every other word out of his mouth was football. It almost became an obsession."

At this time, Carter had dropped out of the football program to make sure he had enough time to get good grades and excel in baseball. But with Kevin as his roommate, the conversation never strayed far from the gridiron—the Wichita Shockers, the NCAA, and the pros.

One day, however, Kevin got hurt. As Carter recalls it, Kevin couldn't even pinpoint when he had suffered the back injury. "He didn't remember how he did it. He doesn't even remember getting hurt. But his back hurt, so he went in to get it examined. The doctors said that if he got one more hit on his back, he'd be paralyzed.

"So now here's a guy who thought about nothing but football, and he's got to give it up," Carter explains. Fortunately, Kevin Scott was able to turn his exuberance from football to something more lasting. Something that Joe Carter had all but ignored as a kid. Something that would finally solve Joe's struggle with the question, "Is that all there is?"

"When Kevin gave it up," Carter says, "he got involved at a church a lot of people in the dorm were going to—Zion Baptist Church. Kevin made a complete turnaround. He went from talking about football all the time to talking about the Lord all the time."

At first, Carter probably wished his buddy would have stuck with football. "I was his roommate, so I had to hear this everywhere I went," Carter recalls. "Personally, I was straddling the fence on the subject, but everywhere he went all he talked about was 'God this' and 'the Lord that' and 'Jesus this.' "

"After a while it became a nuisance. I found out what that line means, 'You can run, but you can't hide.' I would drive around town to get away from him, and I would see billboards that said, 'Jesus Loves You.' I knew that the Lord was definitely speaking to me."

What Carter's parents could not influence him to do as a child, Kevin Scott accomplished with his dedication to telling what Jesus Christ had done for him. Despite Carter's initial irritation with his religious roomie, the message came through clearly.

"It was the first time in my life I made the decision to trust Jesus Christ. Now that I was away from home, I could make the decision on my own and not because somebody else made me do it. For the first time in my life I felt in my heart exactly that love and peace that Kevin Scott was talking about. It gave me a whole different perspective on people and on life."

That unbridled desire to succeed is still there in Joe Carter, but his reshaped perspective has taught him that winning the championship is not all there is. Now he knows that as nice as winning those titles and awards is, life's greatest fulfillment is having a personal relationship with Christ. And because of that relationship, he has found a source of peace, no matter what comes his way. "You know that Satan's out there trying to win a war. So it gives me peace, especially in this game of baseball, to know that I have Jesus Christ in my heart.

"Let's say I hit three home runs in the last three games, and I'm looking good. Well, I get up to bat in the next game and I go hitless. Baseball has a way of humbling you. God gives me the peace to be able to compete in this type of situation."

And as Carter competes—first with the Cubs and Indians, then with the Padres and now the Toronto Blue Jays—he recognizes that thousands and sometimes millions of people are watching. People he can have an impact on. "One thing I like to do," he begins as he speaks of how he can affect the lives of others, "is to lead by example. Some people take Christianity and say, 'Ah, just another religion.' But the real question they want to know is, 'Are you living it?' A lot of people don't want to hear what you have to say—they want to see it in your life."

The best place to start in setting a good example for others, Carter says, is at home. For him, that includes his wife, Diana, whom he met at Witchita State, and their three children. "People can talk and say they are Christians and do this and do that, but nobody knows more than your wife—what you do at home, what you do behind closed doors. That's the real you."

Carter is such a family man that it got him in trouble when he was playing for Cleveland. He wanted his wife—and all the players' wives—to be able to travel with the team on road trips. He was surprised by the uproar this domestic request caused. He knew the kinds of trouble that players sometimes get into on the road, so he couldn't figure out why people would react strongly to a suggestion that would keep players from making big mistakes.

Not that Joe Carter claims to be perfect, for he knows there are other areas of his life he needs to keep working on. "I'll be the first to admit that there's a lot of things wrong with Joe Carter. I'm nowhere close to being the perfect person, and I never will be until Jesus comes back again to take [believers] out. Whenever I do make mistakes, though, I try to learn from them. Sometimes you learn, sometimes you don't, but you try to keep striving."

During Joe Carter's major league career, he has been one of those players who is often a victim of his own talent. Everybody knows how very skilled he is, so they always expect unbelievable things from him. It's almost as if people see what a great athlete he is, watch him play, and then say, "Is that all there is?" It's like wondering what's wrong with Michael Jordan when he scores only 25 points.

It happened in 1990, and Carter is still mystified by it. San Diego had picked Carter up in a trade with Cleveland after the 1989 season. All Carter did for the Padres during the 1990 season was hit 24 home runs and knock in 115 runs. To say thanks, San Diego sent him packing.

Despite the glamor and the high profile of baseball, certain baseball transactions can reduce even the greatest players to the level of a commodity. In Joe Carter's case, the deal sending him from San Diego to Toronto was one of those. Although he is not bitter about the transaction—after all, it sent him to a team that won the 1992 World Series—he was surprised.

"Going from San Diego to Toronto was definitely unexpected," Carter says. "There was nothing we could do to prepare for that. You know, [professional] baseball is very tricky. You can't understand it.

"Being traded from San Diego was probably one of the biggest shocks of my life. It was tough on me. It was tough on my wife. It was tough on everybody. We had bought a home in San Diego and had just settled down."

It's the sometimes forgotten human side of baseball. Forget for a moment that Joe Carter can hit a baseball better than most people alive. Think of him instead as Diana Carter's husband, a guy with a family. A guy who wants to have a place to call home. Like all of us, he wants a degree of continuity and normalcy.

He didn't mind being in a new city. He did mind not knowing he would be traded. After six years in Cleveland, he looked forward to a move, knowing one was likely. Now, however, there had been no warning, and mighty Joe Carter was reminded that ballplayers have no control of their future.

"A lot of people don't realize that baseball players' lives are not stable—as far as the little things, the ins and outs. Like finding a place to stay, trying to find a six-month lease, finding furniture, renting furniture. There are things most people don't really deal with that we deal with every six months."

Referring to the Padres to Blue Jays trade, he explains, "You go someplace where you think you're going to be for at least three years, you buy a house, you spend a whole year furnishing it, you get it all finished—and then you have to move out because somebody changes your plans. It was tough."

It's not for Joe Carter, though, that he is worried. "I know I'm not going to be playing baseball the rest of my life. Sometimes you make a few sacrifices. I think the wife and the kids make more sacrifices than I do because I'm playing the game."

While he is playing the game, Carter maintains a refreshing attitude about the ups and downs that have to come, even for a player who has been able to do the home run trot more than 200 times. It's a perspective that goes beyond helping a baseball player survive a bad day at the ballpark. It has application to everyone. "Let's say I go 0 for 4 or have a bad day or don't do what I'm supposed to do," Carter begins. "I feel kind of bad, and I'm disappointed that we didn't win the ballgame.

"But then I think about the fans. I read in the paper the other day about someone's mother who was hit in the crosswalk. She had a baby who was nine months old. That puts baseball in perspective. Baseball is just a game.

"That woman deserved life, but she can't go on. If I have a bad game, there is always tomorrow. I never lose hope in what I can do tomorrow. Baseball has never been a problem for me if I don't succeed one day, because I know the Lord has given me talent, and He's not going to bring me this far and then let me down.

"We all fall short, but I've got somebody who's willing to pick me up when the going gets tough. Jesus picks me up. I'm playing with the talent that God gave me. If I were not to play up to my ability, it would be an injustice to Him.

"One thing I always say when I talk to kids is that you're going to have trials and tribulations. You're going to be tested. The one thing that God always promised us is victory in the end. But He never promised us we would be ahead at halftime. We may be behind, but when the buzzer sounds, I guarantee we'll be ahead."

Now, after all these years, the sophomore quarterback who became a major league All-Star and who earned a World Series ring knows the answer to the question, "Is that all there is?" He knows the ultimate victory that goes to those who have put their faith in Jesus Christ. And that is all anybody will ever need.

Q & A WITH JOE CARTER

Q: *What do you think about being a role model?*
Joe: I think the role model should always be the parents. Because people just see us for what we do on the field (unless it is something bad, and then it's front page news). But they may never see anything that we do good. If you do something good, then it's always back in the last page, last column in fine print. If you do something bad, it's always on the front in the news story. "Joe Carter does this or does that."

I don't mind being a role model. Kids look up to you and everything. I guess I'm not always going to do everything right, but I'm going to present myself in public without embarrassing anyone—my team or my family or myself or the Lord. I uphold all those conditions and strive to be the best.

Q: *What is your favorite verse?*
Joe: The one verse that I feel says it all is John 3:16. "For God so loved the world that He gave his only begotten Son." When I look at that I look at my son and say, "Would I give my son today for him to die for the rest of the world to live?" I love my son, and it

would be hard to do, but God did that for us. That sums up His love all the way. We're sinners. We all fall short of His glory, yet He saw hope for us. I don't know where, but He saw hope for us. And He sent His Son to earth to die for us—for our sins.

You can't get any more powerful than that. If you sit there and think about the verse—not just say it but think about it—you will be amazed.

MAJOR LEAGUE CAREER PATH

June 8, 1981:   Drafted in first round by Chicago Cubs

June 13, 1984:   Traded with Mel Hall, Don Schulze, and Darryl Banks to the Indians Ron Hassey, Rick Sutcliffe, and George Frazier

December 6, 1989: Traded to the Padres for Sandy Alomar, Chris James, and Carlos Baerga

December 5, 1990: Traded with Roberto Alomar to the Blue Jays for Fred McGriff and Tony Fernandez

THE JOE CARTER FILE

Year	Team	G	AB	R	H	2B	3B	HR	RBI	Avg.
1981	Midland	67	249	42	67	15	3	5	35	.269
1982	Midland	110	427	84	136	22	8	25	98	.319
1983	Iowa	124	522	82	160	27	6	22	83	.307
1983	Cubs	23	51	6	9	1	0	0	1	.176
1984	Iowa	61	248	45	77	12	7	14	67	.310
1984	Indians	66	244	32	67	6	1	13	41	.275
1985	Indians	143	489	64	128	27	0	15	59	.262
1986	Indians	162	663	108	200	36	9	29	121	.302
1987	Indians	149	588	83	155	27	2	32	106	.264
1988	Indians	157	621	85	168	36	6	27	98	.271
1989	Indians	162	651	84	158	32	4	35	105	.243
1990	Padres	162	634	79	147	27	1	24	115	.232
1991	Blue Jays	162	638	89	174	42	3	33	108	.273
1992	Blue Jays	158	622	97	164	30	7	34	119	.264
Major League Career (10 years)		**1344**	**5201**	**727**	**1370**	**264**	**34**	**242**	**873**	**.263**

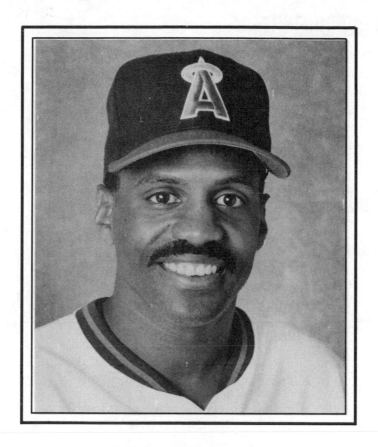

Alvin Davis
Anonymous Superstar

VITAL STATISTICS

Born on September 9, 1960, in Riverside, California
6 feet 1, 190 pounds
Current Team: California Angels/Kinetsu Buffaloes (Japanese Pacific League)
Position: First Base
Graduated from Arizona State University (B.S. degree in finance)

CAREER HIGHLIGHTS

- Rookie of the Year in American League, 1984
- Shares major league record for most putouts by a first baseman in a nine-inning game (22), May 28, 1988
- Shares major league record for most home runs in first two major league games (2), April 11 and 13, 1984
- Selected to American League All-Star team one time

WARMING UP

The numbers, the facts, and the statistics seem to suggest that Alvin Davis would be justified to be an unhappy player—another disgruntled, talented player who doesn't think anyone appreciates him.

But the facts don't add up to that conclusion. Despite the fact that his Sandberg-like statistics have failed to make Alvin Davis a household word, you can detect no hint of bitterness or jealousy from this quiet superstar. Instead you get an intelligent thoughtfulness born of a good education and a supportive mother.

Alvin Davis

Perhaps the best way to begin looking at Alvin Davis is by doing some simple arithmetic. The numbers have been adding up quite nicely for this power-hitting first baseman.

First, add up the numbers from Alvin Davis's eight-year stay in Seattle as the Mariners' first-sacker. Then pick up some numbers that belong to a second baseman who plays in Chicago. Figure out some key numbers for Ryne Sandberg after his first 10 years playing in front of the Wrigley Field faithful.

Alvin Davis averaged 20 home runs, 83 RBI, and batted .281. Ryne Sandberg averaged 20 home runs, 75 RBI, and batted .288.

So what happens in this tale of two cities? For Alvin Davis it was the worst of times as Ryne Sandberg was enjoying the best of times. While the ever-popular Ryno was inking his name to a contract that would pay him more than $7 million a year, Alvin Davis was taking his very similar stats and looking for a new team to play for. Just before spring training began in 1992, Davis signed a new contract to play for the California Angels.

An unusual season of low stats in 1991 after some outstanding years had made Davis expendable for the Mariners. For one season, the numbers were not in his favor, and he was gone. He took his superstar stats and smooth swing down the coast to Anaheim. Once in southern California, where greater media coverage would finally await, Davis seemed to promptly get lost again, agreeing to a contract in Japan with an unknown commodity called the Kinetsu Buffaloes. After batting only 104 times for the Angels, Davis went the way of Cecil Fielder and Bill Gullickson, two players who revitalized their games by playing professionally in Japan before coming back to the majors and establishing themselves as superstars.

Almost 5,000 miles away from home, Davis was playing for the Buffaloes, a team that also featured three former major leaguers. Other former standouts playing in Japan as Davis joined the Pacific League were Lloyd Moseby, R. J. Reynolds, and Jim Paciorek.

As Davis left for Japan, the Angels' vice president of operations, Dan O'Brien, said, "I've known Alvin for 10 years, and he is a consummate professional and outstanding family man. Both of these aspects played a part in his decision." Whether Alvin Davis can return á la Cecil Fielder is unknown, but the statistics suggests we have not seen the last of Alvin Davis.

His outstanding statistics through 1991 followed by the trade to the Angels and his flight to the Orient suggest that Alvin Davis would be an unhappy player—another disgruntled, talented player who doesn't think anyone appreciates him. But the facts—and Alvin's own words—don't add up to that conclusion. Although his Sandberg-like statistics have failed to make Alvin Davis a household word, you can detect no bitterness or jealousy from this quiet superstar. Instead you get an intelligent thoughtfulness born of a good education and a supportive mother.

Listening to Alvin Davis, you get the idea that if he were talking about a totally different kind of statistics, he would be just as comfortable and just as fluent. He has a degree in finance from Arizona State, and we can imagine him chatting about mortgage rates or the stock market with ease and skill. And making the numbers add up right.

After playing in only 206 minor league games, he joined the Seattle Mariners in 1984 and immediately began putting numbers on the board. In his first two games in the majors, he tied an American League record by hitting home runs in each game. "I can still remember my first major league home run," he says. "I can still see that ball leaving my bat."

But he wasn't done after those first two games. He went on to set a Mariner record by hitting safely in his first nine games with the team. By May 12 he already had 26 RBI and was batting .347. While playing in Yankee Stadium, a bad hop ground ball off the bat of Steve Kemp hit Davis in the nose, causing him to miss three games. He came back from that mishap to continue to post some impressive numbers—impressive enough to earn a spot on the All-Star team.

When the season was over, Alvin Davis had earned a spot among such players as Rod Carew, Carlton Fisk, Fred Lynn, Lou Whitaker, and Cal Ripken. His 27 home runs, 116 RBI, 34 doubles, .284 batting average, and .992 fielding average combined to add up to a Rookie of the Year Award for the Mariners' 24-year-old first baseman. He had piled up the most RBIs since Al Rosen knocked in the same number of runs in his rookie season of 1950. And he set a major league rookie record by receiving 16 intentional walks in his freshman year.

What makes Alvin Davis so successful, though, has less to do with numbers than it does to a couple of other factors. It is more related to things like mental and physical toughness and a strong, caring parent.

Davis believes his physical talents have been linked to a consistent discipline. "I think God-given ability is probably the foundation for anybody's success. Put that together with a lot of hard work, physically and mentally. You have to get out there and maintain your skills at a high level and also improve the skills you're not very good at. Make adjustments and bring up certain levels of your game. That's the physical aspect.

"There are obviously people in baseball who are more gifted than others. I think of people like Willie Mays and Hank Aaron, and of course the Babe Ruths, Ty Cobbs, and Ted Williamses. Those Hall of Fame people are gifted athletes; they are better than others. At the same time, we have examples of people like Pete Rose, who maybe was not the best athlete, but his mental attitude elevated him to a level of greatness."

Alvin Davis uses that illustration to underline the aspect of the game that he feels might be just as important as the physical. "With the mental aspect, you have to improve that as you get older. You have to learn different ways of doing things, better approaches. . . . You have to apply the things that you have learned. You have to adjust as the game changes around you.

"There's the chess aspect of baseball. Like when you're facing a pitcher, and he discovers a different way to get you out. You have to adjust in order to continue to be successful.

"A lot of success on this level is the mental factor. Everybody at the major league level has been given a unique set of skills from God. Everybody in the majors has a good work ethic—although some are better than others. The mental aspect is what contributes to a long, successful, consistent career on the major league level.

"It's the ability to adjust and track tendencies during a game. It's the confidence factor—the belief in yourself. Your mental outlook. I think a consistent mental approach can help to eliminate the physical ups and downs that you go through.

"You're not always feeling well. You're not always tracking the ball well. You're not always feeling your strongest. You might have a little pulled muscle or a sore hand that might limit your bat speed. But for the most part, if you can stay mentally on top of your game, it helps to even out the ups and downs physically."

If 1984 was an up year for Alvin Davis, 1986 was definitely a downer. It was a campaign that points out the significance of the mental side of the game of baseball. He lost his manager, Chuck Cottier, with whom he had a solid relationship. As a result, he also lost his mental edge. After 28 games in 1986 the team had only nine wins, and Cottier was released. He had been Davis's manager since the last part of the first baseman's rookie year with Seattle.

"Dick Williams came in and took our team and established a different approach from anything I have ever had," Davis says about the new man on the scene that year. "It was a lot of change. Some of the changes affected me. I spent a lot of time on the bench that year for disciplinary reasons. That was something I had never experienced before. I wanted out. I didn't want to go through and learn those lessons." The mental struggles were taking their toll, and it also had its effect on Davis's physical performance. After hitting 67 doubles in his first two years, he slugged only 18 in 1986. His .285 batting average dropped to .271. Even in the field, he showed the effects, picking up more errors that year than any other season in his career.

He learned some very difficult lessons. "I think in retrospect I'm glad I did," he says now. "I think you can make progress through success, but I don't think you can grow unless you experience adversity. The Bible is very clear about that. The Lord tells us that we will have adversity in our lives, first of all because Christ suffered, and our daily chore is to be more like Him, and second we suffer so we can grow. That is a part of what I went through that year, and what I have gone through at different stages of my career."

Davis survived such a year of turmoil through prayer and perseverance, though he admits it took him time to learn certain truths. "There are a lot of Scriptures in James that talk about trials and that we should pray to the Lord in trial. Other Scriptures tell us to run and not be weary. Just because it gets hot or things are happening that we don't like, we shouldn't quit trusting God.

"Scriptures are very specific about how difficult it will be to be a Christian. A lot of people miss that, and I think that's why Jesus was so specific when He told people to calculate the cost. It's not just what you give up, but what you will encounter along the way. He tells us specifically we will suffer, if for no other reason but for the cause of Christ. It took me a while to understand that."

That learning year of 1986 helps to explain why Alvin Davis can look at his marvelous stats and not be bitter that he hasn't garnered the acclaim and the fame of some less-talented players. His willingness to learn from adversity helps him to see the value of looking past the problem and finding a lesson in it.

Alvin Davis had some help developing such an outlook. And it came from a person who was a pretty good athlete—one of those people he was talking about who have both the physical skills and the mental intensity to make good things happen.

"The number one person who helped me along the way was my mother," Davis declares unabashedly. "And I mean baseball too. She was an athlete. She played softball as a teenager at a very competitive level, and she was very instrumental in my sticking with baseball.

"When I was 13 years old, I was playing Pony League, and I wasn't real happy with the situation we had on the team. We had a coach who I thought was playing favorites, and we had two players who really ran our team. They decided who played and who shouldn't. They ran our practice, and I was very upset with that. I wanted to quit. My mom told me, 'You can't quit. Just because circumstances are such that you don't like them, you can't quit. You stay until this thing is altered.'

"Lo and behold I ended up getting traded. I remember that so vividly. She just let me know that was it: You can't quit. That made such a lasting impression for me throughout my whole career."

And Ma Davis supported Alvin with her physical presence. She moved to Seattle to watch her son play during his final five years there. She lived close to the Davises, "like right around the corner," and came to most games.

A couple of coaches also made an impact on young Alvin Davis as he worked his way up the baseball ladder. The first was his high school coach at John North High School in Riverside, California, where Davis was a two-time all-league selection. "Rich Stalder was a person who laid the groundwork for the work ethic," Davis says of his high school mentor. "He taught me a lot about the physical and mental aspects of baseball. His purpose, as I know now, was to give me those fundamentals to help me be successful in life. He was very instrumental in laying a lot of brickwork to allow me to be successful—to know what it's like to put in a lot of extra work, and to do what it takes to be successful."

In college, Davis ran into a coach, Jim Brock of Arizona State University, who has shaped the careers of many players who are today in the major leagues. "Jim Brock helped me take things to a different level. I think it's important to be able to elevate your skills and your mental abilities to a different level in a situation of higher pressure. He gave me that opportunity and allowed me to have a position of leadership at Arizona State. He made me a captain when I was a junior. He encouraged me with my academics, which has helped me in my career." And most assuredly Jim Brock liked Alvin Davis, for the slugging Californian was named All-Pacific 10 three times and was voted a third team All-American his senior year.

His mother and his coaches. Influences that have shaped the career of a player who understands the combining forces of physical ability and mental acumen, and who knows the importance of not quitting—even when the best you can do is never good enough to please some people.

Major league owners and managers, for instance, often ask the question, "What have you done for me lately?" Management and fans often forget the good years and the big stats and concentrate on more recent failures. Davis thought he heard that question when his numbers slipped in 1986 and again in 1991. He calls it the "stress of having to perform." And it happens "more at the home ballpark than anyplace else," with media, fans, and even teammates accusing the slumping player of not trying.

And then there's the pressure of having a very public career yet wanting to preserve the very private side of life. For Davis, that includes his wife, Kim, and children Jordan, Kayla, and Justin. "When you get home, sometimes you're kind of real quiet, and you're not 100 percent there. That can bring a lot of pressure into your home. That will always be there. So it requires a special group of people in your children and your wife. Sometimes I'm only 98 percent there, but sometimes I'm not."

Davis realizes most families face that pressure, but a professional ballplayer doesn't want to take it onto the ball field. "If you're in the middle of one of those 1-for-38 slumps, you know that you've got to be better the next day, so there's that pressure to succeed." That puts a strain on the player and the family, and it is what Alvin Davis considers one of the high prices major league baseball players have to pay in their occupation.

Another is the separation from Kim and the kids. After a decade of professional baseball, Davis reveals the true, drab colors of a travel schedule that can look inviting to the uninitiated. "Road trips are not what people have glorified them to be, traveling to these great cities. After you've done that for four or five years, how many new restaurants can you find? It can be a grind.

"Now that I have three kids, and my wife's not able to come out on as many trips, there's also that family factor. There's a lot of loneliness. It seems for a ballplayer everything that happens in your family happens when you're on the road. The kids start to talk. They start to walk. It's not all it's cracked up to be. Road trips are a real challenge."

It goes beyond loneliness, especially for Christian players. "There are a lot of temptations on the road," Davis explains. "The biggest is that you have a lot of free time and not much responsibility. I think it is what men do with their free time that shows how deep their faith is or where their priorities are." For Davis the priorities include finding fellowship and studying the Bible.

"Fortunately the Lord has allowed me to meet many good Christian people on the road. I spend my time with them. You establish a pattern as a ballplayer and as a Christian what you will do with your time. I spend a lot of my time in my room or with my friends on the team or friends in the community or family in the community. That temptation to go out is what you have to stay away from. You have to spend a lot of time in the Word. It's an opportunity to spend time with the Lord."

It seems that the Lord has always been important to Davis. Unlike many players who came to faith while in the minor leagues or even in the majors, Davis began a relationship with the Lord as a youngster. As happened with his baseball career that was spurred on by his mom, so did his faith find encouragement at home.

"The foundation for my faith was really the church and the family—a combination of those two. The important thing was the example of leadership from a Christian standpoint that was set by my parents and the people in my church that I looked up to. I grew up in a Christian home, and I grew up in a very strong church. And I think it was a combination of being taught the Word and seeing it lived out in front of me by my parents that really showed me the proper relationship you should have with the Lord.

"If you as a young person attend church, you learn a lot of the basics that are important in building a deep relationship with the Lord. It's important that you know that God loves you. There are a lot of people walking around on the streets who don't know that. I think it's also important to know that there is a God. I mean to really know that He is there. Again, a lot of people are really confused about that. And those were two things that were established in my mind at a very early age."

As a baseball player and as a person, Alvin Davis wants to have a living, walking faith. One way he does that is by joining with some of his fellow major leaguers each fall at the Pro Athletes Outreach convention. While there, the players learn the fundamentals of telling other people about their faith, then they go out and do it. Davis tells about one of those times, when he talked to teenage convicts at a prison.

"We went to a unit for hard-core guys. It was interesting to sit down and see the facade come down. These guys realize that they are in trouble, and they don't have a whole lot of hope. They know that they are going to be incarcerated for a long time.

"It's kind of funny. When you come in, you can see that they have put up this facade. They have this image to project. But when they see that you're sincere, and that you really have something that can help them, that facade comes down and they get very interested. Then you have the opportunity to share with them."

Often, Davis says, the conversation has the desired effect, and the men express an interest in putting their faith in Jesus Christ. "It's exciting to see guys pray and to know that they've accepted the Lord."

Some of the men Davis is talking to know who he is, others don't. That no longer matters to Alvin Davis. After spending most of his years hidden away in Seattle, he knows how it feels to be somewhat anonymous. What matters to Davis is that when they do see him—on or off the field—they can see a man whose faith is genuine, a man who is concerned about living righteously, and a man who will not forget the people along the way who have helped, guided, and encouraged him. And that, in anybody's book, makes a person a superstar.

Q & A WITH ALVIN DAVIS

Q: *What is the best way for you to let others know about your faith?*
Alvin: As a Christian ballplayer, I'm always sharing my faith, every single minute of the day. I know through experience that guys are watching me, and they see how I'm handling every situation in life—success, failure, temptation. People are watching, because they want to see that your faith is real. Even if I fail, the resolution is the most important thing. None of us is perfect. Try as we might, with the Holy Spirit's help, to do exactly what God wants us to do, we are going to fall. I think a lot of times as Christians we can condemn ourselves. We will pray and ask the Lord's forgiveness, but we forget to go the second step, which is to go to the person we've offended and say, "I'm sorry." A lot of times that second step is more important than the first in the eyes of the people who are watching us.

Q: *How do you feel about things that you face that run contrary to Christian standards of morality?*
Alvin: When you're out on the road, there are a lot of things [done by the other players] that the moral guys on the team don't agree with. These are things that go on in the world. They are examples of what things would be like for any of us if we didn't know Christ. I don't look at it in a condemning manner. This is what people do who don't know Christ. That's not to say that everybody gets out on the road and goes wild. But there are a lot of temptations out there.

MAJOR LEAGUE CAREER PATH

June 7, 1982:   Selected by the Mariners in 6th round of free-agent draft
February 13, 1992: Signed by the Angels as a free agent

THE DAVIS FILE

Year	Team	G	AB	R	H	2B	3B	HR	RBI	Avg.
1982	Lynn	74	225	37	64	10	1	12	56	.284
1983	Chattanooga	131	422	87	125	24	3	18	83	.296
1884	Salt Lake	1	3	2	2	0	0	0	1	.667
1984	Mariners	152	567	80	161	34	3	27	116	.284
1985	Mariners	155	578	78	166	33	1	18	78	.287
1986	Mariners	135	479	66	130	18	1	18	72	.271
1987	Mariners	157	580	86	171	37	2	29	100	.295
1988	Mariners	140	478	67	141	24	1	18	69	.295
1989	Mariners	142	498	84	152	30	1	21	95	.305
1990	Mariners	140	494	63	140	21	0	17	68	.283
1991	Mariners	145	462	39	102	15	1	12	69	.221
1992	Angels	40	104	5	26	8	0	0	16	.250
Major League Career (9 years)		**1206**	**4240**	**568**	**1189**	**220**	**10**	**160**	**683**	**.280**

Greg Gagne
All Things Are Possible

VITAL STATISTICS

Born November 12, 1961, in Fall River, Massachusetts
5 feet 11, 172 pounds
Current Team: Minnesota Twins
Position: Shortstop

CAREER HIGHLIGHTS

- Shares major league record for most inside-the-park home runs in one game (2), hit on October 4, 1986
- Drove home the winning run in game seven of 1987 World Series
- Had three 4-hit games in 1989
- Holds Twins' record for consecutive errorless games by a shortstop, 76 (fielding 319 chances without a bobble), and second only to Cal Ripken (95 games) for American League record

WARMING UP

That Greg Gagne had the ability to one day be a World Series hero would not have been a surprise to his friends as he played baseball in Somerset, Massachusetts, during the early and mid '70s.

What may have been surprising to many who knew Greg Gagne during his early teenage years, though, was that it would be possible for him to be both alive and sober enough by 1991 to be a part of that thrilling and sometimes chilling Fall Classic.

Greg Gagne

I t is one of those shining moments that kids dream about but fear is not possible for them. Fifth inning of the first game of the 1991 World Series. The Twins and the Braves are jostling for position, each trying to get the initial edge over the other in this battle of two surprise teams in the annual war for baseball supremacy. Minnesota leads 1-0.

The Twins put two runners aboard. Up to the plate steps shortstop Greg Gagne as the hometown crowd waves their Homer Hankies in anticipation of a big inning.

Gagne is eager for a second chance after striking out during his first at bat. Charlie Leibrandt, the Braves' lefty, throws a soft change-up that catches Gagne off guard; he swings and misses the first pitch.

He steps out and reminds himself, *stay back on the next pitch. Just drive it through the hole.* Leibrandt leans in for the sign, winds, and fires a fast ball. Gagne turns on the pitch and rifles it over the fence. The Twins' infielder has given Minnesota a four-run lead, which would be all pitcher Jack Morris would need to defeat the visiting Braves 5-2. Greg Gagne had delivered the initial winning blow in what would become a World Series unmatched in drama, tension, and pure baseball fun. Later, Gagne would call the World Series home run "the biggest hit of my career."

That Greg Gagne had the ability to one day be a World Series hero would not have been a surprise to his friends as he played ball in Somerset, Massachusetts, during much of the '70s. They had seen the huge Gagne family—there were nine kids in all— compete and compete well. They knew that Mom and Dad Gagne were both fine athletes and that the Gagne gang loved to play ball, whether it was basketball, baseball, or football. The skill level was no mystery to Gagne-watchers.

What may have been surprising to many who knew Greg Gagne during his early teenage years, though, was that it would be possible for him to be both alive and sober enough by 1991 to be a part of that thrilling and sometimes chilling Fall Classic.

Back in the mid '70s, if the folks of Somerset, Massachusetts, would have awarded a Most Likely to Waste a Lot of Talent Award, a top candidate would have been Gregory Carpenter Gagne.

Although he was a fine athlete, his life everywhere else but the baseball diamond was miserable. When he was 11, a time when a young boy's thoughts are generally consumed with important things like learning to hit a curve ball and discovering that girls aren't aliens, he had to worry about his disintegrating family. When his parents decided to get a divorce, life began to fall apart for young Greg, too.

"That caused a lot of problems," he says about the breakup. "A lot of problems for me, because as a kid of 11 or 12, I was immature, and I really didn't care about anything—whether they loved me or cared about me. I didn't want anybody to tell me what to do. I was a free spirit, and no one was going to say anything to me.

"So I ended up having an attitude where I was just going to do my own thing. I took upon myself the freedom to do whatever I wanted to do, and that's when I got mixed up in drinking and drugs and skipping school and all that kind of stuff." He was living with his mother then and was perfecting the art of "getting away with a lot of things," as he puts it.

This life that he thought was so free and easy brought him nothing but trouble, however. He got kicked off the baseball team despite his obvious talent. And his drinking brought him to the brink of death, far before he was prepared to die—far before he could fulfill the hope of his potential.

"One time," he recalls, "I thought about committing suicide. I was just drinking myself to death. Taking Vodka and just downing it. . . . I was very fortunate that night. I remember my friend later telling me that I had flipped in the car, and that I threw up over everything. I could easily have choked on my own vomit."

Fortunately, Greg's father refused to give up on his 16-year-old son. Gagne tells how things began to change. "He brought me into his house and kind of opened up my eyes that somebody really cared about me and loved me. I also had a high school baseball coach and a football coach who saw that I had talent. They said, 'Hey, you've got a talent to play baseball. What are you going to do about it?' They didn't want to see that talent go away, and that gave me a little confidence in myself that I could play baseball, football, in college or on a professional level. So things started to change.

"It was a real testing period for me," he says about his high school days. "It was a real tough time to go through."

With some help, Gagne made it through the testing. When he finally allowed his talent to come to the surface, it earned him All-State honors in both baseball and football. He signed a letter of intent to play baseball at Murray State University in Kentucky, but he also caught the eye of the New York Yankees. Club officials signed Gagne out of high school and sent him to their summer Class A affiliate in Paintsville, Kentucky.

Other changes were coming. Gagne's mom had urged him to do some reading during his free time during his first season in the minors, and one of the books she recommended was written by a noted preacher. Gagne read the book and "found it talking about this faith and this God I did not know. It said that with God, all things are possible. That kind of planted a seed in my life."

The seed lay dormant until the following summer when Gagne had moved up one rung of the baseball ladder. On one of those notorious minor league bus rides—the kind where bored players read, sleep, talk, play games, or stare out the window—he spotted three players in the front of the bus reading the Bible.

"I was just looking out the window, just spacing out, not really thinking about much, and those guys up there were talking about Jesus and the Bible and eternal life, and reading out of the Bible.

"I said to myself, 'I ain't doing nothing, I think I'll go up and talk to them.' I went up there and we just started talking. They were reading some verses out of the Bible that say everybody is a sinner. They were talking about eternal life and salvation and all these things I had never really heard about. So when they were talking about that, I could relate to it.

"I thought, *Yeah, that makes sense. I feel like I'm definitely a sinner. There's no doubt about that. I felt like, yeah, I want forgiveness, yeah, I want eternal life.* A light just went on inside of me. I thought, *This is real to me. This is truth. I want to do that.*"

That night when Gagne got home—on the road in Greensboro, North Carolina—he threw himself on the bed and cried. "I wept like I had never wept before. I confessed all my sins and asked Christ—this God that I really didn't even know—to come into my life. And He did. That's when I was born again. I let Jesus Christ into my life, and that's when my new life started. That's when things really changed for me."

As someone who nearly destroyed his life by living a destructive lifestyle as a teenager, Gagne knows the dangers that face today's young people. And he knows what can help them. Despite the fact that he was able to escape tragedy long before he became a Christian, he feels that the only real answer is Jesus Christ.

"I really didn't have Christ in my life at a young age. I knew a little about Christ, I went a little bit to church, went through catechism and first communion. So I knew a little bit about it. But it was a shock to hear the things my teammates said on that team bus, because I really didn't hear that as a kid.

"The most important thing for today's young people would be for them to look at Christ, look at His Word, and see what He says. I look at it as a road map to life, on how to live, how to treat people."

When Greg Gagne talks about a subject like substance abuse, people should listen. He's been through it. It almost killed him. Yet he takes a bit of a different approach from the one most popularly preached—the "education will solve everything" theory. He says that the message needs to go beyond educating the mind. It takes something more spiritual to change kids.

"On TV, the ads say stay away from drugs and drinking, but then what does a kid turn to? Sure, I believe we need to tell the kids to stay away from drugs and drinking, but we also need to tell them to turn to Jesus. That's the main thing that we need to look at.

"We need to look at Jesus and what Christ proclaimed and said in His Word, and to do that, and nothing else really matters. The answer is Jesus, it's not education. Even though education is good, they have to take . . . Jesus into their hearts . . . and then live a Christian life.

"When I was a kid growing up, I just didn't have Christ, so I didn't have any direction in my life. I mean, the direction I took was just drugs and drinking, to have a good time, to get along with my friends. I didn't listen to my family, which is something the Bible teaches we should do."

There is no doubt in Gagne's mind that faith is the answer to life's most difficult questions, but he also found out soon after his Greensboro experience that things don't always go smoothly for believers.

"As a newborn Christian, I felt different, like a new person. I was really high on Christ for that first week or two. Then the trials and tests came to my faith." He discovered the sobering truth that becoming a Christian does not prevent problems, nor does it keep anyone from getting things out of proportion—like the time he almost let hot weather destroy his baseball career.

He was playing Double A ball during a long, hot summer in Orlando. (The Yanks had traded him to the Twins.) The stifling heat had Gagne thinking he might as well hang up his glove. When his dad came down to Florida to watch, Greg was honest.

"Dad, it's too hot. I can't play down here."

"Well, what are you going to do, go home?" his father asked. "And what are you going to do back home?"

After thinking for a moment about the possibility of returning to civilian life, Gagne decided it wasn't so bad in Florida after all.

"Yeah, you're right," young Gagne admitted, and stayed the summer. In Orlando he set records in several categories, including most at bats, most home runs, and most RBIs by a shortstop, as well as most assists.

That season in the sun was the last tropical stop for Greg Gagne. He was off the next year to Toledo, where he spent parts of two seasons, before moving even farther north to Minnesota. There he became a mainstay in 1985.

"In the minor leagues your goal is to get to the big leagues, and once you get to the big leagues, then you've got to produce at the big league level with all the best players in America," Gagne says as he describes the dilemma a young player faces after he finally arrives in the majors. "One of the most difficult things is that you are playing with guys [a lot older.] I was 23 when I first came up."

Veterans, rookies, and the players in the middle of their careers—all were competing. No longer the everyday player, new rookie Gagne found the adjustment tough. One day in the lineup, the next day on the bench. Over time, though, Gagne adjusted, handling the pressure and soon becoming a regular starter.

Gagne knows how to handle the pressure, whether the bad times come—as they have done for Gagne in the form of hitless streaks like his 0-for-32 in June of 1991 and 0-for-30 in September of 1987—or the good times come—the two World Series and his chance to participate in the 1988 U.S.-Japan Baseball Summit.

"The Lord has blessed me," he says. "But He has helped me a lot through some hard times—times when I was not succeeding in the world's eyes. I just feel that if I can please my Father, and keep my eyes on God and what His Word says to do in this very visible area, then that's all I would ask. Then I can have peace and not really worry about things.

"God is in control," he says with confidence. "That's my perspective because there is a lot of pressure up here, and you can easily get discouraged and frustrated. I still do, but when my eyes are focused on God and His Word, I can overcome the discouraging times."

One of the times Gagne feels most discouraged is when he has to board the plane again and leave his family behind while he goes off to play baseball. It troubles him to be without his wife, Michelle (Mickey), and their two boys, Zachary and Lucas.

Michelle is, in a sense, Greg Gagne's childhood sweetheart. Yet just as Gagne spent a good portion of his teen years running from reality through substance abuse, he also spent those years without Michelle. "We dated a little bit in middle school," he explains, but the relationship cooled to nothing more than a friendship for several years. Their on-again, off-again romance got a bumpy second chance after Greg's first year of pro ball. He returned to Somerset to work at a restaurant washing dishes. In December he invited her to the restaurant's Christmas party. But he didn't have a car, so he had to ask Michelle to drive over and pick him up. "I felt bad, and I felt embarrassed. But we had a great time."

Not only did they find each other again, but they also discovered to their delight that they had both found the Lord. It wasn't long after that inauspicious, backwards date that Michelle and Greg decided to get married. "I felt that the Lord was leading me to marry her. She was a Christian, and we had the same values in life."

The two boys are the Gagnes' joy, and Greg misses them greatly when playing away from home. Sometimes Zachary and Lucas cry as Daddy leaves. "The toughest thing is being away from home for a long time. . . . It's also tough on my wife. I know, because she has to watch the kids during the day, so sometimes she needs to get a babysitter so she can go work out or just have some free time. It's a balancing act for her, and sometimes she just needs to get away. When I'm on the road, I have a job to do and I try to do that with the pressures I face. That's a little different from the pressure my wife has."

To maintain some semblance of normalcy for the family during those long stretches, he calls the family "to see how things are going."

Things went especially well for Gagne during a 76-game stretch in 1991 when he put together the second longest errorless streak in American League history for a shortstop. As the streak reached near-record proportions, though, it added a new pressure to Gagne's life—increased media exposure. And that added its own level of anxiety. "Some days you feel it more than others," he says about the pressure of such a streak. "Most of the time you try not to think about it, but the media is always there asking questions."

The key to error-free fielding is an alert mind that keeps the infielder anticipating, according to Gagne. The shortstop has to ask himself many questions: *Does this hitter pull the ball? Does our pitcher throw outside or inside? What base do I go with the ball? Will the runner be going? Who will cover second? Is it a bunt situation?* Mental alertness, then, is what every good fielder needs. Ironically, as the knowledge grew that he was approaching Cal Ripkin's record 95 games, a simple mental error cost Gagne his streak.

Here's how he describes the play. "The ball was a high hopper that I had to charge. I probably shouldn't have thrown the ball because I wasn't going to get the runner anyway. But I threw it, and it went past the first baseman."

The play ended a remarkable string of flawless efforts in the field for Gagne—another reason for young baseball fans to respect him as an important part of the Minnesota Twins' success.

And that is exactly what Gagne would like them to do. "I look at the younger kids, those are probably the ones who look up to us and really think something of us. I want to be a role model to the kids. To go out there and work hard. I can influence them more in the way I walk than in what I say."

One way Greg Gagne's "walk" caught the fans' attention has been through his major role in bringing to Minnesota the first World Series title the franchise has enjoyed in more than 60 years. Before the crew of Puckett, Gagne, Hrbek, Gladden, and company won the Series in 1987, the Washington Senators–Minnesota Twins organization hadn't captured the ultimate victory since the Senators defeated the New York Giants in 1924. In 1987, Gagne won the Charles O. Johnson award as the Most Improved Twin. He helped the Twins get into the World Series by hitting .278 against the Tigers in the playoffs with a couple of home runs and three doubles. And in 1991, he had that remarkable streak of 76 errorless games and posted the second best fielding percentage in the league among shortstops. As he has done his entire career, he worked hard, and he did everything he could to help the cause.

And then there he was in his second World Series, a seven-game war that he calls his biggest thrill in baseball, because the Twins were again victorious. "I think the second [World Series] was a little sweeter because the games were tighter." And, just maybe, because of that three-run homer that reminded the world and the people of Somerset, Massachusetts, that indeed with God nothing is impossible.

Q & A WITH GREG GAGNE

Q: *How have people tried to tease you about your faith and your new lifestyle?*
Greg: Someone once put a sign on my locker. It said, "Get drunk and be somebody." I had already done that and being on drugs and running away from home and skipping classes. I don't have to do those things because I know who I am in Christ Jesus, that I am a new man now.

Q: *As a single man, what were you looking for in someone to marry?*
Greg: I definitely wanted to marry a girl who had the same beliefs as I had, who was a Christian. The Bible says, "Be not unequally yoked." It meant to me having a Christian wife. I was taught in church to marry someone who had Jesus in her life. That was one of the number one priorities—finding a girl who had those qualities, someone I could share my life with.

Q: *What goals have you set for your baseball career?*
Greg: It's tough to really set goals. I just try to go out there and play hard day in and day out and if I feel like I did the best I can, I feel that's good enough for me. I really don't know how long I'm going to play this game; only God knows. So I just have to trust in Him and be thankful for today.

Q: *What do you think of the money situation in baseball today?*
Greg: I never thought I'd be making this much money. It's a business. The players see all that money, and they want a piece of the pie. Careers aren't that long, so they want to get as much money as they can. That's the nature of baseball right now. There's a lot of different feelings toward this, mostly that players make too much money. But we only play a short time. I don't think you can really blame the players for getting as much as they can, because they don't really know how long they are going to be in the game.

Q: *Would you approach the club to renegotiate your contract?*
Greg: I feel that if I signed a three-year contract, I signed a three-year contract, and I have to live up to it. That's basically it for me, but if they come to me and say, "We'd like to change that," then fine. I feel like when I sign something I've got to live with it.

MAJOR LEAGUE CAREER PATH

June 5, 1979:   Selected by the Yankees in the 5th round of free-agent draft

April 10, 1982: Traded to the Twins with Ron Davis and Paul Boris and cash for Roy Smalley

Year	Team	G	AB	R	H	2B	3B	HR	RBI	Avg.
1979	Paintsville	41	106	10	19	2	3	0	7	.179
1980	Greensboro	98	337	39	91	20	5	3	32	.270
1981	Greensboro	104	364	71	108	21	3	9	48	.297
1982	Fort Lauderdale	1	3	0	1	0	0	0	0	.333
1982	Orlando	136	504	73	117	23	5	11	57	.232
1983	Toledo	119	392	61	100	22	4	17	66	.255
1983	Twins	10	27	2	3	1	0	0	3	.111
1984	Toledo	70	236	31	66	7	2	9	27	.280
1984	Twins	2	1	0	0	0	0	0	0	.000
1985	Twins	114	293	37	66	15	3	2	23	.225
1986	Twins	156	472	63	118	22	6	12	54	.250
1987	Twins	137	437	68	116	28	7	10	40	.265
1988	Twins	149	461	70	109	20	6	14	48	.236
1989	Twins	149	460	69	125	29	7	9	48	.272
1990	Twins	138	388	38	91	22	3	7	38	.235
1991	Twins	139	408	52	108	23	3	8	42	.265
1992	Twins	146	439	53	108	23	0	7	39	.246
Major League Career (10 years)		1140	3386	452	844	183	35	69	335	.249

Brian Harper
Sacrifice at the Plate

VITAL STATISTICS

Born October 16, 1959, in Los Angeles, California
6 feet 2, 208 pounds
Current Team: Minnesota Twins
Position: Catcher

CAREER HIGHLIGHTS

- Second team Associated Press All-Star for 1991 season
- Batted .381 in 1991 World Series
- Hit .307 in 1992, ninth in the American League

WARMING UP

After the 1985 season, Brian Harper evaluated his talents and concluded the best position in the big leagues would be catcher, his position both as a youth and in the minor leagues. The on-again, off-again utility player began to pray. "Lord, if there is any way that I could get a chance to catch in the big leagues, please make it possible."

During spring training, a confident Harper approached the Cardinals' manager and asked for a chance to catch. Weeks later, he was released.

"I was totally shocked. I had a real good spring training, and I had never even thought about getting released. I finally realized that God was in control and that God could work things out for the good, so I had to take Him at His word."

Brian Harper

I t wasn't always easy for Brian Harper to sacrifice. Take the time, for instance, when his first manager in professional baseball called on him to lay one down to move a couple of runners over. The skipper was Larry Himes, a rookie manager who eventually made good as the Chicago Cubs' general manager.

Seventeen-year-old Brian Harper stepped to the plate with runners at first and second. His Idaho Falls team was up by a few runs. Harper looked down at Himes and saw something he had never seen before. Himes was flashing the bunt sign.

"I wiped across my chest," Harper recalls, indicating that he wanted his boss to repeat the sign. "He gave me the bunt sign again. I stepped out of the batter's box and thought, *I've never bunted in my life. How can he give me the bunt sign? This is ridiculous.* So I wiped again."

By now, Mr. Himes was not growing in his admiration for this kid from San Pedro, California. Not backing down, he flashed the bunt sign again, and this time Harper finally believed it. He stepped in and laid down a great bunt, moving the runners to second and third. But the incident wasn't over.

"As I went back to the dugout, I was just kind of laughing at myself, saying, 'Man, I can't believe it.'" Himes watched Harper and misread him. What had been Harper's disbelief that he could actually lay down a good sacrifice although he had never bunted before, Himes thought to be a bad attitude. Himes figured that Harper had laughed because he had been instructed not to hit.

"After the inning was over and I was putting on my catcher's gear, he came over, picked me up by my chest protector, and said, 'Who do you think you are? This isn't high school anymore. You think you're too good to bunt?' And he fined me $25. So I never questioned another sign after that."

Several times in his career, though, Brian Harper would question whether it was worth the trouble to hang around trying to get another shot at the majors. And each time he came to a crossroads of decision about giving it up or not, it always led to what Harper calls a time when "I sacrificed my career."

Brian Harper says that he has had two careers in baseball. The first took him from that initial rookie season in 1977 through a devastating release from the St. Louis Cardinals in 1988, and the second began with a chance given him by a minor league team and culminated in his highly successful tenure with the Minnesota Twins. Those two careers were separated by a winter of loading dock work in Chico, California.

What accounts for his turnaround and his eventual success with the Twins? "I really feel that the secret to my success lately has been that I surrendered my career to the Lord and have learned to trust in Him for all things. When I was young, baseball was so important to me that it was my god. But now I've learned to surrender my career to the Lord."

Surrender. Sacrifice. The words keep appearing.

It was in the early part of Harper's "first career" that he began to sense the importance of giving up his own dreams and ambitions to Someone who had a better view of things than he did. He was 20 years old, recently married to another young Christian, and playing Double A ball for the California Angels. Then he hurt his arm throwing to third base.

"I was playing 'burnout' with the third baseman. I was trying to throw the ball real hard and a bone popped in my elbow. I ended up having to go to the Angels' doctor. And he told me, 'It doesn't look like you'll be able to throw again, especially as good as you have before.'

"Basically, he was telling me that my career might be over. I was devastated. I was 20 years old, and I wasn't going to be able to play baseball anymore.

"I was moping around for a couple of weeks, feeling sorry for myself. And the thought popped into my head, *What's more important, God or baseball?* That was the first time I realized that if I was the greatest catcher who ever lived and made it to the Hall of Fame, but didn't serve God, then what good does it do? That was the first time I really put the Lord first in my life."

Obviously, the arm got better, and Harper continued his climb through the minor leagues until he reached the majors briefly in 1979 and then off-and-on in the '80s.

The dreams and ambitions of Brian Harper created in him a drive to succeed. Perhaps that's because he knew it would take extra effort and complete dedication to realize his goal of playing in the majors. He acknowledges he had limits even in his days playing sandlot baseball. "I wasn't a great athlete as far as strength or speed or anything like that. I made the All-Star teams, and was always one of the better kids on the team. But I wasn't a superstar."

To compensate for what might have stopped some youngsters from reaching that elusive goal of pro baseball, he followed some advice. "My dad told me when I was young, 'If you work hard enough at anything, anything is possible. If you work hard enough, you can be anything you want.'"

So young Brian went to work. He would swing the bat hundreds of times, do pushups, even spend five nights a week at the batting cage hitting baseballs. At one point he would sleep with his baseball bat during the season.

He devoured books about baseball and began doing the drills that he heard a major leaguer talk about. He loved squeezing handgrips. During football season, as he watched the Sunday NFL games on TV, he squeezed handgrips 10 times between every play.

And then there was the competition. As a teenager he played several leagues at a time: Mickey Mantle, Colt, American Legion, and Connie Mack. As a high school senior he had a strong year and was drafted in the fourth round by the California Angels.

"I was 17. I had a scholarship to go to Pepperdine but chose to sign a contract because that was my dream."

It looked like a dream career lay ahead for Brian Harper. Great skills. Good work ethic. The desire to succeed. Yet this is not a Dwight Gooden, success-at-teenage kind of story. No, the Brian Harper road to the majors, stardom, and World Series fame was one that had as many detours, dead ends, and roadblocks as a Chicago expressway in the summer.

In his first season in professional baseball—the year he was introduced to Larry Himes and the sacrifice bunt—he unpacked in Idaho Falls and met his new roommate, another recent high school graduate, Jeff Conners.

Conners, Harper noticed, had a strange habit. Every night after the team came home from the ballpark, he would open his Bible and read it. This was something new to Harper. "I kind of figured the Bible said, 'You can't do this and you can't do that. You can't have any fun.' I had never read the Bible."

So Harper asked his roomie why he read the Bible.

"He started telling me about John 3:16, how God sent His Son to die for us so that if we believed in Him, we'd have eternal life."

The words "eternal life" touched a hot button. As a high school senior Harper had been stunned when a good friend died in an auto accident. "When my friend was killed in a car accident, I really began thinking about what happens to you when you die —sort of a scary thing for a teenager. Here I was in high school wondering about what happens to you when you die.

"As soon as Jeff Conners said, 'Eternal life,' I said, 'Wait, wait. Tell me more about this.' So he shared the gospel with me.

"I told him, 'That's what I want.' I wanted eternal life, and I knew that what the Bible said was true, so I believed in Jesus Christ. I trusted Him as my Savior in July 1977."

So, Harper's career in baseball and his life as a Christian began at about the same time. And in both baseball and the Christian life, Harper would have ups and downs along the way.

In 1979, for instance, Harper was called up to the Angels, spent a month with the team, and played in only one game. That was a valley, but at age 19 he couldn't have expected more. Then came a mountaintop experience. In 1980, the year he first was willing to sacrifice his career for God, he also achieved a personal victory. He married his high school sweetheart, Christine.

Now there were two of them to travel the minor league circuit together. First to El Paso and then to Salt Lake City. On to the Big Show for occasional stops in Anaheim, Pittsburgh, St. Louis, Detroit, and Oakland. Here and there more farm team visits in Portland and Nashville and San Jose. Throw in the winter baseball excursions to Puerto Rico, the Dominican Republic, and Venezeula and you have an itinerary that looks more like it belongs to a traveling salesman than to a catcher.

The traveling show was wearying at times. There was nothing to suggest that Brian Harper would ever become more than a journeyman ballplayer. Still, there were bright spots:

- Leading the league in RBI with Quad Cities in 1978
- Stroking 37 doubles for El Paso in 1979
- 192 hits, 122 RBI, and a .350 average for Salt Lake City in 1981
- A World Series appearance with the Cardinals in 1985

But something kept stopping the major league clubs from letting him use his skills. Each time he made it to the Angels or Pirates or Cardinals, he was viewed as a utility player. He was a designated hitter and outfielder for the Angels. For Pittsburgh, mostly an outfielder. The boy who would be catcher had become the man who would play anywhere.

After the 1985 season, Harper evaluated his talents and concluded the best position in the big leagues would be catcher, his position both as a youth and in the minor leagues. The on-again, off-again utility player began to pray. "Lord, if there is any way that I could get a chance to catch in the big leagues, please make it possible."

During spring training, a confident Harper approached the Cardinals' manager and asked for a chance to catch. Weeks later, he was released.

"I was totally shocked. I had a real good spring training, and I had never even thought about getting released. I finally realized that God was in control and that God could work things out for the good, so I had to take Him at His word."

About three weeks later, the Detroit Tigers signed Harper and sent him to their American Association team in Nashville. They thought he should work on his catching. And Harper thought he might have found a home.

"The Detroit situation was a big faith-building process in my career," Harper explains. "I started catching in Triple A for Detroit. I had a really good year catching."

The next year in spring training Detroit had Harper on the roster as a catcher. But management soon asked him to return to Triple A for seasoning. With four years' experience in the big leagues, Harper had the right to say no. "I really strongly felt—my wife and I both did—that the Lord had something else for me. So I told them, 'No. I'm not going to Triple A—go ahead and give me my release.'" They did.

It looked like the end of the line. After 10 years in pro baseball and less than 400 major league at bats, the career seemed over. "No one would sign me." Harper sighs. "I could not get a job anywhere.

"For 40 days I was out of baseball. For 40 days I was out looking for someone to sign me. That was another big learning experience. I began to think, *You know, I can live without baseball.* I had been playing since I was 17. But I [realized I could] live without baseball."

For Brian Harper, it was another sacrifice. A good sacrifice. "I sacrificed my career on the altar again. I thought, *Hey . . . the Lord loves me. I have a great wife. I have great kids. I can make it without baseball—no problem.*"

As soon as Harper sacrificed his ambition he was ready for a phone call. The lowly San Jose Bees—an independent team that had a lot of guys who had been in trouble—called asking him to join their Single A club. He agreed, played there for one week, and then the Oakland A's signed him and sent him to their Triple A club.

But the long wait was not over yet. "This was probably the biggest time when I sacrificed my career. I was really struggling, and I just felt like maybe it was time to quit. Here I was 27 years old, and I was going backward and wasn't doing good in Triple A [at Tacoma]."

He sought God's guidance. He prayed for a sign. None appeared, but Brian felt certain God wanted him to continue. And Christine also felt that her husband must continue playing. So Harper prayed once more, fervently, but with peace: "OK, Lord, it's yours. I'm done putting baseball as such an important priority in my life. I'm going to work hard, but I'm going to put You as Lord of my baseball career."

He even began to make definite plans about what he should do if his career was indeed at an end, considering youth ministry and enrolling in some college courses. Still, Christine and Brian felt God wanted him to keep playing baseball.

The next year Harper signed with the Twins, "and from then it's just been nothing but blessings." Harper explains. "On May 28, 1988, I got called up to the big leagues in Minnesota as a catcher—not as a utility player, but as a catcher—and I caught my first game the next day with the Twins. I realized that the Lord had answered the prayer that I had prayed back in the winter of 1985. He got me to the big leagues as a catcher."

And what a catch Brian Harper has turned out to be for the Twins as a catcher. His batting averages of .295, .325, .294, .311, and .307 have opened a lot of eyes in major league baseball. "Where did this guy come from, and where have the Twins been hiding him?" people are asking.

The years of sacrifice and wondering and questioning—as well as the uniform switching and bus riding—have paid off for Brian Harper. But for Harper, the payoff has come in ways that far exceed what has happened on the field. He has been an impact player for God. As teammates ask him questions about his years in the minors and his relationship with God, the Twins' catcher has been able to talk about his faith.

Take Gary Wayne, for example, a young Twins pitcher who has been up and down with the Minnesota organization. Though Brian never discussed the Lord directly with him the whole year, Wayne watched his actions closely.

"He told me that he watched me all year, and he watched how I was with my kids and my wife. He watched how I treated other people, and at the end of that year, he decided that he wanted to be a Christian because of the way that I acted. I was really thankful, because sometimes we think it's because of what we say, but a lot of times, it's because of what we do."

And then there is the story of Brian and his roommate, Allan Anderson, who was also with Minnesota. Anderson became a Christian at the end of the 1990 season after three years as Brian's roommate. They had been best buddies, and Harper had talked often about the Lord. Eventually Anderson began to read the Bible and pray. Then one night in Anaheim, California, after playing the Angels, a tired Harper turned down an invitation from Anderson. He laughs as he recalls his reaction.

"I was really tired; I could hardly walk. And I just lay on my bed.

"Allan said he was going to go to Gary Gaetti and Greg Gagne's room, because they were going to talk to him about the Bible. And he asked, 'Do you want to come?' I told him I'd love to, but I was too tired. So here I was his roommate for three years, and he's going to talk about the Bible with some other guys.

"At about four in the morning, he comes in the room just singing and happy. He kind of woke me up, and he said, 'I just accepted the Lord. I'm born again,' Just like that. That was a great night."

In a sense, Harper sees this kind of activity as his mission, perhaps the reason his perseverance finally paid off in a successful career. "As pro athletes, we are role models for kids. Not only that, I am able to share my faith with guys who won't even go into a church. So, it's almost like professional athletes who are Christians are missionaries to pro athletes who would not go into a church."

But even missionaries run up against obstacles. And Harper knows that one of the biggest roadblocks any person in professional sports faces is temptation. "There are some definite temptations. There is a lot of sin right around you."

Harper, though, has a way to escape. "The way I look at it, sin is fun for a short time, but the destruction that it causes is not worth the short time of fun. I see what the guys are doing, and I say, 'You know what, going out and goofing around and getting drunk and doing the things that some of the guys do, it's not worth ruining my marriage and ruining my family and doing something that I would regret the rest of my life.' So I handle the pressures of the temptation by just realizing that's not where it's at.

"I enjoy waking up in the morning and having peace with God and knowing that I don't have anything to feel guilty about. And then coming home from a road trip just waiting to see my wife . . and . . . [my three] kids. I don't have to feel guilty."

When Brian Harper talks about his family, you can see why he doesn't want to jeopardize his relationship with them, and why he can't wait to see them.

"My family, besides my relationship with the Lord, is the most important thing in my life. If I don't succeed as a husband and a father, I'm a failure, because that's the most important thing we can do.

"I think that is a lot of the problem with kids today. They didn't have a good example as a father. We have a responsibility to be good examples. Not that we are perfect—only God can be, but we need to be good examples, good fathers."

Of course, that too requires a sacrifice, But for a man who has made several serious sacrifices in his career, he knows it's well worth it. He recognizes that as he gave up things for his family, his baseball career, and his God, that the Lord has honored those sacrifices and kept his dream alive.

Q & A WITH BRIAN HARPER

Q: *What was one of the funniest incidents in your career?*
Brian: When I was with St. Louis, basically my job was to warm up pitchers in the bullpen. We were in the pennant race, and it was late August or early September in St. Louis. Joaquin Andujar was pitching, and he would warm up 5 or 10 minutes before the game. That's all he would need. When he was warming up, there were already 20,000 or 30,000 people in the stands. As I was jogging down to the bullpen to warm him up, I heard a girl up in the stands call out, "Hi, Brian, how ya doing?"

Man, I must be looking pretty good, I kind of thought to myself. So I waved up at her in the stands, "Hi, how ya doing?" and as soon as I did that, I tripped on the Astroturf and fell right on my face. That was my most embarrassing moment. Pride comes before the fall.

Q: *How do you handle the highs and lows of major league baseball?*
Brian: I use Christian music to help me. I bring my cassette player to the ballpark, and if I have a bad game where I'm really feeling down, I'll just put in a worship tape that will remind me how great God is and how much He has done for me. The next thing I know, instead of feeling down, I'm feeling great because of what God has done for me. So I use Christian music as a big uplift for me in the down times.

No matter how bad the down times get in baseball, I can always think of the positive things. I have a God who has forgiven me of all my sins, He's given me eternal life freely. I have a wife who loves me, and kids who love me.

Q: *What problems has fame caused for you and your family?*
Brian: It's kind of hard on the kids. A lot of times they'll get friends just because their dad's a big league ballplayer.

It's really hard on my wife. To be a pro ballplayer's wife, I think the divorce rate is like 80 percent. The ballplayer is looked on as such a great guy, and he's looked up to. And the wife is kind of looked at like "Oh, that's Brian Harper's wife." Kind of second class.

I realize that the fame and all these things we have are only temporal. Except for a few guys, the Hall-of-Famers, once you're done playing, it goes. The only thing that is eternal is what you do for the Lord. Besides that, I'll be with my wife and my kids a lot longer than I'll be with baseball. So I have to check my priorities.

Q: *How do you view the big money major leaguers make?*
Brian: As a pro ballplayer, and as a Christian, I feel that it's my duty as a Christian to try and make as much money as I can. The Bible doesn't say money is the root of all evil; it says that the love of money is. The Bible says [we shouldn't] try to be rich, that shouldn't be a goal. The more money I make, the more generous I

can be with not only my giving of my tithes and offerings, but in helping people out. I feel like if I didn't try to make as much money as I can, I would be cheating. This is one way I can help the gospel, by giving money to God's work. We have tithed since the day we were married.

Q: *What's it like to face Nolan Ryan?*
Brian: Nolan Ryan can be very intimidating, and he knows it. So he tries to intimidate hitters by giving them a glare or kind of walking toward them while he's rubbing the ball up. It's really not as bad as you think. When you go up against a guy like Nolan, you say, *This guy has struck out 5,000 batters, so what do I have to lose if he strikes me out?* Well, he's got 5,000 other guys, so what's the big deal? It's almost a relaxing thing when you're facing such a good pitcher, because even if he makes you look bad, he's made others look just as bad.

Q: *What is your favorite Bible verse?*
Brian: Psalm 37:5. "Commit your way to the Lord; trust in Him and He will do this." I feel that's been the story of my career, where I've had to commit it to Him and just watch Him work things out. He's worked my career out better than I could ever imagine.

MAJOR LEAGUE CAREER PATH

June 7, 1977:	Selected by the Angels in 4th round
December 11, 1981:	Traded to Pirates for Tim Foli
December 24, 1984:	Traded to Cardinals with John Tudor for George Hendrick and Steve Barnard
April 1, 1986:	Released by the Cardinals
April 25: 1986:	Signed by the Tigers
March 23, 1987:	Released by the Tigers
May 3, 1987:	Signed by San Jose (minor league)
May 12, 1987:	Sold to the Athletics
October 12, 1987:	Released by the Athletics
January 4, 1988:	Signed by Portland (Twins' minor league team)

Year	Team	G	AB	R	H	2B	3B	HR	RBI	Avg.
1977	Idaho Falls	52	186	28	60	9	3	1	33	.323
1978	Quad Cities	129	508	80	149	31	2	24	101	.293
1979	El Paso	132	531	85	167	37	3	14	90	.315
1979	Angels	1	2	0	0	0	0	0	0	.000
1980	El Paso	105	400	61	114	23	3	12	66	.285
1981	Salt Lake	134	549	99	192	45	9	28	122	.350
1981	Angels	4	11	1	3	0	0	0	1	.273
1982	Pirates	20	29	4	8	1	0	2	4	.276
1982	Portland	101	395	71	112	29	8	17	73	.284
1983	Pirates	61	131	16	29	4	1	7	20	.221
1984	Pirates	46	112	4	29	4	0	2	11	.259
1985	Cardinals	43	52	5	13	4	0	0	8	.250
1986	Nashville	95	317	41	83	11	1	11	45	.262
1986	Tigers	9	36	2	5	1	0	0	3	.139
1987	San Jose	8	29	5	9	0	0	3	8	.310
1987	Tacoma	94	323	41	100	17	0	9	62	.310
1987	Athletics	11	17	1	4	1	0	0	3	.235
1988	Portland	46	170	34	60	10	1	13	42	.353
1988	Twins	60	166	15	49	11	1	3	20	.295
1989	Twins	126	385	43	125	24	0	8	57	.325
1990	Twins	134	479	61	141	42	3	6	54	.294
1991	Twins	123	441	54	137	28	1	10	69	.311
1992	Twins	140	502	58	154	25	0	9	73	.307
Major League Career (13 years)		**788**	**2363**	**264**	**697**	**145**	**6**	**47**	**323**	**.295**

Howard Johnson
No Reservations

VITAL STATISTICS

Born November 29, 1960, in Clearwater, Florida
5 feet 10, 195 pounds
Current Team: New York Mets
Position: Third Base/Center Field

CAREER HIGHLIGHTS

- Holds National League record for most home runs as a switch hitter in one season (38) in 1991
- Led National League in home runs (38) and RBI (117) in 1991.
- Second player in major league history to achieve three 30-homer, 30-steal seasons.
- Named to All-Star team twice

WARMING UP

Detroit Manager Sparky Anderson still admits to watching the scoreboard and noticing with some chagrin every time it says in the summary of home runs: "NY Mets 20 HR." Number 20, Howard Johnson, has pounded out almost 200 home runs since joining the Mets.

Although Anderson and the rest of the Detroit contingent once had reservations about Howard Johnson—enough so that they dealt him off to the Mets for Walt Terrell—not many people in New York feel that way now. The two-time All-Star third baseman has hit with consistency and power since joining the Mets.

Howard Johnson

Detroit Manager Sparky Anderson probably has stayed at a Howard Johnson's lodge sometime in his long career of traveling the world with baseball teams. Whether he was happy that he stayed at HoJo's we don't know. But one thing is sure. He is not very happy that he didn't stay with Howard Johnson, the former Detroit third baseman now finding success with the New York Mets.

The Tigers skipper still admits to watching the scoreboard and noticing with some chagrin every time it says in the summary of home runs: "NY Mets 20 HR." Number 20, Howard Johnson, has pounded out almost 200 home runs since joining the Mets.

Although Anderson and the rest of the Detroit contingent once had reservations about Howard Johnson—enough so that they dealt him off to the Mets for Walt Terrell—not many people in New York feel that way now. Look at what the two-time All-Star has done since joining the Mets:

- Between 1987 and 1991 he averaged more than 30 home runs a year.
- In 1991 he lead the league in home runs, RBIs, sacrifice flies, and extra base hits.

- In 1991 he made the 30-30 club for the third time (30 home runs and 30 stolen bases). Only Bobby Bonds did it more times (5). Another fellow who spent some time in center field in New York, Willie Mays, did it just twice.
- He became the second Met to hit home runs from both sides of the plate in one game.
- He has climbed to second on the Mets' career home run list.

Imagine what the Detroit Tiger lineup would have been like in 1991 if you would add Howard Johnson's 38 home runs to Cecil Fielder's 44 and Mickey Tettleton's 31 and Rob Deer's 25 and Lou Whitaker's 23. It would have been bombs away.

Sending Howard Johnson packing after just one full season with Detroit was surely a bomb of a deal for the Tigers, coming as the trade did on Pearl Harbor Day in 1984, but for the Mets and HoJo, it's been the best thing since room service. "When I first got traded, I was a little disappointed," Johnson admits. "But I looked at it as an opportunity to play with a team who wanted me. They traded for me. It was a good deal for both teams."

Most important for Johnson, the trade gave him a chance to play regularly. During 1984, his one complete season with Detroit, he hit 12 home runs in 355 at bats for the Tigers during their awe-inspiring sweep through the American League schedule; yet he appeared in only one game against the San Diego Padres in the World Series that followed. In the Fall Classic, third base was mysteriously handed over to Marty Castillo, who never batted 355 times in his whole major league career. A couple of months later, the Tigers put out the no vacancy sign for HoJo, and he was off to open up a new Howard Johnson's in New York.

So what happened? What turned the spurned Tiger into a player so good that he has outlasted such marquee stars as Gary Carter, Darryl Strawberry, and Keith Hernandez? A player who in 1991 won two-thirds of the National League triple crown (home runs and RBIs, missing only in batting average)? A couple of things come to mind for Johnson.

First, the work ethic. "I just work hard and try to improve my skills constantly, not trying to just sit back and take it easy. I'm always trying to improve."

That was evident in 1992 when new manager Jeff Torborg asked HoJo to change rooms. He wanted his slugging infielder to pack up and move to the outfield. Although Johnson is not noted for his fielding prowess at third, the suggestion to switch to center field would have caused most superstars who had led the league in home runs and RBIs to start complaining and acting like a bell-boy who didn't get a tip.

Not Howard Johnson. "I've always enjoyed a challenge," he says as he recalls that spring training 1992 request. "And that to me was another challenge. The older you get in baseball—with the repetition, the travel, all the things that are bad—it's nice to have something new to look forward to every day. This was defini-tely new, and I was certain I could do it. It's just a matter of apply-ing myself and proving to myself that I could do it, and to help our ballclub as well."

It's not as if Johnson had never been in the outfield. He had played outfield off and on during his amateur days, and he also had spent some time out there early in his career with the Mets. It almost seems that Howard Johnson doesn't care where he plays, as long as you hand him the bat.

A second reason HoJo has been able to stay with the Mets has been his maturity. "When I was with Detroit," he recalls, "I was pretty young. As you get older, you physically get stronger, and you ask questions of the veterans. You watch them play, and you learn how to play the game the way it should be played. Then it's just a matter of working and trying to bring each talent up to [a higher] level."

Early in his career, there was one place Howard Johnson knew he didn't want to stay, the minor leagues. Yet to his utter horror, that is where he found himself in 1983—after having made the big team in the previous year. In his second year in Detroit, he was hitting only .212 after 27 games, so he was sent to Evansville.

Evansville's a nice town and all, but for a young player who didn't know what the future held, it was devastating. "Getting sent down early in the season after I had made the club in Detroit was probably the worst thing that ever happened to me," Johnson re-calls. Then, to make the situation more grim, he injured a finger and missed almost the whole Triple A season. At Evansville he appeared in only three games before the injury.

He had been in the land of generous meal money and of hotels better than his namesake. He had hit .316 in 1982 with the big club. And now he faced the disabled list and uncertainty.

At the end of the minor league season, he was not called up. It was almost like starting over. "I had to go to the Instructional League and winter ball and just keep playing. I didn't know where my career was going." But within a year he was going to New York. The hard work and patience he spoke of soon would pay off.

When HoJo landed in the Big Apple in 1985, he took with him two very important mementos of his stay in Detroit. His World Series ring and his wife. If you watched the 1991 All-Star game, you may remember the night she came into your living room on CBS. As her husband was making his second appearance at the summer classic, she was just about ready to make her third appearance in a maternity room. The roving Pat O'Brien found Kim in the stands rooting her hubby on, and he treated the viewers to an interview that made him seem more uncomfortable than she must have been.

Clearly concerned that Kim seemed to be in the wrong place to be experiencing her last days of a pregnancy, O'Brien asked her if perhaps she was taking a chance by coming to the game in her condition. Relaxed, she replied simply and eloquently, "No, everything is in the Lord's hands."

And indeed it was. The baby was born three days later, just 20 minutes after Daddy arrived at the hospital, directly from Shea Stadium.

On the night their daughter Kayla was born, Johnson got word that his third child was coming as the Mets were locked up in a battle with the Padres. He told teammate Kevin McReynolds about it, and while HoJo knelt patiently in the on-deck circle, McReynolds lashed a single to score the winning run.

HoJo was out of Shea in a flash and soon at the hospital to welcome Kayla into the family. The Mets beat the Padres, Daddy beat the traffic to the hospital, and Kayla joined brother Glen and sister Shannon as part of the Johnson team.

The family has taken on new significance for Howard Johnson in the past few years. And it is largely due to the influence of Kim. One reason she could tell O'Brien so confidently about God's control is because she has seen what He has done for her husband.

"I came to Christ in 1990," Johnson says, without reservation. "My wife was a big part of that. She was really concerned about how we would bring our children up. She wanted to bring them up in a Christian home. With the way the world is today and all the things that are going on, that's the only way. One thing you want to make sure of is that the children are looked after and are well cared for. It was really Kim's nudging me and the Holy Spirit's working in her that got me going. I finally made my decision to trust Christ as my Savior in October of 1990."

That step of faith has made a big difference for the Johnsons, Howard says with thankfulness. "It has brought us a lot closer. It put that trust in the relationship that I think the Lord intended all along. It's still tough on family life because the kids don't get to see their father as much. In the times when I'm at home, though, I think less of what I want to be doing and I think more about spending time with them and with Kim and trying to be a good husband and father."

As workmanlike as Howard Johnson is at the ballpark and at home, and as much as he has become a symbol for the working man in New York because of his diligence, there is one thing about the workingman's life that he envies.

"People work from nine to five, and they come home. But my kids don't have me around very much. In an ideal situation, you spend the weekends and as much time as possible with your family. Spending time with them is our only legacy.

"My greatest hope is that my children grow up knowing the Lord, being strong Christians, and will pass it to their kids. The Bible speaks about building families on the faith generation upon generation. That's important to me. The hard part about it is that I need to be the disciplinarian and father and love them all at once, and be the spiritual leader. Because I have to be gone so much, it can be difficult, but we do the best we can."

The Howard Johnson who sat on the bench during the 1984 World Series and who later played only a bit more in the 1986 showdown between the Mets and the Red Sox is far different from the one who patrols the outfield today. He's been remodeled, renovated, and rebuilt. Instead of the single, wondering, youthful third baseman that he was then, he is today the happily married father—the confident outfielder whose faith has given him a new outlook on his family and life in general. He has played in the World Series and the All-Star Game. He has broken records and led the league in all kinds of stats. He's been Player of the Month, a member of the National League Silver Slugger Team, the Associated Press and *The Sporting News* All-Star third baseman, and twice named Sports Channel's Leukemia Society Man of the Year.

So which of these things does he call his greatest thrill? None of them. He refuses to select one simple event or award. Remember, his worst moment was the time he wondered within himself whether he might never return to the majors after a couple of short stints with the Tigers. Instead he points to his now steady career as a ballplayer. "My greatest thrill is being able to play this long and being successful. I think the longer you play, the more you appreciate being able to play a long time and being successful and meeting a lot of good people. You meet some friends, and you have a relationship with some friends for times out of baseball, and that's been very rewarding. I wasn't always a Christian as a ballplayer, but it's really helped me now because I'm in the back third of my career. I want to really do it right. It's just been a lot of fun."

Like his namesake motor lodge, Howard Johnson the man looks pretty good, even from a distance. And about this man's heart and soul nobody needs to have reservations.

Q & A WITH HOWARD JOHNSON

Q: *How do you share your beliefs with others?*
Howard: According to Scripture, there are going to be some who plant the seed and others who water it and nurture it, and others harvest. I'm more the one who nurtures it along and waters it.

We've got a good group of guys on our team. Some have been Christians a long time. Others haven't been Christians long at all, and I can relate really well with them. All I can try to do is show them what God has done for me and give them answers when they have tough questions.

Q: *How do you handle it when things happen that go against your standards?*
Howard: That's tough. First, you have to pray about those situations. In your own strength, the natural tendency is to be angry and frustrated and look at that person in a really ugly way. Instead, you've got to love the person as Christ loved us, because we were once like that. Even though we're saved and we know the Father, we look at things from a different perspective than they do. It's up to us to know that and recognize that when we deal with them.

Q: *What goals have you set for your career?*
Howard: I don't have number goals. As you play and you go along, you reach certain milestones that are nice. The danger is making those things the focal point of your game. My goal has always been to win and to help our team win, and I get frustrated when we don't win. That's why it's important that I have friends on the ball club who feel the way I do. So that if I have a problem, we can relate together. To me that's rewarding.

Q: *What do you think you would have done if you hadn't played major league baseball?*
Howard: I really don't know, but I always had an interest in NASA [the National Aeronautics and Space Administration] and the space program. Also, I had an interest in architecture.

Q: *Who is the toughest pitcher you ever faced?*
Howard: The most difficult guy has been Orel Hershiser before he got injured. Tom Browning is another guy who can give me some problems.

Q: *How do you view the responsibility of being a role model?*
Howard: Being a role model isn't portraying an image to the fans. As a Christian, being a role model is being what the Lord wants

me to be. The world has standards, and a lot of the standards are never met. I try to do the best I can and be obedient.

MAJOR LEAGUE CAREER PATH

January 9, 1979:   Selected by Tigers in secondary phase of free-agent draft
December 7, 1984: Traded to Mets for Walt Terrell

THE JOHNSON FILE

Year	Team	G	AB	R	H	2B	3B	HR	RBI	Avg.
1979	Lakeland	132	456	49	107	9	6	3	49	.235
1980	Lakeland	130	474	83	135	28	1	10	69	.285
1981	Birmingham	138	488	84	130	28	7	22	83	.266
1982	Evansville	98	366	70	116	16	4	23	67	.317
1982	Tigers	54	155	23	49	5	0	4	14	.316
1983	Tigers	27	66	1	14	0	0	3	5	.212
1983	Evansville	3	9		2	1	0	0	0	.222
1884	Tigers	116	355	43	88	14	1	12	50	.248
1985	Mets	126	389	38	94	18	4	11	46	.242
1986	Mets	88	220	30	54	14	0	10	39	.245
1987	Mets	157	554	93	147	22	1	36	99	.265
1988	Mets	148	495	85	114	21	1	24	68	.230
1989	Mets	153	571	104	164	41	3	36	101	.287
1990	Mets	154	590	89	144	37	3	23	90	.244
1991	Mets	156	564	108	146	34	4	38	117	.259
1992	Mets	100	350	48	78	19	0	7	43	.223
Major League Career (11 years)		**1179**	**4309**	**672**	**1092**	**225**	**17**	**204**	**650**	**.253**

Kevin Maas
The Education of a Ballplayer

VITAL STATISTICS

Born January 20, 1965, in Castro Valley, California
6 feet 3, 206 pounds
Current Team: New York Yankees
Position: First Base/Designated Hitter
Attended University of California, Berkeley

CAREER HIGHLIGHTS

- Hit 3 home runs in 3 successive games during first year in the majors
- Averaged 18 home runs per year in first 3 years in major leagues

WARMING UP

In just 79 games at the end of the 1990 baseball season, Kevin Maas's newfound power took him from Columbus to Yankee Stadium to fame in two and a half months.

But it almost never happened.

Just a year earlier, Maas found himself on the disabled list—a minor league player with a bum knee and a date with a surgeon. "I didn't know if I would ever play again," he confesses.

Kevin Maas

He seemingly came out of nowhere to challenge the friendly right-field fences at Yankee Stadium and to awaken memories of the glory years in the Bronx. Blessed with a style reminiscent of DiMaggio, and equipped with a home run proficiency that recalled the Babe, Kevin Maas nearly grew into a legend before he grew accustomed to wearing pinstripes.

In just 254 trips to the plate in his rookie season, the man with the degree in mechanical engineering banged out 21 round trippers. Only the Detroit Tigers' one-man wrecking crew named Cecil Fielder, who had 51 home runs in 573 at bats, had a better home-run-to-at-bats ratio (11.2 for Fielder to 12.09 for Maas).

Maas's major league debut exceeded all expectations. The most home runs he had ever hit in a minor league season was 16, in Double A ball. But in just 79 games at the end of the 1990 baseball season, Kevin Maas's display of power took him from Columbus to Yankee Stadium to fame in two and a half months.

But it almost never happened.

Just a year earlier, on July 27, 1989, Kevin Maas found himself on the disabled list—a minor league player with a bum knee and a date with a surgeon. "I didn't know if I would ever play again," he confesses.

How does a young player deal with the strong possibility that his dream of big league baseball is dead? "The Lord gave me a lot of strength," Maas explains. "I turned to Him in every way. I trusted Him for patience, just letting things happen and not worrying. I wasn't worrying about playing baseball again."

As he prepared for crucial reconstructive surgery on his knee, Maas ignored his long-term goal of being in the big leagues in two years. Instead he channeled his energy to a full recovery, so he could play any baseball once more. "I tried not to think about the baseball field until I was able to get on it. When I got to the point where I saw my leg recovering, I began to see that the Lord did have plans for me to get back on the ballfield. I knew this was going to a big turning point in my faith and in terms of building my trust in God, and that's really what it did."

Kevin Maas also prepared for the worst, as he took steps to cover his possible retirement at age 24. He returned to college and earned his engineering degree. If his career ended, he would have joined an engineering firm, perhaps "Bechtel, McDonnell-Douglas, Rockwell, or some smaller engineering firm. That's what I really enjoyed doing in college. I also really enjoy business." And when Maas's major league career does end, "I might go back to school and get an MBA or something."

If this sounds like someone who is not overly impressed with himself, perhaps it comes from the stability he had learned—and still experiences—through his family. At an age when many people are so wrapped up in creating their own niche in life that they easily forget who got them where they are, Maas still values his family ties. He praises his parents for supporting his dreams and attending athletic contests while he was still a youth.

"I can't recall a single day, when I was growing up, when my dad was not at one of my games—whether basketball or baseball. And even to this day, he's willing to take any time out of his day to hit with me or to go over our hitting practice. He's pretty much my hitting mentor. We work out all the time in the winter, and he spends so much time with me. My mom's the same way. They invest above and beyond the amount of time required of parents, and I really think that's one reason I'm where I am today—because of their love and support."

Growing up in the supportive Maas family with older brother Jason, who played minor league baseball, Kevin was given every opportunity to excel at both baseball and basketball. But in neither sport, he admits, was he the team superstar.

"I was somewhere between star and superstar," he says about the growing up years. "I wasn't a superstar. I was always one of the top couple of players on every team, but there always seemed to be maybe another guy who would outshine me." Among those to whom young Kevin Maas took a back seat in baseball was Lance Blankenship, who has spent several years with the Oakland Athletics. And in basketball, where Maas was an All-Northern California selection in his senior year, he was eclipsed by guys like Brian Shaw, who now plies his trade in the National Basketball Association.

In fact, Maas thinks that the kids he played with in youth baseball are probably quite surprised to see their old teammate hanging around places like Yankee Stadium.

"I was always a good player, but I was a late bloomer, and I came into my own late in my college career. I didn't begin to mature physically and mentally and really put it together until late."

It wasn't for a lack of effort that Kevin the Kid didn't remind his friends of Reggie Jackson. After climbing through the ranks of Little League and Babe Ruth Leagues, high school ball and American Legion, he played on a traveling summer league that "played over 100 games for three summers in a row. At least one game a day. Sometimes we would play five games in one day. We would go from one doubleheader to the next doubleheader. We were playing, playing, playing.

"Those were the first times when we traveled and got away from home. It was just a great experience. I didn't know that it was preparing me for the minor leagues, because I didn't have any visions that I was going to be a professional player. I was having fun, and I was good at it. I have a lot of good memories with the guys. A lot of camaraderie that we built as we traveled together."

The baseball lessons Kevin Maas learned during those summers of playing amateur baseball in California, Wisconsin, and

Alaska paid off in June of 1986 when he was selected by the Yankees in the free agent draft. That began his three-year climb through the minors that had him reaching for the final rung of the ladder when the knee injury toppled him.

Being that close to seeing his major league dream realized, and then watching it almost fade away, has given Maas a perspective on baseball—and life.

"It's understandable for someone to say about me, now that I'm in the big leagues, 'Oh, sure, it's easy to say that you're at peace and everything.' But that's not true at all. I've been through some trials that were really threatening, and it's those times that really make you the strongest in your faith. And you realize, when you come out of it, that it's almost a blessing that you went through it, because you're a much stronger person for it. And I think my knee injury was a big example of that."

After the surgery, of course, Maas came back stronger than ever. After only 57 games of the 1990 minor league season, the Yankees called. Maas answered with a show of rookie power that in some ways was the greatest of all time. By mid-August, after only 114 at bats, he had more home runs than Kirby Puckett, Robin Yount, and George Brett, all of whom had been playing since April. He slammed out 10 home runs in fewer at bats (78) than anyone in major league history, a phenomenal 7.8 ratio of home runs to at bats.

Suddenly Maas was a media darling. And he began to receive a new kind of education. Coming back from knee surgery is one thing, but suddenly becoming the object of attention in media-rich New York is entirely different. Life could have easily flown out of control for Maas as the hordes descended with their microphones and notepads.

"As great as things went in 1990, it was really tough just to concentrate on baseball," he says about those glory days of being called the next Lou Gehrig. "I became in pretty high demand for appearances and for people who wanted me to come out and sign autographs here and there during the season."

He's not complaining. Or bragging. Just trying to explain the distractions that sneaked up on him because of his power surge. The previous winter he had been just another kid sitting in an engineering class at Berkeley. The only autograph that meant anything was his name on the top of his assignments, and the only interviews he did were with his academic counselor, making sure he would graduate. And suddenly he's in the middle of some intensive summer school classes in Superstardom 101.

"Right before the game—even during the game—the media would be out there," he recalls incredulously. "They want interviews up until 20 minutes before you play the game, practically. And they want their own exclusive report after the game. People are tugging on you this way and that way to come down and speak to their kids at the local high school or whatever. And they're all things that you want to do because you feel like, 'Hey, I'd love to help. Or I'd love to be able to share this.'

"But you realize too that your number one goal—the thing that got you here—is to play baseball. And not necessarily to do that interview with this newspaper or whatever. And so you've really got to have a fine balance of the two, and to know when to say yes and when to say no."

Balance. As in engineering? As in making one side of the equation equal the other side? Maybe.

But more probably, it's a balance that has nothing to do with what he learned at U. C.–Berkeley. It is more related to something he began learning about during his second year of professional baseball. A balance between the everyday and the enduring matters of life.

The scene was Ft. Lauderdale. As first baseman for the Ft. Lauderdale Yankees, Kevin Maas was struggling with the long bus rides, the minimal pay, and the selfish, get-ahead attitudes as every player tried to get to the big leagues. It was his first extended period away from home. "Ft. Lauderdale, Florida, is a long way from California," Maas says simply.

Looking for that little bit of home that going to church might give him, he began to attend Baseball Chapel. "That was my church. Growing up going to church on Sunday was something I did. It was part of me. I always went to church on Sundays in college. It was something I wanted. Something I needed.

"It wasn't until then that I really began to look for something more secure in terms of not having to worry about going 0-for-4 every day. I came across some wonderful people through Baseball Chapel. I felt that they really had something that I wanted, and that was a personal relationship with Jesus Christ."

One day the leader of his minor league Baseball Chapel, Bill Watts, asked Maas, "If you were to die, are you sure beyond a shadow of a doubt that you would go to heaven?" Maas didn't know how to reply.

"I didn't know that answer. It was something I didn't want to be unsure of. I had never really been asked that question up front, and I wasn't really sure if I was going to heaven. I started reading the Bible at that point and understood that Christ died for me on the cross and that by receiving Him into my life, I could make sure I was going to heaven.

"I accepted the Lord that summer. Once I accepted Christ into my life personally, it became such a relief for me, knowing that I really did have a direction, and that the Lord really did have a plan for my life. Since then, everything that I've seen happen in my life has been a real blessing, one way or the other."

Blessings, yes. A smooth ride on this new road? No. "There's no question that I was confronted in different ways by distractions and temptations," Maas says about those first months as a follower of Jesus Christ. "It was something that I had to deal with. It wasn't maybe the alcohol, or it wasn't the women. But I think it was the distractions that really kept me from trying to do my best on the ballfield, things that would have limited my success and would have limited my ability to share my faith."

Which takes us back to those hectic days of 1990, when the area around Kevin Maas's locker was a highly popular stopping-off point for reporters, and when the whole world wanted a piece of the action from this young Yankee phenom. New to it all, Maas was trying to use his faith to balance the demands.

"I really felt the Lord working, that He was guiding me according to when to say yes and when to say no. And that's the most important thing. That year was kind of a tug of war for me. But now I feel more firmly rooted in terms of where the Lord wants me to go."

There have been times, Maas admits, when he has learned the hard way that not everyone who asks for a favor of Kevin Maas has the most honorable intentions. Once while playing the Brewers in Milwaukee, he answered a phone call from a woman claiming she was with a local charity, wanting him to sign several baseballs. She planned to drive 10 hours to have Maas autograph the balls in the hotel.

Maas agreed, thinking it was for charity. She arrived, he let her in the room and was about to sign. "Five minutes after she came into my room, I got a knock on the door," Maas recalls. "It was one of the players. He said this lady was a scam artist, and that I better get out of my room or I'd be caught in a compromising situation that I didn't want to be in."

Later the hotel manager showed Maas a *Sports Illustrated* story on the Pete Rose scandal, pointed to the woman's picture and said, "Yeah, there she is." "That was the same one he had seen in the lobby going up to my room," Maas recalls.

The classroom of major league baseball also has taught Maas that it's not just people from the outside you have to watch out for. Just as happens with anybody in any walk of life, you must be careful who you hang out with.

"I try to avoid bad company," Maas explains. "The Bible says, 'Bad company corrupts good character.' And I firmly believe that. That's one thing that has helped me stay on the right track in terms of the way I want to live my life—hanging around the right people, hanging around my Christian brothers, or not even so much that, it's just staying out of awkward situations.

"I don't drink, and if I'm going out at night with my friends that I know feel the way I do, I know I'm going to stay out of trouble. In the clubhouse when things get a little nasty, I expect that. I've grown up in the game long enough to know that things get raunchy at times, yet the guys can be a lot of fun at different times."

Maas knows young people want positive models. A couple years ago he appeared on the cover and in a feature article in *Breakaway* magazine, a teen-oriented publication for boys that attempts to show them how to live a life that honors God.

"I think being a role model is great," Maas says with the confidence of someone who knows how important it is to provide a good example for those who watch him. "I think it is a privilege and an honor to have kids look up to me—to see me as somebody they want to be like."

Maas holds up a letter from a boy living in South Florida. "He says he wants to be just like me. For me, that's exciting. I know some people would say that's no big deal, but that's exciting for me. I accept that, and I think it's great.

"The image I try to project is really just me. It's real. The way I perceive myself on the field or project myself in the media is just the way I am, and that's someone who loves the Lord Jesus Christ very much and is trusting Him as my Lord and Savior. Someone who believes a lot in family and hard work—and [believes] that nothing's for free. You've got to put in your time and your energy. Someone who feels that an education is as important as anything."

Again he comes back to education. Maas believes in learning—learning from family, from church, from school, from mistakes, and from others.

And others are learning from Kevin Maas—learning about a personal faith in God. "I've had a great opportunity as a major league baseball player to give my testimony. It's not always what I say that counts. A lot of times it is how I act, what I don't say on the field. But there are times in the off-season or occasionally during the season when I can speak to kids, whether at a church or at a card show. I tend to write Bible verses under my autograph or the sign of the fish, which is used as a symbol of [faith in] Jesus Christ. It raises questions, if nothing else. It's a good way to raise people's awareness of what I'm about, and hopefully they will see a difference in me.

"I've had a lot of opportunities to speak at retreats, rallies, things like that. And not because of me, but certainly because of the Lord, a number of people have come to accept the Lord through my testimonies. The Lord has really opened up some avenues and changed some lives through my testimony. That's been exciting for me to see that the Lord can change lives that way."

Maas recalls a couple at his home church who listened to his testimony at a retreat. The husband became a Christian as a result. "Subsequently, his marriage, which was in trouble, came back together when they put all their faith in God. That was exciting for me to see."

There are other lessons Maas is learning in this education of a ballplayer, lessons about fame and expectations.

"Fame leads to an invasion of your private life." He is not so much complaining as explaining. "It's an invasion of your quiet time. It's an invasion on your personal time. It's an invasion of your relationships. Everybody wants a piece here and there. People wanting interviews. People wanting autographs. People wanting photographs. That's the biggest thing—once you go from the minors to the majors—the demand on your time."

And in the vicious circle that is professional sports, the better you play the worse the problem becomes. You can't be good without having to put up with the bad. "That's just the way it is," says Maas of this law of growing demands. The demands are magnified in New York because it is a media center, he says, and "When you are going good in New York, they want you. . . . I think it is something that you deal with every day—dealing with those expectations, and the pressure. The thing that helps me get through is to only do what I know I can do, and not try to be anyone else."

That first year in New York awakened some great expectations that Kevin Maas has had to try to forget about. Still, the year was full of marvelous moments, and it is certainly his most cherished season so far.

There are favorite single moments that he likes to remember about 1990. "Hitting a home run off Nolan Ryan. My first home run off Brett Saberhagen—on the Fourth of July, 1990. Having two home runs and five RBIs on Oldtimers' Day at Yankee Stadium in 1990. Those are big moments. Setting three or four major league records was a dream. It's something I'll probably have to try to live up to—or something I'm expected to live up to."

But people wanted more. They wanted 40 home runs. A hundred runs batted in. It was just something else Maas had to learn to respond to. Speaking of those great expectations everyone else had for him, he says, "It bothered me in the sense that I got away from myself—my game. Away from what I know I can do. And that is definitely not hitting record rates of home runs. That did kind of get to me during the [1991] season. I felt that if I didn't hit a home run I wasn't pleasing the fans or the management." But he has learned. "I can't try to be Babe Ruth or Lou Gehrig or Joe DiMaggio—any of the people they tended to compare me to in my first year. That's not me. When I step to the plate, it's just me against the pitcher. I'm not trying to think about how many people are in the stands or how many home runs I have. I really just try to take it one pitch at a time. In that sense, I try to put the distractions behind me."

Distractions such as setting goals. "Setting goals is for me not the best thing. That's long term, and I've always been a short-term-goal person. By short term I mean literally day to day. I want to go into each game and get a couple of hits, get a couple of RBIs, if the situation presents itself, and be prepared for that. And as the season progresses, those things will just come. I've found out that setting long-term goals sometimes gets me in trouble."

The education of a ballplayer that began with supportive parents, the minor league decision to trust Christ, and a knee injury continues today. By enduring the good and the bad with the right attitude, Kevin Maas is learning another lesson: patience. "Patience in letting things happen. Patience in not worrying about anything else, anybody else. Not worrying about players in front of me or behind me. Just worrying about myself. Playing my game. In spite of injuries, which I've had, or setbacks. Just letting the Lord take over and bring me along as fast as He wants to bring me along."

That's a lesson that is not just for ballplayers.

Q & A WITH KEVIN MAAS

Q: *Why did you pursue a degree in mechanical engineering?*
Kevin: I was really curious about how things worked—why planes flew and how cars ran. I think also why it made a difference was I look up to my older brother, Jason. He's about a year and a half older. He started out in college in engineering. We're so similar in a lot of ways, that I think his direction gave me a nudge. . . . And

more than anything else, I think engineering was something I really wanted to do.

Q: *What organizations helped you during your minor league days?*
Kevin: There are so many guys in the minor leagues who are searching and don't have direction in their lives—who don't have Jesus Christ. . . . I think Baseball Chapel is a great organization. Certainly it's one that puts Jesus Christ first in your life. So I've gotten tremendous direction and support from Baseball Chapel, as well as from some of the other ministries, including Athletes in Action and Campus Crusade for Christ. These are the organizations that really have one purpose in mind, and that's to put Christ first and to preach His Word.

Q: *As a Christian, do you feel competitiveness is wrong?*
Kevin: Oh, I don't think so at all. I really feel that I was spoiled in the past. I've been on so many winning teams. In Single A we won a championship. In Double A we won a championship. In Triple A, before I got hurt, we were in first place. And my whole career I've been on winning teams. So this has been a challenge with the Yankees to try to pick this team up and put us in championship form. I've had to reach down deep for a little extra competitiveness and pick everybody up in that sense. So I think it's been a real positive thing.

Q: *How should a Christian play the game?*
Kevin: Christ would only expect us to play at 100 percent. He would expect us to take out that second baseman as hard as we can when we're going in there. Not with the intention of hurting anybody, but with the intention that *it's my job, and I'm going to save that runner at first base*. And when you're up at the plate, the only thing in your mind is doing some damage with that baseball—hitting it as hard as you can. I don't think the competitive spirit is anything but a positive factor to the believers who are playing this game.

Q: *What do you think of salaries in baseball today?*

Kevin: The sad part about it is that . . . raising all these ticket prices [is] making it so families can't afford to come to games. Salaries are going through the roof, but to bring a family of four to the game it's now costing over $100. And that's frustrating to see. When I was a kid, going to the game was so much fun, and I got such a thrill out of it. I'd hate to have that be such a burden for families.

MAJOR LEAGUE CAREER PATH

June 2, 1986: Selected by the Yankees in the 22d round

THE MAAS FILE

Year	Team	G	AB	R	H	2B	3B	HR	RBI	Avg.
1986	Oneonta	28	101	14	36	10	0	0	18	.356
1987	Ft. Lauderdale	116	439	77	122	28	4	11	73	.278
1988	Prince Williams	29	108	24	32	7	0	12	35	.296
1988	Albany	109	372	66	98	14	3	16	55	.263
1989	Columbus	83	291	42	93	23	2	6	45	.320
1990	Columbus	57	194	37	55	15	2	13	38	.284
1990	Yankees	79	254	42	64	9	0	21	41	.252
1991	Yankees	148	500	69	110	14	1	23	69	.220
1992	Yankees	98	286	35	71	12	0	11	35	.248
Major League Career (3 years)		**325**	**1040**	**146**	**245**	**35**	**1**	**55**	**139**	**.236**

Matt Nokes
Catching On in the Real World

VITAL STATISTICS

Born October 31, 1963, in San Diego, California
6 feet 1, 191 pounds
Current Team: New York Yankees
Position: Catcher

- Named to the All-Star team in his rookie year
- Hit 32 home runs in his first year in the majors
- Led the Yankees in home runs (24) in 1991

WARMING UP

We go through hard times. We have a choice," Nokes says in his characteristic straightforward style. "What do we do? Well, we let God comfort us. We don't avoid the hard times; we can't avoid them."

As Matt Nokes talks about life and the tough realities of it, he exudes a confidence and intensity that lets you know this is serious stuff to him. When he holds court on vital issues of life, he looks his visitor in the eye, almost imploring him to understand, to get it. He has a message to convey. As he talks and gestures and speaks with passion, you know he is a student of life in the real world.

Matt Nokes

ormer catcher and current manager Jeff Torborg was onto something when he quipped about his old position, "There must be some reason we're facing the other way."

Catchers are a breed apart. Think about it. How many humans can catch a 90-miles-an-hour fastball? Or squat for three hours without ripping out their knees? Or block home plate as someone like 6 feet 6, 220-pound Dave Winfield comes careening around third with nothing but scoring the tying run on his mind?

The mask, the shin guards, the chest protector. Nobody earns the privilege of wearing the tools of ignorance and being the most active athlete on the field without going through the school of hard knocks. Matt Nokes has been to school—and survived the education. Perhaps the classroom of life prepared him for his future catching career with the Detroit Tigers and New York Yankees. The world of Matt Nokes has always been a world where the lessons of stark reality could not be ignored.

Trouble began when Matthew Nokes was in elementary school. "In 1970," Nokes recalls of those grade school days, "my mother had cancer, and they gave her about eight weeks to live."

His mother was a woman of faith, so she did the only thing she could do that might help. "She got the prayer groups all together," he recalls. As they were gathered and praying, "she felt like something happened in her body." She went back to the hospital, and said, "I'd like a complete reexamination." To humor her, they did.

She was standing outside the X-ray room when she heard the excited X-ray technician: "It's a miracle, it's completely gone! She has no more cancer."

Unbelievable as it sounds, they were right. Matthew Nokes's mom got better. "God had something else for her to do," he says with conviction. "From that time on, my mom knew that her time wasn't up, and she had some things she had to go do."

Perhaps the most important thing she had to do was to help take care of her son's spiritual needs. And she did that first through the way she conducted herself—through what Matt could observe in her a few years later as a result of a change in her life.

"The Scripture says in John 3:8 that the wind blows where it wishes," Matt begins. "You can hear the sound of it, but you don't know where it's going. So it is with those who are born in the Spirit of God." I was in junior high. Obviously, I couldn't see the Spirit, but I could see the effect He had on my mother's life—the change in her life. And I could just see her, and I knew God was working, just through the example that she led. She really showed me and showed other people in my family that Jesus loved me for who I was and that He had died for me.

"My mother pointed me to the Bible. She let me read it. She let me investigate it. She let me see the effect that God could have on my life. Growing up, I remember times where I would wake up in the middle of the night. I knew there was some kind of emptiness. I knew there was something I didn't have. Because of that, I got interested, and I accepted Christ. I started reading the Bible and started feeling that God had a plan for me. That He loved me."

The trouble wasn't over, though. When Matt was in the ninth grade, the miracle that his mother had experienced several years before ended. A new kind of cancer struck her, ravaging her body and putting her at death's door. Her health declined quickly, and soon she could not speak. Matt was at her bedside the day she died.

"Seconds before she died, she said, 'Jesus, Jesus, Jesus.' It was special—the time we could spend together."

Her swift, painful death could have embittered young Matt. As has happened with many people, he might have turned his back on God in anger, blaming Him for his mother's death. Or he might have given up on himself because the tough times were too difficult.

He might have. But he didn't. Instead, he came to a conclusion that is still affecting his life today as a major league baseball player. "I realized that I not only needed to make [Christ] my Savior, but I needed to really sell out and make Him the Lord of my life. He gave me meaning and purpose and direction in life that I never thought possible. I know, because of the friends I used to hang out with and stuff, I would not be here [in the major leagues]."

In his mother's death Matt began to learn invaluable lessons from God. "I used to go through a lot of hard times during high school. But one thing God showed me was that He was going to be my very best friend. I could always come to Him."

He wants to pass on to others the lessons of God's comfort. One of Matt's favorite verses is "Praise be to the God and Father of our Lord Jesus Christ, the Father of compassion and the God of all comfort, who comforts us in all our troubles, so that we can comfort those in any trouble with the comfort we ourselves have received from God" (2 Corinthians 1:3).

"We go through hard times. We have a choice," Nokes says in his characteristic straightforward style. "What do we do? Well, we let God comfort us. We don't avoid the hard times; we can't avoid them."

As Matt Nokes talks about life and the tough realities of it, he exudes a confidence and intensity that lets you know this is serious stuff to him. When he holds court on vital issues of life, he looks his visitor in the eye, almost imploring him to understand, to get it. He has a message to convey. As he talks and gestures and speaks with passion, you know he is a student of life in the real world.

"We look at life and everyone thinks it's going to be a bowl of cherries. No, there are going to be a lot of hard times—hard things that happen, even if you are a Christian. Sometimes it's worse for believers. So what do you do? We have the greatest gift—we have the gift of God comforting us as that verse says. And that's supernatural. We see God work, and through that, we grow and we mature. We become people who have substance.

"Life's not easy," Nokes continues. "There are tough times. But . . . God is there and He loves us; He's the one who made us. He knows how to handle any situation. He knows how to handle it for us."

In Matt Nokes's career as a baseball player, he has had to endure a variety of situations—ranging from stunning success to deep discouragement. Perhaps the most astounding year of his major league life was his first full year in the big time. After a short stint with San Francisco in 1985 where he hit his first two major league home runs, he became a not-so-famous part of a big trade to Detroit that was supposed to bolster the Tiger pitching staff.

But it was not Eric King or Dave LaPoint who stole the show in Motown in 1987. Matt Nokes shocked everybody, including Manager Sparky Anderson, by putting together a phenomenal rookie year. Among other things he clubbed 32 home runs, batted .289, batted in 87 runs, made the American League All-Star team, hit a home run in the playoffs against the Minnesota Twins, and was named to *The Sporting News* American League All-Star team.

Matt Nokes is being realistic when he says that "life's not easy," but for one season it sure looked like it wasn't all that tough. In a few short months Nokes went from obscurity to fame. He seemed to be the catcher of the future for Detroit.

Yet like the boy Nokes watching his mother experience a miracle and then succumb later to a different form of cancer, the adult Nokes saw his grand debut with Detroit end with disappointment. The next year his home run production fell by half, the batting average fell by 38 points, and the RBIs dropped by 34. About the only thing Nokes had more of was errors.

But if 1988 was a bad dream, 1989 was a nightmare. Not only was Nokes foundering, but the whole Tiger team was sinking like a rock. Just two years before, they had overtaken the Toronto Blue Jays in the final week of the season to win the division. But in this dreadful season they could manage only 59 victories in 160 games. Nokes missed seven weeks of the season with a knee injury, and when he returned he hurt his shoulder and had to settle for duty as a designated hitter. As he watched his once-promising career begin to appear a mere flash in the pan, Nokes lost his starting job behind the plate to Mike Heath. That exciting promise of 1987 seemed to be nothing more than a tease.

Finally, in June of 1990, his Detroit days ended. The Tigers received two pitchers as Matt Nokes was traded to the New York Yankees. From the outside, it might have looked as if Sparky Anderson had given up on Nokes, much as he had dismissed Howard Johnson in 1984 to that other team in New York. But Nokes doesn't see it that way.

"It was a little more than giving up," Matt explains. "He saw that I wasn't enjoying catching anymore. And he didn't know what he could do. He really didn't know what to do."

Obviously not all baseball trades are made in heaven, but Matt Nokes is convinced that this one originated from on high. "Really, it was an act of God that brought me over here, and the Lord brought me somebody—bullpen coach Marc Hill—who understood. He spent the time with me. He taught me how to do it, how to go through hard times. Through that, a real miracle took place."

It sounds as though Nokes couldn't be happier. "Playing in Yankee Stadium and playing with the Yankees," he says, "is a dream come true." From the nightmare of 1989 to the dream come true of the '90s, Matt Nokes has faced the down times and has survived. His 1991 stats (24 home runs, 77 RBIs) didn't quite match the great year of 1987, but he served notice that he had returned.

It takes a person with a clear view of reality to overcome the roadblocks and come back as Nokes has done. A player of lesser intensity and a more idealistic look at life would have given up or perhaps would have been unable to survive the competitive fires that burn in major league clubhouses and dugouts. But Matt Nokes understands something about the mental aspect of baseball that may always remain a mystery to those who are not first-hand participants.

Nokes is intense, competitive, and genuine. Some might expect a Christian ballplayer to act sweet and mild, but Matt Nokes has a different perspective. It is a realistic view that some might find troublesome, yet the intensity is convincing, as Nokes presents it.

Baseball players are part of a rough-and-tumble family, according to Nokes. For six months they work and even room together. They have no weekends off. "It's not like when you're at your workplace where you see your fellow employees at your work from nine to five and that's it. It's like you're in the army together. You're in the trenches. You see each other when you're frustrated. You see each other when you're excited. When you're happy, when you're sad, the whole gamut.

"You've got to be real. By being real, you can be approachable. If you're not, if you put on this fake, sweet attitude and they don't see the real you—if you're putting on an act, they see through that immediately. Basically, you're being weird. It doesn't fit."

As Nokes explains this philosophy, he is sitting in the home locker room before a game at Yankee Stadium. Sitting next to him is Tony Kubek, who is waiting to interview him for television. Yet Nokes stays focused on this topic, speaking about it with passion and concern, punctuating his thoughts with strong hand motions and intense eye contact. Even with others listening in who might not understand, he continues to give his heartfelt perspective on Christians in sports.

"Now, if you're going through a hard time, and you're struggling, and you're being sweet and weird, what kind of witness is that? Your teammates want to see a real person. When they see you being real—and they see some frustrations from time to time—but they watch you deal with them and see that you have a greater perspective on life, then they will respect you.

"But if you strike out and you come back to the bench smiling or no big deal, they're thinking, *What*?

"In fact, everyone is looking for an excuse to say, 'Christian ballplayers aren't the hard-nosed type of players.' I'm going to be the last one they're going to be able to say that about.

"When they see that you're a scrappy, hard-nosed player, then when they go through hard times, they're going to come to you. There's no fooling anybody. When you're out on that baseball field or when you're going out to dinner with someone's family, when you see them relating to you personally, they want to see some strength of character, not some plastic person. They want to see you putting your nose to the grindstone, being a scrappy player, doing whatever the scrappiness of the game calls for.

"A lot of people won't understand this is the way we feel, but if I have a hard at-bat, or I'm struggling, I'll grab my helmet. The fans aren't going to understand, so I'm not going to make a fool of myself by throwing my helmet [in front of them]. But I'll go down in the dugout, in the runway, and I'll destroy something. I'm walking back there and my teammates are laughing, because everyone does this. And I come back and I'm laughing too, because it's no big deal.

"Be real. If you're happy, say it. If you're mad, say it."

It may seem to be an unusual way to let others know about faith, this reality approach, but Matt Nokes is convinced it is what works, and he wants it to be used for God's glory. "Anybody I come in contact with," he says, "I hope they will know I'm a Christian. When I earn the right to speak with them, then the conversation will sometimes end up on that. I've never heard anyone coming to Christ without anyone saying anything to them. You have to talk. You have to share your faith. You have to back it up with who you are. And in sports, it means you have to be real."

Watch Matt Nokes play and you'll notice something that goes beyond his ability to reach the right field fence in Yankee Stadium and throw runners out at second. You'll notice that he is one of the most intense competitors on the field, determined to show anybody who is watching that he has a realistic view of who he is and what he has to do. And as you watch, if you're curious enough to want to know about his source of strength, he'll tell you that it's Jesus. Really.

Q & A WITH MATT NOKES

Q: *What is the most important thing to you today?*
Matt: My number one priority is my relationship with the Lord, and then from that spins the rest of my life. Life is all relationship-oriented.

Q: *Since you said being a Yankee was a dream come true, who did you enjoy watching in baseball as you were growing up?*

Matt: I wasn't a spectator of any kind. I didn't watch sports—still don't watch a whole lot. I'd rather be out playing sports, basketball, baseball, football than watching. I'd rather be watching a science fiction movie than watching a baseball game.

Q: *What was the worst thing that ever happened to you?*
Matt: When my mom died in 1977. That was very hard. Also there have been a lot struggles in baseball that have been very, very hard. The Lord protected me from that when my mother passed away. He healed all the wounds—He didn't leave any scars. But it was a year before I could really talk about it.

Q: *Do you have a family?*
Matt: My wife's name is Christy. We have four children: Corey, Hannah, and the twins, Hillary and Heather.

Q: *How do you handle the ups and downs that come with playing major league baseball?*
Matt: It's kind of an attitude that you have when you're hitting. Just strap it on and go. You wouldn't be there if you didn't have this attitude. You have to go out there and bring it to them. You've got to be intensive. You've got to have grit. You need perseverance and desire.

Q: *What is your favorite verse?*
Matt: Philippians 1:6: "Being confident of this, that He who began a good work in you will carry it on to completion until the day of Christ Jesus."

MAJOR LEAGUE CAREER PATH

June 8, 1981:   Selected in 20th round by Giants
October 7, 1985: Traded with Dave LaPoint and Eric King to the Tigers for Juan Berenguer, Bob Melvin, and Scott Medvin
June 4, 1990:   Traded to the Yankees for Lance McCullers and Clay Parker

THE NOKES FILE

Year	Team	G	AB	R	H	2B	3B	HR	RBI	Avg.
1981	Great Falls	44	146	14	33	6	2	0	13	.226
1982	Clinton	82	247	19	53	12	0	3	23	.215
1983	Fresno	125	429	62	138	26	6	14	82	.322
1984	Shreveport	97	308	32	89	19	2	11	61	.289
1985	Shreveport	105	344	52	101	24	1	14	56	.294
1985	Giants	19	53	3	11	2	0	2	5	.208
1986	Nashville	125	428	55	122	25	4	10	71	.285
1986	Tigers	7	24	2	8	1	0	1	2	.333
1987	Tigers	135	461	69	133	14	2	32	87	.289
1988	Tigers	122	382	53	96	18	0	16	53	.251
1989	Tigers	87	268	15	67	10	0	9	39	.250
1990	Tigers/Yankees	136	351	33	87	9	1	11	40	.248
1991	Yankees	135	456	52	122	20	0	24	77	.268
1992	Yankees	121	384	42	86	9	1	22	59	.224
Major League Career (8 years)		**762**	**2379**	**269**	**610**	**83**	**4**	**117**	**362**	**.256**

Jody Reed
Patrolling the Infield

VITAL STATISTICS

Born July 26, 1962, in Tampa, Florida
5 feet 9, 165 pounds
Current Team: Boston Red Sox
Position: Second Base
Graduated from Florida State University in 1985 (B.S. degree in criminology)

CAREER HIGHLIGHTS

- Played in two championship series, 1988 and 1990
- Hit two doubles in one inning to tie a major league record
- Averaged 40 doubles per year, 1989-1992

WARMING UP

When you put a team in Fenway Park, you'd best not be doing too much running around lest you run your team right out of the chance for a three-run blast over the Green Monster. The Red Sox generally are not a team that spends much time worrying about stealing bases.

For a player like Jody Reed, that's just fine, for he does so many other things to help his team. Like spraying doubles throughout Fenway and scooping up hot ground balls between second and third base. Besides, he really is an honest man in the true sense of the word. He values his role as someone people can look up to. There really is no "larceny in his heart." With a college degree in criminology, he keeps the other team honest as he patrols the infield.

Jody Reed

Jody Reed doesn't steal many bases. There's little need to. He gets plenty of base hits (ninth in the American League in 1990 with 173). But he also bangs out lots of doubles (first in the American League in 1990 with 45 and seventh in the league in 1991 with 42). He accumulates putouts by the hundreds (278 in 1990).

All those doubles may explain why he swiped only 16 bases in his first five years with the Boston Red Sox.

Of course, Reed may not be a base theft for another reason, his educational background. Perhaps all those courses in criminology he took at Florida State University have kept him from stealing bases. Or maybe Jody Reed fits the description of old-time baseball writer Arthur Baer, who once wrote of a player, "He had larceny in his heart, but his feet were honest."

But probably his limited base-stealing exploits arise from playing in Fenway Park. When you put a team in Fenway Park, you'd best not be doing too much running around lest you run your team right out of the chance for a three-run blast over the Green Monster. The near left field wall, only 315 feet away from home plate, invites and rewards long-ball hits. Therefore, the Red Sox generally are not a team that spends much time worrying about stealing bases.

For a player like Reed, that's just fine, for he does so many other things to help his team. Like spraying doubles throughout Fenway and scooping up hot ground balls between second and third base. Besides, he truly is an honest man in the real sense of the word. He values his role as someone people can look up to. There really is no "larceny in his heart."

With a college degree in criminology, he keeps the other team honest as he patrols the infield. Yes, Jody Reed is the kind of person you could leave the keys with when you lock up the stadium at night. He's one honest cop.

For instance, look at the soul searching he put himself through because of the high salaries baseball players receive. He's not one to just take the money and run. He wants to handle it right.

"I have spent many nights reading in the Bible about money and what I should do," he explains. "I've spent many nights reading about how the Lord doesn't want you to make money your idol. There's the verse that says it's tougher for a rich man to get to heaven than for a camel to get through the eye of a needle. I've read that, and I think I understand it."

Then there is the sensitive area of knowing that when you make a large salary people will be after you to get a piece of it. "There are people out there who are in need, and they ask you for money. The tough thing to figure out is whether this person really needs help, or if this person is sincere. Sometimes they are, and sometimes they are not. You've got to use your head in a situation like that."

Several years ago, Detroit Lions running back Barry Sanders surprised a lot of people when he signed a huge contract with the Lions and announced that he was giving 10 percent of his salary to his church. To many people who heard about it, it seemed like a rare, even newsworthy achievement. But what a lot of people don't realize is that many athletes do that.

Here's how Jody Reed arrived at the conclusion that some of his money should go to the church. "I read the part in the Bible where it says they were questioning Jesus about paying taxes, and He said, 'Is that Caesar's face on the coin?' and they said, 'Yeah.' So Jesus said, 'Give Caesar what is his and give Me what is Mine.' That's what we do—my wife and I—we tithe every year, and we think that's important. God says, 'You tithe for Me and show me that money is not your god, and I will return it to you many times over.' And it feels very good to do that.

"Sometimes money is a problem," he says, echoing a feeling most people have, no matter which side of the money ledger they find themselves on. "Sometimes you put more of a priority on it than you should. But for the most part, when you get into the Bible . . . you start to realize that money is nice and it's there for a reason, and you earn it for a reason."

If you listen to Jody Reed very long, you get the idea that this is a man who doesn't like conflict. Take for instance his opinion about what could be done to improve baseball. It's no give-me, give-me plea. No call for better clubhouses or smaller strike zones. It's a call for unity among the factions in baseball that are most often at each other's throats.

"I would like to see some type of situation where there would be more harmony between the proponents of the game. The owners, the players' association, and the umpires' association. I hate to see the discord between any of those groups. Nobody likes to see that. I wish there was some way we could work more closely together and be in more harmony to the public." This man shouldn't be playing second base. He ought to be running for commissioner.

If there's anybody in a community that you want children to look up to, it's the men and women in blue—the police force. Since they enforce the laws, they should always be setting the example for others. They should be role models. Patrolman Jody Reed of the infield precinct is just such a person.

"Being a professional athlete sometimes thrusts people into a role model situation when they are not comfortable or ready to be a role model," Reed begins as he talks about this extra responsibility that comes with the territory of sports stardom. "People put a lot of blame on and have a lot of negative talk toward some of these athletes, because they are not acting appropriately in a role model situation. Maybe they're not ready to be a role model. Maybe they are not comfortable being that.

"I myself feel comfortable that people can look at my life and see the happiness that I get, and the joy that I get through the Lord. I think that's one of the purposes He has for me. It's like

He's saying, 'I want you to go out there and play and do with your abilities that I've given you, and shine for Me and let people see that you're happy and you glorify My name. And be a role model.'

"Some people can be doctors, some people can be lawyers. God has given everybody certain abilities, but I was blessed with the ability to play baseball—physical ability, and I'm hoping I can use that to show others that Jesus is the source of my happiness. I love what I do. . . . A lot of people aren't able to do what they love to do for a profession. I think I was allowed to because I'm going to go out there and glorify God and give Him all the credit."

Jody Reed has not always been so confident. In fact during his early years of minor league baseball, he was struggling with this new world that was opening up before him. The concept of God was not new to him, for he was brought up going to church. But he had never gotten anything out of his church experience that prepared him or would help him when he took off to play at the lowest level of professional baseball: the Single A Florida State League Winter Haven Red Sox.

"All of a sudden you go from college—sort of a sheltered-type situation with not too many responsibilities—to being away from home on your own," he explains about the transition to life as a minor leaguer. "You have bills to pay. You have to perform. It's more pressures than you're used to. You feel very alone, don't know where to turn."

Teammate Chris Cannazaro, a Christian, invited Reed to join him for the Winter Haven Red Sox's Baseball Chapel, and thinking it would make up for missing church during the season, he said yes. After the first chapel, Jody agreed to attend another and then another. Soon he was telling Chris about his worries and the heavy burden he felt. His teammate opened the Bible to 1 Peter 5:7 and read, "Cast all your anxiety on Him because He cares for you."

"The Lord says we should put our burdens on His shoulders so we can do His will," Chris explained. That caught Jody's attention.

"You mean I can ask Him to take all these problems and deal with them His way? That way I can concentrate on what I've got to do down here?"

"That's it," Chris answered.

Later in the season, the Winter Haven Red Sox were in Tampa, ready to play the Tampa Tarpons. Seated on a bench in the bullpen, Jody and several other minor league players listened to a guest at the Baseball Chapel meeting. When he finished his message, he invited the ballplayers to accept Christ as their savior.

I want it, I feel right doing this, Jody said to himself. "That's where I turned my life over to Christ," he recalls.

"That's not to say that I saw sparks and things like this," Reed says about this time of coming to faith, "but I felt a certain comfort immediately after. In my Christian life, there's been ups and downs, certainly. But now I feel like I'm finally making some ground. I feel very fortunate to have been introduced to and to have accepted Christ."

His life changed, but perhaps in ways he alone could recognize. He didn't have a wayward life that needed turning around, but something happened in his attitudes and behavior that becomes clearer as he explains it.

"I wasn't the social, party-type person. I got more disciplined. Maybe I had some resentments, wishing I could do what others could do. Things like that. Once you start reading the Bible, you realize that that's not what God wants you to do. He doesn't want you to want what they have.

"At first, I was slow to read the Bible. I might have a good week and then a bad two weeks. But the more I read the Bible, the more I realized how God wants me to be. That's the thing that has changed me the most—getting into the Scriptures and reading my Bible and learning about how I'm supposed to be."

One place where Reed has no doubts about how he is supposed to be is on the baseball diamond. And as you would expect a person of his demeanor to be, he is grateful for the guidance of those who got him where he is. He realizes that his being in the major leagues is a combination of hard work, good coaching, and God's guidance, for no one ever confused Jody Reed with Jose Canseco.

"I don't think I'm one of those guys with an abundance of talent, so I'd have to say [my success is due to] a lot of hard work, a lot of perseverance. Just a love for the game."

It wasn't that he wasn't good, because he was. But one thing he wasn't was big. In fact, his lack of size made him switch positions one year in high school. "I was always a shortstop—until my sophomore year when I was in high school. I wasn't strong enough to play shortstop. I couldn't compete against juniors and seniors who were more advanced than I was. I had to play second that year, until I grew a little more over the summer. Then I went back to shortstop as a junior." He wouldn't play second base again until 1989 with the Red Sox, when his double-play partner, Marty Barrett, got hurt and Reed filled in for him.

What he might have lacked in strength as a kid, he surely made up for in drive, determination, and love for the game. "I lived and breathed baseball, I loved the game. Recognizing his limitations, he says, "You have to stay within the limits of your capability. If you try to do more than you're capable of, you're not going to be as successful."

What Jody Reed knew he was capable of was concentrating on the task at hand. "The thing that sticks out about high school, college, minors, and even pro ball is focus. I had to stay very focused. I couldn't just show up and go out there and dazzle people. I had to really concentrate and play hard every day. And that was just to get a little recognition by scouts and coaches—just to get a chance to play pro ball.

"And once I got into the minors, I had to go even harder and concentrate even more to make it from level to level."

From his days as a high school player in Florida to the summers in places like Winter Haven and Pawtucket, this young man who "breathed baseball" drove himself, listened to his mentors, and patrolled the infield with such skill that he finally was stationed in Boston, beginning in 1987.

Besides that inner drive that burned inside him and the focus that he maintained, Jody Reed knows he had another advantage: a unique ability to hit doubles. In only five full years in the major leagues, he has made it safely to second 180 times. Rickey Henderson steals bases, Cecil Fielder hits home runs, Ozzie Smith makes circus catches, and Jody Reed hits doubles.

Reed modestly describes his doubles as "singles that get by the outfield." Concerning his marvelous 45 doubles during 1990, which tied for the league lead, he says, "I was fortunate. I wasn't going up to the plate to hit a double. I was just trying to hit the ball hard."

There is no special formula for becoming a doubles hitter, according to Reed, who denies it takes "special skill for hitting doubles." Placement, though, is important for this 5-feet-9 batter. "I hit most of my doubles down the left field line, and also in the left-center alley." And that often lands him back at second base, which makes sense. It is his zone of patrol, offensively as well as defensively.

In major league baseball, however, every player will struggle, no matter how hard he concentrates or how hard he works. In 1992, for instance, the entire Boston team was in a slump, with the team batting a meager .246 and ending the year at the bottom of the American League East division. For Reed, that falloff even affected his doubles production. He had 27 two-baggers, second on the team but below the 43 he averaged the previous three seasons.

Because Reed cares so much about this game, times like that are probably more nettlesome for him than for most. He tells about another of those times. "I was in a bad slump for about a month. I felt anger. I felt impatience. I felt resentment. I felt all those things. But every time I felt those things, I opened up my Bible to find out what God says about it, what He wants me to do about it, how He wants me to feel about it.

"I would go and read and find the section or verse or chapter, and I'd say, 'OK, this is how You want me to be; this is how I'm going to be.' I felt it was a trial that God was putting me through to teach me something. I think it was a time when He wanted me to learn patience, perseverance, overcoming. Through that I think I've become stronger. That's what life is all about. We're going to go through trials and tribulations."

But trials much worse than being unable to connect against Jack Morris have come into Jody Reed's life. Trials that might cause some people to reject God, be bitter toward Him, or curse Him. "My wife, Michelle, miscarried two times," Reed says. "Our losing those two pregnancies was the worst thing that ever happened to me. It hurt. And it was very confusing. You just don't know why it is happening. I feel there was a definite purpose. It was a tremendous learning experience for us. And obviously there was a reason for that to happen. It brought us extremely close.

"Things like that really draw on your relationship and your trust in God. It was comforting to be able to give it to Him and say, 'It's Your will. We're going to stick close to You, and we're going to get through this with Your help.' Without a doubt, those were the toughest times either one of us has ever had." One way God helped them get through that tough time was to answer their prayer for a healthy baby, which the Reeds celebrated during the summer of 1992.

The next time you see Jody Reed patrolling the infield, think about all that has gone in to making him the kind of person he is. The drive to succeed. The life of following Christ. The appreciation of being able to live out a dream. The constant faith despite tragic setbacks.

And think about this final word, which gives you an idea of how arresting a testimony can be when it comes from someone with a real love for God. "It's very comforting to know that you have accepted Jesus Christ and you have eternal life, but also you are in a position to help others. Nothing will make you feel better than to know that you've had a hand in helping others find Christ. Once you've accepted Him, that's the ultimate sacrifice and conviction."

Q & A WITH JODY REED

Q: *How do you feel about sharing your faith with others?*
Jody: I'll talk to anyone. I used to be a little shy about it and a little hesitant. But I'm getting to the point where I feel very open about discussing any questions about my beliefs in Christ. I feel very confident in talking about it. I think that will help the people I come in contact with.

Q: *What kinds of things do you see at the ballpark that are funny?*
Jody: Each day you're going to have something funny happen. The things that stick out the most are the things the fans do. For

instance we were in Yankee Stadium in 1990, playing a night game. A fan jumped from the upper deck onto the screen behind home plate. He bounced on the screen like it was a trampoline. In Boston a guy got on the retaining wire that holds the screen and scaled it hand over hand like a cat burglar.

Q: *What is the most important thing in the world to you?*
Jody: My relationship with the Lord. There was a point when I would have been a little shy to say that because I was afraid of what people might think. But the things that the Lord has shown me and the way He's led my life [makes that relationship] number one, without a doubt. Certainly there are times when I don't feel like I'm worthy—a lot of times. But He's been there each and every time I've needed Him.

Q: *If you were the commissioner of baseball, what would you change?*
Jody: I would resolve the designated hitter rule, one way or the other. I think it would be in baseball's best interests to make the leagues uniform as far as that goes. The experiment has been either successful or not successful, and you need to go one way or the other.

MAJOR LEAGUE CAREER PATH

June 4, 1984: Selected by Red Sox in 8th round of free-agent draft

Year	Team	G	AB	R	H	2B	3B	HR	RBI	Avg.
1984	Winter Haven	77	273	46	74	14	1	0	20	.271
1985	Winter Haven	134	489	95	157	25	1	0	45	.321
1986	New Britain	60	218	33	50	12	1	0	11	.229
1986	Pawtucket	69	227	27	64	11	0	1	30	.282
1987	Pawtucket	136	510	77	151	22	2	7	51	.296
1987	Red Sox	9	30	4	9	1	1	0	8	.300
1988	Red Sox	109	338	60	99	23	1	1	28	.293
1989	Red Sox	146	524	76	151	42	2	3	40	.288
1990	Red Sox	155	598	70	173	45	0	5	51	.289
1991	Red Sox	153	618	87	175	42	2	5	60	.283
1992	Red Sox	143	550	64	136	27	1	3	40	.247
Major League Career (6 years)		**715**	**2658**	**361**	**743**	**180**	**7**	**17**	**227**	**.280**

Harold Reynolds
Pointing the Way

VITAL STATISTICS

Born November 26, 1960, in Eugene, Oregon
5 feet 11, 165 pounds
Current Team: Seattle Mariners
Position: Second Base
Attended San Diego State University, Canada College, and California State University

CAREER HIGHLIGHTS

- Shares the major league record for assists by second baseman in one game (12), August 27, 1986
- Led American League in stolen bases in 1987 (60)
- Led American League second basemen in double plays in 1986, 1987, 1988, and 1991
- Named to All-Star team two times

WARMING UP

I went to the White House and got time with him," Harold Reynolds begins as he talks about his visit with the most powerful man in the world. "We spent about 10 to 15 minutes—just the president and me—in the Oval Office. We talked about the Lord, believe it or not. It was really neat."

Harold Reynolds

Second basemen don't often get invited to the White House. Especially those whose teams don't win the World Series. But All-Star second sacker Harold Reynolds earned his way into the Oval Office—and he did it more for what he accomplished off the field than for what he was able to do on it.

To be sure, Reynolds is no slouch around second base. He has led the American League in assists several times. He has combined with his Seattle shortstop to record the most double plays in the league on three occasions. And he is nearly always near the top in putouts.

But the White House didn't call because of Reynolds' glove. They invited him to meet with the President because of his heart. He received President George Bush's 195th Point of Light Award for his work with kids.

It was September 1990, and the Seattle Mariners were playing in Baltimore. Answering the invitation from the point man himself, Reynolds took a side trip to Washington, D.C. "I went to the White House and got time with him," Reynolds begins as he talks about his visit with the most powerful man in the world. "We spent about 10 to 15 minutes—just the president and me—in the Oval Office. We talked about the Lord, believe it or not. It was really neat. He'd had Billy Graham there the night before, and the Kuwait situation was just coming up.

"I told him before I left that I was going to be praying for him, and that changed our whole conversation. I ended up staying about another 10 minutes just talking about what our relationship is with Christ."

What was it that got the president's attention at a time when the Middle East was on the verge of war? What could Reynolds have done that would result in his recognition as one of the most caring, compassionate people in the United States? What does Harold Reynolds have going for him?

A few years earlier Reynolds followed the lead of Milwaukee Brewers' player Cecil Cooper, who brought an antidrug message to children in the inner city. "Coop's Kids" featured sports stars speaking to children in schools and the community. Cooper invited Reynolds and teammate Alvin Davis.

"I really didn't know what to say, so I shared the gospel—I started just sharing about my relationship with Jesus. About 50 of those kids got saved that day."

When he returned home Reynolds told himself, *I must start this program in Seattle. But it's going to be strictly to share the gospel.* The following year he began the program, bringing in athletes from different teams to give their testimony. More than 2,000 youngsters came during the next couple of summers. They heard the gospel, and Reynolds estimates three-quarters of them "got plugged into churches and got saved."

The program soon expanded, and Reynolds began a children's foundation. The foundation addresses drug abuse and other dangers children face. "I continue to try to reach kids that are in need to give them direction in their lives and also to give them the opportunity to get to know who Jesus Christ is."

Although Reynolds doesn't have any children of his own, he has decided to take an entire stateful of kids under his wing. The Washington state organization, called the Harold Reynolds Children's Foundation, sponsors baseball clinics for children and a speakers' program at local schools. Reynolds' foundation also produces children's literature that helps them tackle some of the big problems they face. Among the booklets the Reynolds' group has sponsored and underwritten are the antidrug stories called *What Mary Found* and *Hands to Love.* These are not just pamphlets that give kids 10 reasons to stay clean; they are well-crafted stories, for Reynolds feels that just as Jesus got His point across by telling stories so can anyone who wants to help children.

Another project Reynolds devotes time and effort to is Role Models Unlimited. Wayne Perryman, a former gang member and the author of *What Mary Found,* is cofounder of Role Models Unlimited, a group designed to help black children aspire to success. In 1990 the two men held a banquet for black businessmen in an attempt to motivate them to return to the inner city and help the neighborhoods they left behind when they moved up the economic ladder. One thousand men showed up.

Long before Harold Reynolds became one of Seattle's top citizen activists and proponents of children, back when he was just a tenderhearted kid growing up in Corvallis, Oregon, he had two lights of his own to point the way for him—his mother and his grandmother. Together they reared Harold and his seven brothers and sisters. Their influence is now felt in the lives of the thousands of young people Harold reaches out to each year.

How did they do it? What did Mom and Grandma have that helped them bring up someone with the social consciousness and spiritual concern of Harold Reynolds? They had a Bible verse: "Train up a child in the way he should go, and when he's old he will not depart from it" (Proverbs 22:6).

That's not an easy verse for a parent to depend on when all is going against her. And Harold's mother could have easily felt that way. She and her husband parted company when Harold was only three, leaving Mom and Grandma to rear the family through a variety of jobs. Besides that, hers was one of only four African-American families in town, a situation that surely caused its own share of difficulties.

Yet she was the strength that kept the family moving on up. "She had a tremendous influence on my life," Harold says of his mom. "She did everything she could to make sure we had what we needed. She really showed what it meant to be committed to her kids. She sacrificed her whole life to make sure we had what we had."

Her work has definitely paid off. All eight of her children graduated from college. Harold is a major league ballplayer and two brothers, Don (1978-79 Padres) and Larry (1979-84 Rangers and Cardinals), also played professional baseball.

In the noise and constant activity that must have characterized the Reynolds household of eight children, there were constants—such as church, sports, and the positive influence of the brothers and sisters on each other.

"I grew up going to church," Reynolds recalls. "I can remember Sunday mornings when I was a kid, my mom coming in and waking us up and saying, 'Hey, come on! Get dressed! It's time to go to church.'

"There was a lot of training in our household that developed a lot of characteristics that are in me today. I encourage parents with that. Even though your kids may fight and fuss and not want to [listen to you], when they're older, they'll look back on a lot of different things and appreciate them."

The influence of sports on Harold's life began early, what with all those older brothers and sisters around. Though the starting age for youth baseball was six, he began playing at five. Still, he made the All-Star team. Growing up, he always played with older kids, starting with his four older brothers. The older brothers had a big influence on Harold. As high school ballplayers, they participated in the Fellowship of Christian Athletes. Young Harold wanted to tag along. "I figured, hey, they're doing that, so I'd like to go and check it out." And they welcomed him.

"My brothers and sisters, through their own trials, continually came back and refreshed my mind that it was important to continue to put the Lord first. When you see it in somebody's life at an early age, you start to understand it yourself. . . . When I got to an age where I knew I needed to make a commitment, it was something that I wanted to do and I needed to do."

Through all of those influences, Reynolds recalls, "the seeds got planted at an early age for me. When I was about a junior in high school, I realized that I was one of the older guys in our FCA huddle group. The speaker was talking to us about a personal relationship with Jesus Christ, and I said, 'Man, I don't have that.'

"It wasn't a matter of having to go through a traumatic experience to come to know Jesus. It was more natural. I was basically living off the relationship that everybody else in my family had.

"I think what happens with a lot of kids that are brought up in that kind of environment is that people just assume they're Christians, because that's the environment they are in. And it doesn't become personal. I really got on my face before the Lord and asked Him to come into my heart. That was the time that I really made a commitment to God and really started to walk with the Lord."

It was no dramatic turnaround for this future All-Star. He had spent his childhood wondering about God and desiring to know more about Him. The influence of a godly mother and grandmother prepared him. Once, at age six, he was watching TV when a man declared in an interview that God had died. Harold walked outside, fearful and confused. His grandmother was working in her rose garden when she heard young Harold sniffling.

"What's wrong?" she asked.

"Well, the man on TV said God died."

"Grandma sat me down and started showing me all the roses, and she started showing me all the trees and how the wind was blowing in the trees. She pointed to those trees and said, 'That's the breath of God, and if God was dead none of these things would be alive.'

"At that early age I started having a different perspective. I really wanted to know this Man. Not just know Him, but I wanted to know Him intimately. When I was 17 and making that verbal commitment of asking Jesus Christ into my heart, it was more like saying, 'OK, now I know,' but when I was little, I think I already really understood the concept of who He was."

Not only was Harold a bit ahead of others in his thoughts about God, but he was usually ahead of everyone else in baseball too. Besides beginning his career in organized baseball at age five and having the advantage of playing against his older brothers, he and his brothers would practice with the Oregon State baseball team. The son of the head coach was one of Harold's best friends.

All that experience of being the youngest kid playing helped Harold when he left Corvallis for Southern California to play baseball at San Diego State, although the competition was a bit stiffer now. "The biggest thing was getting over the intimidation factor of playing with older guys. To me that was natural, that was normal."

Of course the biggest challenge was yet to come: professional baseball. Especially since there were two things that his coaches saw in his game that they wanted to change when Harold Reynolds showed up at that level. First, they moved him in from the outfield and made him a second baseman. The second alteration was to make him into a switch-hitter.

"I developed a lot of work habits when I was a kid," Reynolds says about all those hours he spent playing on the Corvallis sandlots, "but I had to really work when I got into pro baseball." The hard work did not go unrewarded. He spent parts of five seasons in the minors, but Harold Reynolds finally stuck with the Seattle Mariners in 1986.

After playing baseball since he was five and having achieved major league status, Reynolds could have been smug and satisfied. After all, how many boys grow up to play baseball for a living? But he has a couple more urgent missions. First, "I'm here to win people to Jesus. And that's what it's all about." His second mission has been partially accomplished: to be an All-Star second baseman.

He began thinking about the possibilities of making the All-Star team in the winter between the 1986 and 1987 seasons. "I had hit .222 [in 1986]," Reynolds begins. "All winter long I worked out and I prayed that God would give me some vision. I felt like this was the year that really turned things around for me."

Before this winter of his discontent, he says, "I was just happy to be in the big leagues—just glad to get my letterman's jacket, so to speak. But I wanted to be more known so I would have more of a platform. I felt that being an All-Star would be the best way. I heard a guy preaching about having vision for your life. And it just grabbed hold of my heart. Proverbs 29:18 says, 'Where there is no vision, the people perish.'"

So all winter Reynolds worked out with a vengeance. On every jerk of the weights, he would think, "This is an All-Star lift."

"That was my goal. I wanted to become an All-Star. I wanted to go from just existing to being an All-Star. But I wanted to do it in a righteous way, not for my own vanity."

By midseason, he "had the stats and everything to make the All-Star team." But there was a glitch in the plan. "Being in Seattle, I didn't get voted in. Lou Whitaker got picked ahead of me. I was outplaying him, and I should have made the team. Then all of a sudden Lou hurt his back." Just a few days before the All-Star game, the Boston Red Sox were in Seattle to play the Mariners. John McNamara, the manager of the Red Sox and the American League team, walked up to Reynolds and asked him what he was planning for the day of the All-Star game.

"Probably watching the game," Reynolds replied.

"How about coming to Oakland with me? I'm putting you on my All-Star team."

"To me that was confirmation from God," Reynolds says. "It was something that I really laid before Him and earnestly desired. That was my biggest thrill in baseball because it was God who did it, not John McNamara."

After earning the label "All-Star second baseman," Harold Reynolds has not backed down from his pledge to use his recognition as one of the best players in the game as a testimony for Jesus. Sometimes it happens without his having to leave the stadium. Once Reynolds and then-teammate Mike Kingery were taking early batting practice in Baltimore. During a break Reynolds went into the locker room to get a Bible. He returned, and as Kingery sat with him in the stands before the fans arrived, an usher walked by.

"Hey, you're Mike Kingery." Then seeing the other Mariner, the usher exclaimed, "You're Harold Reynolds!"

"He sits down, and I closed the Bible, and we start talking," Reynolds recalls. "He says, 'Man, I go to church a little bit. How do you become saved?' So I just started talking to him about how to come to know the Lord in a personal relationship. That blew my mind, because a lot of people want to know what it means to be saved or born again, but they don't necessarily ask. They seek, but they don't necessarily ask." Here was an opportunity for Harold Reynolds to fulfill his mission simply because someone recognized him.

As helpful as Reynolds finds the spotlight in enabling him to spread the good news, at times that spotlight can be downright humbling. Although things like this probably happen only once in a career, he remembers one humorous incident while playing Milwaukee in the Seattle Kingdome.

"I made this great play. I went up the middle and jumped and spun around and threw Glenn Braggs out. I thought, *Man, it doesn't get any better.* I thought I was cool. I was jogging off the field—we had a big crowd that night—and right before I got to the dugout, I tripped.

"I'm strutting in, thinking I'm cool, and I trip. My glove and my hat fly off, and I'm laying there just flat on the turf. I look up, and everybody is looking at me! Here they were cheering the play, and I'm coming off thinking I'm cool, and I fall flat on my face. Sometimes God humbles you."

Most of the time, however, Harold Reynolds proves that God uses you. Uses you to influence others for good. Uses you to help kids avoid what is bad. Uses you to point the way for those who are searching for direction.

It is ironic that a man who was reared successfully by a single parent has become so involved as a spokesman for the need for men to get interested in children's lives. He recognizes that he is one of the fortunate ones and that his situation is not at all typical. It is almost as if God has specially picked him out to do this work.

As a founder of Role Models Unlimited, he recognizes his own influence as an example. All baseball players "have a special, unique platform as athletes. And I understand the importance of trying to live right and being a role model, but I feel like the greatest role models are the ones who are in the homes." Reynolds desires that those who spend the most time with children—the parents—would be the role models. He recalls how as a child he idolized Gus Williams, the high-leaping forward for the Seattle Supersonics. Young Harold tried to emulate his hoops hero and wanted to be like him. But whenever he would be out playing and get hurt, he says with insightful simplicity, he would go running to his mom, not Gus Williams, for sympathy. It is those who actually touch the children's lives who really need to maintain their position as people to look up to.

If Harold Reynolds can help people to see that—and to help them see that the only real answer in life is Jesus Christ—he will be successful in pointing the way.

Q & A WITH HAROLD REYNOLDS

Q: *How do you deal with the highs and lows of professional baseball?*
Harold: The main thing is prayer. Through spending time getting to know God's heart I can deal with things. I want to have the heart of Jesus and that intimacy with Him. So you've got to stay in prayer.

Q: *What about the fame of playing major league baseball bothers you?*
Harold: The thing that I have problems dealing with is that so many people think they know you but they don't really know you. I'm very personable. I allow people to come up and talk to me. I don't block my calls when I'm on the road, stuff like that. I am real to people. But a lot of people will assume that they know you, and sometimes that bothers me.

Q: *What goals have you set for your career?*
Harold: I haven't really thought about career goals. The main thing I want to to do is just stay healthy. If I stay healthy, the numbers and statistics will be there. I guess the main thing I want to do is always improve on the year before.

Q: *What do you think about playing in Seattle?*
Harold: I love Seattle. Seattle's been home for me. I grew up in the Northwest, in Oregon. In my heart, I would really like to stay in Seattle.

Q: *What would you be doing today if you had never played in the major leagues?*
Harold: I probably would have been working with some kind of youth ministry.

Q: *Who is the toughest pitcher you've faced?*
Harold: In 1991, we faced Bret Saberhagen [who was then pitching for the Kansas City Royals] when he had everything working. To me, that was the toughest game I ever had. He struck me out three times, and it wasn't even close. That was a rough game.

Q: *If you were commissioner of baseball, what would you change?*
Harold: I think a lot of problems in baseball are caused [by] the publication of [salaries]. I don't think it's right. I think it's an invasion of privacy. You don't print what doctors make. I think it's ruining the game to print what certain guys make.

Q: *How do you want people to remember you?*
Harold: As a man of God who really tried to do what was right, who tried to walk right.

MAJOR LEAGUE CAREER PATH

June 3, 1980: Selected by the Mariners in secondary phase of free-agent draft

THE REYNOLDS FILE

Year	Team	G	AB	R	H	2B	3B	HR	RBI	Avg.
1981	Wausau	127	493	98	146	23	3	11	59	.296
1982	Lynn	102	375	58	102	14	4	2	48	.272
1983	Salt Lake	136	534	84	165	20	9	1	72	.309
1983	Mariners	20	59	8	12	4	1	0	1	.203
1984	Salt Lake	135	558	94	165	22	6	3	54	.296
1984	Mariners	10	10	3	3	0	0	0	0	.300
1985	Mariners	67	104	15	15	3	1	0	6	.144
1985	Calgary	52	212	36	77	11	3	5	30	.363
1986	Calgary	29	118	20	37	7	0	1	7	.314
1986	Mariners	126	445	46	99	19	4	1	24	.222
1987	Mariners	160	530	73	146	31	8	1	35	.275
1988	Mariners	158	598	61	169	26	11	4	41	.283
1989	Mariners	153	613	87	184	24	9	0	43	.300
1990	Mariners	160	642	100	162	36	5	5	55	.252
1991	Mariners	161	631	95	160	34	6	3	57	.254
1992	Mariners	140	458	55	113	23	3	3	33	.247
Major League Career (10 years)		**1155**	**4090**	**543**	**1063**	**200**	**48**	**17**	**295**	**.260**

Scott Sanderson
Enjoying the Ride

VITAL STATISTICS

Born July 22, 1956, in Dearborn, Michigan
6 feet 5, 192 pounds
Current Team: New York Yankees
Position: Pitcher (right-handed)
Attended Vanderbilt University

CAREER HIGHLIGHTS

- Has compiled 10 winning seasons as a starter in the major leagues
- Has struck out more than 1,300 batters
- Selected once to the American League All-Star team

WARMING UP

Baseball threw Scott Sanderson a sharp-breaking curve after the 1990 season. That year was almost a storybook campaign for him. He won 17 games for the Oakland A's and helped them get into the World Series. But as 1990 wound down, on the last day of the year, he was sent packing to the New York Yankees, a team that had won 67 games and finished last. In one move, Scott Sanderson moved from a contender to a cellar dweller.

Scott Sanderson

Scott Sanderson has an attitude.

A good one.

A lot of professional athletes do their best to try to make fans feel sorry for them. They moan because they have to ride on scheduled airplane flights instead of charters. They whine because their contract ends after the season and pays them only a million and a half dollars. They gripe about the schedule. They grouse about the manager.

The more they fuss, the less the fans like them. Then they complain because no one appreciates them.

Thankfully, not all athletes are like that. Some are like Scott Sanderson.

Take, for instance, the way baseball threw him a sharp-breaking curve after the 1990 season. That year was almost a storybook campaign for Sanderson. He won 17 games for the Oakland A's and helped them get into the World Series. But as 1990 wound down, on the last day of the year, Sanderson was sent packing to the New York Yankees, a team that had won 67 games and finished last. In one move, Scott Sanderson moved from a contender to a cellar dweller.

But remember, Scott Sanderson isn't just any baseball player. He knows how to enjoy the ride, even when it gets bumpy. He will not complain about his coast-to-coast transition. "Instead of being bitter at the Oakland A's or anything like that, I look at [the trade] just the opposite. I was so fortunate to play there even one year. A lot of guys go through their career and don't get to play for a team quite like Oakland was.

"They don't get to play for an organization that has as much class as they do, and play for a manager like Tony La Russa, and have the expertise of a Dave Duncan as a pitching coach," Sanderson continues, careful not to burn any bridges. "Even though it was only for one year, I really have become a better ballplayer for it. I'll be forever grateful that I got to go there even for one year."

Yes, this really is an honest-to-goodness major league baseball player sounding appreciative, gracious, and grateful. But Scott Sanderson doesn't take credit for that great attitude. He knows it comes from Someone else.

"That's not a perspective I would come up with on my own," he explains. "I just thank the Lord for laying that on my heart and giving me that attitude. Although I would have preferred to stay [with Oakland], I think it allowed me to leave there feeling pretty good about everything."

Maybe Scott Sanderson is onto something. Maybe a happy pitcher is a successful pitcher. And Sanderson certainly seemed to be both for the Yankees during his initial year in pinstripes. In his very first outing for the Yanks, he nearly no-hit the Detroit Tigers, holding them hitless until late in the game. From that point on, Sanderson was by far the ace of the staff. He won 16 games, twice as many as his nearest challenger on the team. He led the team in strikeouts, starts, complete games, and innings pitched. He also made the All-Star team.

Of course, there's more to baseball than stats. A player also has to survive and try to thrive in the environment of the city he lives in. For Sanderson, the move from Oakland took him into a situation that many players fear: New York City and the Yankees. The city has ruined many attitudes along the way. There's the allegedly hostile press. The demanding fans. The specter of controversy. Scott Sanderson knew what he was getting into.

"As a visiting player, I heard it said over and over again, 'Boy, this would be a tough place to have to play.' But I don't find it any tougher than anywhere else," he says with his characteristic ease. "If you pitch well, or if you perform well, the fans are going to like it, and if you don't—you have a bad game—they're not going to like you. I don't think that really changes anywhere. I think because of the size of the city and the amount of maybe more intensive media coverage, people get an idea that it's tougher to play there."

Although negative press might be one of the main reasons some athletes don't like to play in Gotham, it never bothers Sanderson, and it never will.

"One thing I learned earlier in my baseball career," he explains, "is that I don't read the newspapers and I don't listen to the radio—the call-in shows. It is very seldom that I will even watch the sports replays on TV." It might affect his game, he argues, so he chooses to shut those kinds of things out.

"It is mostly because I think the players sometimes can get their own sense of value a little screwed up, depending on what some reporter or some call-in show will say about them. I think early in my career that happened one time. I got really upset by something I read in the paper, and it probably took away from my game because I was so upset about it. So now I just leave all that kind of stuff alone."

This is not the arrogance of a player who won't talk to reporters or the sarcasm of an athlete berating reporters. It is simply a matter of avoiding unnecessary distractions. Sanderson just doesn't need anyone to tell him how he is doing. He has been around long enough to know how to prepare and what to do, so he will not spend time worrying about what observers say about him.

"The most important thing for me," he explains, "is that I know what kind of effort I'm putting into the game. I know the talent that God's given me is a gift, and I know that it is my responsibility to continue to develop that talent as best as I can. And that means to be intense about it."

A great attitude and intensity. It's an unbeatable combination. Sanderson has parlayed those two traits into a career that has brought him more than 140 victories. "As a Christian ball-player, I don't think we're called on to be soft," Sanderson explains as he extols a work ethic that has allowed him to succeed. "I don't think we're called on to just roll over and let people walk over us. I think it's quite the opposite. When I go through my workouts and I prepare for a game, and I'm pitching a game, to me nothing is more important than that moment right there, and being as intense and as competitive as I possibly can be."

"Nothing is more important" in baseball, he says. But outside baseball, he reserves his most ardent affections and support for a tiny group of people far different from the New York Yankees or the Oakland A's: his wife, Kathleen, and their two children.

"There are hours set aside in a day for baseball," Sanderson explains, "and there are other hours that I set aside for being a father and being a husband. [That's the time for] letting Kathleen and the kids know they're the most important thing to me."

It's not always easy to find those hours when the schedule dictates that between March and October Daddy will be out of town half the time. This is the part of the road that is filled with potholes—the part of the ride that he might find difficult to enjoy—so he tries to negotiate it the best he can.

"It is a challenging part of the game of baseball—the fact that we're away from our families," Scott says, but having cited the problem he lets his ebullient attitude of acceptance show through. "But as in every profession, there are pluses and minuses. The plus side is that during the off season you get four months of being home, if you so desire to be home 24 hours a day, seven days a week for four months in a row. I mean, that's a pretty long vacation time to get to be home.

"What we try to do, Kathleen and I, is to balance it. When I'm home, I spend as much time as I can with her and the kids, helping out, whether it be taking them to the park or all of us going out to breakfast together. We just try to spend as much time as we can together.

"I know there is also a need for Kathleen, because she is in charge of taking care of the kids and has the sole responsibility when I'm on the road. When I come home off the road, and I've been eating out every night and been in hotels, and I'm so happy to be home, I like to stay home. But there's a need for her also to get a break, to get out alone with me. We're not just parents; we're husband and wife also."

To some athletes, their idea of coming home after a road trip is to unload the suitcase, throw the golf clubs in the trunk, and head for the course—neglecting the responsibilities and joys of being a dad and a husband. One football player reportedly went from the Super Bowl to the links and didn't come home for several weeks. That's a road Scott Sanderson won't travel.

"I like the responsibility of being a husband," he says without apology. "You know, taking over the leadership of the family spiritually and decision-making—all that kind of stuff. I like that. I like to work together with Kathleen." The Sandersons accept their role as spiritual leaders of their children, though they know at times it's a challenge.

"We're conscious, each and every day, of the instruction that we give our children, the amount of time we spend with them, the love that we give to them. We know in these early formative years that that's really where the groundwork is laid for what they're going to be like and what their hearts are going to be like. It's a great responsibility, but it's one that I just love. I realize that I can't do it by myself and that God has given me the direction."

It's not natural, one could assume, for a star athlete to have such a good outlook about everything. Handling career changes without complaint. Playing with intensity and tenacity in spite of obstacles. Being a loving father and husband. Letting God direct his ways. These are not things most men do naturally. But for Scott Sanderson, a supernatural transformation took place in his life several years ago that accounts for his positive outlook and inclination to do the right thing.

Let's go back before the Oakland A's, the Chicago Cubs, and the Montreal Expos. Even before West Palm Beach in the Florida State League. As a kid growing up, Sanderson went to church, but only because his parents insisted. When he entered Vanderbilt University in Nashville, he was ready to make his own decisions, and not just about church.

"For the first time in my life, the decisions I made—even whether to get up that day and go to class or not [were mine]," he recalls. "Mom and Dad aren't there to say, 'Come on, son, get out of bed. Let's go.' My senior year in high school I couldn't have stayed in bed all day long if I wanted to. My freshman year in college—six months later—if you want to sleep all day, and if it's raining outside or cold or whatever, there's no one there to tell you that you must do something.

"That carried out to my personal life, my academic life, my social life—everything. It also was true of my spiritual life. No one was there saying, 'Scott, you have to go to church. You have to do this. You have to do that.' "

Ironically, though, it was an invitation he received—not a forced command to attend a religious meeting—that turned things around for Sanderson spiritually. To be sure, it was an invitation with some very strong incentives for this kid fresh out of high school baseball, but it was an invitation.

"The two senior captains of the baseball team at Vanderbilt invited me early in my freshman year to a Fellowship of Christian Athletes' meeting," Sanderson recalls. "And I didn't even hear that it was an FCA meeting. All I knew was that two senior captains of the baseball team were inviting a freshman to go somewhere, and I was going to go. I didn't care where it was. It could have been to a bar for all I cared, and I was going to go, just because they asked.

"At that meeting and at the next few FCA meetings after that, I was presented with a question. What was I going to do with this Man, Jesus Christ? And I think that it hit me at this time that God had prepared my heart to hear this message, and I was ready for it. It was the first time that I was out there on my own to make a decision on my own.

"At that point I did decide to accept Jesus Christ as my Savior, and so from that point on (1974) it's been a gradual growing process.

"I'd like to say that as a freshman I got my life squared away right then and never had any slip-ups or anything, but that's not the case. I will say that after being married for more than 12 years and having two children, I think the responsibility of being a husband, being a father—that in and of itself has made me be very introspective in my spiritual life. I try to be the man that God would have me be—not only in a baseball uniform, but more important, at home."

Part of the growth for Kathleen and Scott Sanderson came during a long nine-year stint in their lives when they feared that they would never have any children. Kathleen explains the trauma of that waiting period. "When I was first married, I thought, *This is great, just the two of us. I could have this forever, this is fine.* But I knew that Scott really wanted a family, and I prayed for that desire to be a mother. The Lord gave it to me so strongly that even through the infertility, I knew that He would bless us with children, one way or the other. People we didn't even know across the country were praying for us to have a baby.

"I think the Lord used that time in our lives to help me relate to other women who are going through the same thing. And I've seen it a lot in baseball, a lot of women are going through that, and I've been able to empathize with them in a way that if you haven't been through it yourself, you can't."

When the children came, both Scott and Kathleen felt a sense of completeness. And their two children have smoothed the ride even more. "They can take Scott's mind off of baseball and the ups and downs better than anything," Kathleen says. "They are the perfect thing for him. And so that has helped a lot. Scott also does a real good job of trying to maintain an even keel when he comes home, and not bring the ballgame home. He really doesn't talk about the games—win or lose—that much at home.

"When I talk to other women, I think I've noticed that he doesn't talk about it as much as some of the other husbands might. And I think that helps him, so it helps us to maintain a normal life at home, rather than getting keyed up after a good game and too down after a loss. And I think he couldn't do that without his spiritual life, without maintaining that and keeping in the Word steadily."

It's not hard to see why Scott Sanderson appears to be enjoying the ride so much. He keeps his perspective of life uncomplicated. "I know how my family feels about me," he says, summarizing his outlook. "I try to do the best I can for God, and I care what He feels about me and about what I'm doing." That's a perspective that almost guarantees a smoother road ahead.

Q & A WITH SCOTT SANDERSON

Q: *What's tougher—a 3-2 count, bases loaded, and facing Jose Canseco, or changing diapers?*
Scott: Well, I'll tell you what's more fun. I think changing diapers is a lot more fun. Anything I can do for my family, I just take great joy in that. They're the most important thing to me. But I also praise God and thank Him every day for giving me the ability to come out here and play baseball for a career. My goodness, it's a dream that a lot of people have, and I realize that I'm lucky enough to be able to carry it to fruition out here on the field.

Q: *How do you share your beliefs with others?*
Scott: I try to do that daily. Since I'm a baseball player, I am with my teammates 200 days a year. And not all teammates are going to be believers. I would say daily I share my faith with nonbelievers because that's part of my job.

Q: *How do you like being a role model?*
Scott: I love it. I'm thankful that God has given me the talent to play this game of baseball. And I take very seriously the fact that we are role models, that there are kids out there who look up to us, not because of who we are as individuals but because of what we do for a living—we play baseball. That doesn't mean that any one of us is any better than anyone else.

MAJOR LEAGUE CAREER PATH

June 7, 1977:	Selected by the Expos in 3d round of free-agent draft
December 7, 1983:	Traded with Al Newman to the Padres for Gary Lucas
December 7, 1983:	Traded to the Cubs for Carmelo Martinez, Craig Lefferts, and Fritz Connally
December 7, 1988:	Re-signed by Cubs after free agency
December 13, 1989:	Signed by Athletics after free agency
December 19, 1990:	Re-signed by Athletics after free agency
December 31, 1990:	Sold to Yankees

Year	Team	G	IP	W	L	H	SO	BB	ERA
1977	West Palm Beach	10	57	5	2	58	37	23	2.68
1978	Memphis	9	58	5	3	55	44	19	4.03
1978	Denver	9	49	4	2	47	36	30	6.06
1978	Expos	10	61	4	2	52	50	21	2.51
1979	Expos	34	168	9	8	148	138	54	3.43
1980	Expos	33	211	16	11	206	125	56	3.11
1981	Expos	22	137	9	7	122	77	31	2.96
1982	Expos	32	224	12	12	212	158	58	3.46
1983	Expos	18	81	6	7	98	55	20	4.65
1984	Cubs	24	141	8	5	140	76	24	3.14
1984	Lodi	1	5	0	1	7	2	0	3.60
1985	Cubs	19	121	5	6	100	80	27	3.12
1986	Cubs	37	170	9	11	165	124	37	4.19
1987	Cubs	32	145	8	9	156	106	50	4.29
1988	Peoria	1	5	0	0	4	3	0	0.00
1988	Iowa	3	13	1	0	13	4	2	4.73
1988	Cubs	11	15	1	2	13	6	3	5.28
1989	Cubs	37	146	11	9	69	86	31	3.94
1990	Athletics	34	206	17	11	205	128	66	3.88
1991	Yankees	34	208	16	10	200	130	29	3.81
1992	Yankees	33	193	12	11	220	104	64	4.93
Major League Career (15 years)		**410**	**2227**	**143**	**121**	**2192**	**1443**	**571**	**3.74**

Kevin Seitzer
Playing for All the Right Reasons

VITAL STATISTICS

Born March 26, 1962, in Springfield, Illinois
5 feet 11, 180 pounds
Current Team: Milwaukee Brewers
Position: Third Base
Graduated from Eastern Illinois University (B.S. degree in indus-
  trial electronics)

- Had six hits in one game on August 2, 1987
- Tied for league lead in hits in 1987 with 207
- Hit .323 in his first two years in the major leagues (1986 and 1987)
- Selected to American League All-Star team once

WARMING UP

Probably the hardest thing I had ever gone through was when I lost my job," Kevin Seitzer says about that forgettable 1991 season. "I got benched. I was in pain. At the end of the year, my wife was pushing me out the door to go to the ballpark."

While Lisa Seitzer never gave up on her husband, the Royals did, so Kevin and his agent started the 1992 campaign in search of a job. But they did not embark on the search alone. "I prayed that the Lord would make it very clear to me where I ought to be."

At first it looked like "where he ought to be" might not be in a baseball uniform. "When I was released, there were four teams that were looking for a third baseman. The Yankees, Cubs, Dodgers, and Padres were looking at third basemen. We put calls in to all four teams, and none of them were interested. I thought my career was over."

Kevin Seitzer

It looked like the end of the road for Kevin Seitzer.
Despite a career batting average approaching the .300 mark, Seitzer had been released by the Kansas City Royals. After banging out more than 800 hits for the Royals in only four full seasons and parts of two others, he no longer fit into the Royals' plans.

After all, they reasoned, he had undergone the knife during the off-season, suffering through a double knee operation that was designed to take care of the wear-and-tear damage that nearly 30-year-old knees sometimes incur. Even Seitzer admits that the operation "didn't go quite as they hoped. It wasn't as slick an operation as they thought it was going to be. The doctors were pretty confident that it was something that could be taken care of and I would be back out there, but it didn't go quite as they hoped."

In addition to the surgery, the Royals were undoubtedly influenced by Seitzer's uncharacteristic 1991 season in which he played only 82 games and batted only .265. For a player who had posted marks of .345 and .348 in the minors and back-to-back .323 years in his first two major league campaigns, the pain of his injured knees and the pain of his unproductive season were undoubtedly comparable.

"Probably the hardest thing I had ever gone through was when I lost my job," Seitzer says about that forgettable 1991 season. "I got benched. I was in pain. At the end of the year, my wife was pushing me out the door to go to the ballpark. She'd never done that before. I didn't want to leave her because that was the only place that I really felt secure. At home I felt like a little kid. I just wanted my wife to hold me and not let me go."

While Lisa Seitzer never gave up on her husband, the Royals did, so Kevin and his agent started the 1992 campaign in search of a job. But they did not embark on the search alone. "I prayed that the Lord would make it very clear to me where I ought to be."

At first it looked like "where he ought to be" might not be in a baseball uniform. "When I was released, there were four teams that were looking for a third baseman. Yankees, Cubs, Dodgers, and Padres were looking at third basemen. We put calls in to all four teams, and none of them were interested. I thought my career was over.

"Twenty-four hours later, the Brewers traded [Gary] Sheffield," Seitzer explains, "and they were in contact with my agent. They said, 'We're interested in taking a look at Seitzer.' It was unbelievable."

The Milwaukee Brewers was a team Seitzer thought he could feel at home with. He knew that several of the members of the team were Christians, including the general manager, and with the trade of Sheffield, he knew a spot was open in the infield.

"It was where the Lord wanted me to be," he says without reservation. "It is incredible. You talk about being totally at peace and just knowing that that's where you're supposed to be, it wasn't even funny. I was ecstatic."

Contract negotiations came next, and Kevin Seitzer's story contradicts the more typical tales of signings that stall because of high salary demands. Here was a player who stood for integrity more than money.

Soon after he found out about the opening in Milwaukee, Seitzer asked his agent, "Well, what kind of salary are they looking at?"

"I don't know," the agent replied honestly.

"You got any idea?"

"No."

At this point, we are used to hearing high-priced athletes trot out their statistics and their egos and say something like, "Well, whatever it is, you make sure you get as much as you can, 'cause I'm worth it." But that wasn't Kevin Seitzer's line.

"I'll tell you this. Whatever they offer, take it," Seitzer instructed his agent. "I don't care if it's the minimum. Take it. . . . If I deserve more money, I'm going to make it next year after my free-agent year. If I don't deserve more money, then nobody's going to be able to accuse me of stealing."

That is astounding enough, but the story doesn't end here. Milwaukee wasn't the only team who had designs on this third baseman. While Seitzer was in the Brewers' camp, ready to sign, his agent called. The Cleveland Indians had just contacted him and wanted Seitzer to sign with them. Seitzer's response was immediate and direct: "No way."

That may be understandable, since Cleveland players usually have to play in front of 80,000 empty seats in cavernous Municipal Stadium. But then his agent told him how much money the Tribe was holding out for Seitzer to take. "They were talking about triple the money that the Brewers were offering me. When he told me that, the flesh said, 'Whoa!' And my heart said, 'No.' " So he called his wife for advice. "Honey, this is the situation," he said. "What do you think?"

"If you think Milwaukee is the place you ought to be, then let's go to Milwaukee."

So he signed with the Brewers for the minimum salary. "I felt fine about it. It didn't bother me in the least."

Kevin Seitzer had traveled a long road from those heady days of 1987 when he banged out 207 hits for the Royals to that frightening spring of 1992 when he faced retirement at age 30. Yet along the way he had experienced something that would allow him to handle both the good things and the bad things that major league baseball offers. It was a personal relationship with Jesus Christ, and it made the disaster of being released bearable. "All I can say is that without Christ, I never could have made it," Seitzer concludes about spring training 1992.

His statement contains great irony. In 1988, he was at the top of his game, yet he was a most miserable person. In 1992, he was at the bottom, yet he was able to survive without despair. In 1988 he had baseball right where he wanted it, but he didn't know Jesus Christ. In 1992, he almost didn't have baseball anymore at all, yet he had Jesus Christ as his Savior and Lord. How could this turnaround occur?

It wasn't because Kevin Seitzer was looking for it.

"As a kid growing up," Seitzer explains as he talks about that happy-sad year of 1988, "I always thought that if I had a lot of money and success, I'd be the happiest person on earth. But after my second year in the big leagues, I had a lot of money and I had a lot of success, but the pain and misery were a lot worse than even before.

"It was the biggest letdown in my life. I had everything I ever wanted, but I was so miserable. It just wasn't what I expected it to be, and I really felt a sense of emptiness. It almost felt like I had a sense of failure. I felt I had failed, when I hadn't. And I didn't know why.

"I told my wife that I needed to find something else to do during the season to get my mind off baseball. Take up a hobby or something that would just give me another interest. The winters were so miserable for me when we weren't playing ball. That was when I took up hunting. I figured that would give me something else to do and make me happy. I enjoyed it, but it wasn't what I was needing."

What he needed he found at a place he didn't know he was going to. His former teammate Mike Kingery had invited Kevin and Lisa to attend a conference in November sponsored by Pro Athletes Outreach, a group that ministers to professional athletes. Seitzer did not know PAO was a Christian organization.

"We were having some family problems, and we went down there to get some counseling," Seitzer recalls, "but if I would have known it was a Christian conference, I never would have shown up. We just thought it was a conference for ballplayers where you can go down and kind of lay your problems on the line and get some advice from different people.

"Mike Kingery and I came up through the minors together, and we were real close. He was a Christian, and I wasn't, but I really had a lot of respect for him. I loved his attitude, and the way he raised his family, and the type of person he was. I just always looked up to him. When he told me about the conference, I asked my wife if she wanted to go, and she said yes.

"Both of us were pretty shocked when we walked in and found out it was a Christian conference. That night, I was pretty miserable.

"The first night of this conference, the speaker was speaking right to me," says Seitzer. "There were 150 people there, but he was speaking right to me. He was really just dictating my life right to me. He was saying, 'This is how you can change your life and the way you are feeling—through a personal relationship with Jesus Christ.' He went on to explain how you would go about praying and receiving Christ as your Savior and asking Him to come in and take over your life."

The explanation made sense, but the ballplayer thought he would be forced into changes he didn't want to make. "I had a drinking problem at the time, and I couldn't control my language, and I thought, *I can't do this stuff. If I become a Christian, I've got to stop this and this, and this and this, and I enjoy that. Those are the only things that are fun for me.* I figured, *I'm not going to make a very good Christian, so I don't think it's very smart for me to try it.*"

This idea of becoming a follower of Jesus Christ was not exactly new to Seitzer. He had heard it before in Sunday school where his parents sent him, and he knew "the whole story about Jesus and how He had died on the cross for our sins and had arisen the third day. My idea of receiving everlasting life was just on believing in Him. And I thought that's all you had to do. I believed in God. I believed He created everything, and I believed in Jesus. I thought that was good enough."

But this PAO conference speaker was challenging Seitzer with a new concept. "I found out that you had to ask Him to come in and take over your life, and you had to give your life to Him. That night I decided to pray to receive Christ."

The reluctant guest, who thought he could find happiness with an off-season hobby, discovered the answer to his difficulties. "All I can say is that my marriage was saved, my family life was saved, my life was saved."

The next day, his wife, Lisa, rededicated her life to God. Apparently she had first become a Christian soon after she and Kevin were married, but he had not received the news very favorably at the time. She had begun attending Bible studies, but, "I put a stop to that in a hurry," Seitzer recalls. Lisa had brought a Bible home and began to raise Kevin's interest, but Seitzer quickly told her he didn't want any more Bible reading.

"Get it out of here," he had told her.

Seitzer understands now why he was so reluctant to have his wife read the Bible. Now that he has had his share of opportunities to watch people respond to his faith and his love for the Bible, he knows why they seem to be so much against it. "People are intimidated by the Bible. They are intimidated by religion. That's a very powerful word to people: religion.

"They don't understand what Christianity is all about. It's a relationship, not a religion. People don't understand that, they think *freak*."

That's what he had thought a few years earlier when his wife wanted to read the Bible. "I thought, *Freak, Bible-thumper. Keep that thing out of my face. You're not going to convince me to tell me how to live my life by telling me I can't do this or I can't do that.* It's really a false stereotype of what Christianity is. Until you live it, you don't know what you're missing."

Kevin Seitzer may no longer be missing the spiritual joy that can come only to those who have peace with God, but he has learned to live with one less important goal that he realized long ago he could never achieve: playing professional basketball.

His childhood dream was to play for a team like the Milwaukee Bucks, not the Brewers. Although he grew up playing baseball from the Little Leagues through high school, he achieved what he calls "the greatest thrill in high school" on the basketball court. As a senior guard for Lincoln High in Springfield, Illinois, he made it to the state championships. He received many scholarship offers, many more to play basketball than to play baseball. "I was a shooting guard, from long range," Seitzer recalls.

So why isn't Kevin Seitzer bombing three-pointers for somebody in the NBA instead of playing third for somebody in the major leagues? "I stopped growing while I was in high school," he says in disgust. "It ticked me off. It was the hardest thing for me because my boyhood dream was to play in the NBA. That was always what I wanted to do." But when the growth chart topped out at less than 6 feet, Seitzer knew the dream was over.

He still enjoyed baseball, but for him it was a summer diversion. "Basketball was what I really lived for, but I didn't want to play it in the summer. As soon as baseball was over and it was time to play basketball, I got a lot more fired up."

Fired up about baseball or not, he must have done something right on the baseball diamonds at Eastern Illinois University. After his junior year as a Panther, the Kansas City Royals came calling. Although Seitzer had grown up rooting for the other major league team in Missouri, the St. Louis Cardinals, he subdued his loyalties and signed with the team from K.C. When he made it from the minors to Royals Stadium in 1986, he missed by one summer what would have been quite a thrill for him—the Royals and the Redbirds battling for the championship in the 1985 World Series.

When Seitzer signed with the Royals, though, he didn't really have World Series thoughts. In fact, he had pretty much convinced himself that he would never even make it to Royals Stadium. "When I signed," he remembers, "I really wasn't thinking about the big leagues. It's such a long haul, it's really difficult to make it. Just a really small percentage of people who get into pro ball make it to the big leagues. I just set my mind to doing the best job that I could at whatever level I was at.

"I was always content with wherever I went. If I had stopped at Double A, I could tell my grandkids that I had played pro ball and made it to Double A, and I would have been proud of that. That was kind of my approach all through the minors. I never really thought about the big leagues until I was here. That was when it was really exciting for me."

After seven seasons in the big leagues, Seitzer's goals are simple yet significant. When Seitzer does flag down his last line drive and pound out his last hit at the end of his career, he hopes he is remembered more for who he is off the field than for what he has done on the field. "I'd like to be respected for the way I live my life. I'd like to be remembered as a good father and a good husband. And somebody that had my priorities in line: God, family, and baseball." During the off-season and those rare days off during the baseball schedule, he enjoys time with his Lisa and their two boys, Brandon and Cameron.

But while he is still active, he enjoys telling people about what happened to him at that 1988 PAO conference, how Jesus Christ has changed his life. He presents his life-changing story to athletes and neighbors alike. He remembers, for instance, the sad/sweet story of a fellow minor leaguer with the Royals, a player who was a "real good friend" when Seitzer was in the Royals' farm system.

"He had a chemical imbalance. It was depression," Seitzer explains. "He had a lot of problems with this thing. I guess there are other people in his family who have it also, and it ended up costing him his baseball career. He had been fighting it for years. He had been to all kinds of therapists, to counseling, and to doctors to try to figure out what to do to resolve it. I witnessed to him, and he gave his life to the Lord. He didn't have any more problems with his depression after a while. It's a pretty neat story."

People in his community know where Kevin stands. "My wife passes out my testimony tracts at Halloween, along with some candy. A pastor at one of the churches in our neighborhood came to a breakfast that I was speaking at and he told me that two kids came walking in with these tracts and wanted to know how they could come to know the Lord. That was pretty powerful. That meant a lot to me."

Yet for all of the things Lisa and Kevin Seitzer do to spread the Word and to tell others the gospel, they don't intend to do it so others can tell them how great they are. "You never know who you are touching by living your life and doing little things," he says. "I don't like to take any credit for people coming to know the Lord through my testimony or anything like that. All I am is a seed planter. If it's somebody's time, it's not just because it's what I said. It's because of the things they have heard in the past and the Lord was ready for them, and He said, 'Now's the time.'"

Such off-field stories are close to Seitzer's heart, yet one remarkable on-field story will remain in his memory and those of Kansas City fans for a long time, the day he stroked six hits and batted 1.000.

The prairie sun blazed that early August day as the Royals faced the Boston Red Sox. Boston pitcher Bob Stanley faced the Royals' hitters, a pitcher who had won 100 games in his career but was struggling this season. Seitzer stepped in to face Stanley, who would later complete the year with a 4 and 15 mark.

Stanley fired a pitch inside, and it jammed Seitzer, who fought it off and fisted the ball through the middle of the infield for a hit. It was the beginning of an unbelievable afternoon for the Royals' 25-year-old third baseman. As the temperature rose on the Royals Stadium turf that day, so did Kevin Seitzer's batting average.

The next time up, Seitzer hit a home run. His third and fourth times to the plate resulted in singles. He was four for four.

But he wasn't done. At-bat number five produced his second home run of the game.

By the time he stood in for his sixth at-bat that day, it was late afternoon and the sun was low in the sky. Seitzer swung at an outside pitch and lofted it toward right field. Mike Greenwell looked up—and saw nothing but sun. He lost the ball in the glare and it bounced into the stands for a ground rule double.

Kevin Seitzer stood on second with one of the rarest feats in baseball. He had gone 6-for-6. When the game started, he was hitting .304. By game's end, he was hitting more than .320. "I was pretty locked in," he says now about that career-in-a-day afternoon. And he apparently stayed "locked in," for he went 6-for-9 in his next two games combined. That adds up to 12-for-15 in three games, a phenomenal batting average of .600.

Seitzer may never top that outstanding performance in his new post–Kansas City career, but the Brewers and anybody else who ever hires Seitzer to hold down the hot corner know that they have a man who goes all out on the filed. "I don't want anyone ever watching me play and saying that Christians are wimps," he says.

Seitzer's strategy is clear on and off the field. "I really try not to compromise. I don't like fence walking. If you believe in one thing, then do it. I've got an owner's manual that tells me how I'm supposed to live my life now, and I try not to veer off that. My wife and I have made a commitment to the Lord that we're going to try to live our lives that way and raise our kids that way, and be a good witness. People ask me what my goal is in life, and my only goal is that when I stand before the Lord at the judgment seat, I want Him to say, 'Well-done, thou good and faithful servant.'"

No wonder the Brewers wanted Kevin Seitzer. He does things for all the right reasons.

Q & A WITH KEVIN SEITZER

Q: *What has been the secret to your success?*
Kevin: That's a tough question. Well, probably a lot of hard work and discipline. I've caught some breaks when I've needed to. That's a key. There's a master plan in everything, and it's kind of neat just living your life and waiting to see what the Lord's got planned for you.

Q: *Who is the toughest pitcher you've ever faced?*
Kevin: Probably Roger Clemens. He's got a nasty slider that gives me some problems and a little two-seamer forkball that he throws in there, too. Randy Johnson, on a given night, can be the best pitcher I've ever faced. Jim Abbott can be the best. Clemens, though, probably more times than anybody else, is the best pitcher. There are times when other guys can be off and on, but you know that about 98 percent of the time you're going to get Clemens's best stuff. He ain't gonna be off. That's just the way he's been. That's why he's got the Cy Youngs [best pitcher awards] and the great reputation. He's a great pitcher.

Q: *What are your greatest thrills in baseball?*
Kevin: There are probably two of them: The All-Star game in 1987 and my 6-for-6 game in the same year.

Q: *How would you change baseball if you could?*

Kevin: I'd shorten spring training. Also, right now, I'd eliminate the DH [designated hitter], because I'm not one. Seriously, it bothers me that pitchers are out there throwing at guys and they don't have to get a bat in their hands and go to the plate. Maybe you could change it and have the pitcher bat and still have a DH.

MAJOR LEAGUE CAREER PATH

June 6, 1983:   Picked by the Royals in the 11th round of free agent draft

April 8, 1992:   Released by the Royals

April 15, 1992: Signed by the Brewers

THE SEITZER FILE

Year	Team	G	AB	R	H	2B	3B	HR	RBI	Avg.
1983	Butte	68	238	60	82	14	1	2	45	.345
1984	Charleston	141	489	96	145	26	5	8	79	.297
1985	Ft. Myers	90	290	61	91	10	5	3	46	.314
1985	Memphis	52	187	26	65	6	2	1	20	.348
1986	Memphis	4	11	4	3	0	0	0	1	.273
1986	Omaha	129	432	86	138	20	11	13	74	.319
1986	Royals	28	96	16	31	4	1	2	11	.323
1987	Royals	161	641	105	207	33	8	15	83	.323
1988	Royals	149	559	90	170	32	5	5	60	.304
1989	Royals	160	597	78	168	17	2	4	48	.281
1990	Royals	158	622	91	171	31	5	6	38	.275
1991	Royals	85	234	28	62	11	3	1	25	.265
1992	Brewers	148	540	74	146	35	1	5	71	.270
Major League Career (7 years)		**889**	**3289**	**482**	**955**	**163**	**25**	**38**	**336**	**.290**

Frank Tanana
Class Act

VITAL STATISTICS

Born July 3, 1953, in Detroit, Michigan
6 feet 3, 195 pounds
Current Team: Detroit Tigers
Position: Pitcher (left-handed)
Attended California State University at Fullerton

CAREER HIGHLIGHTS

- American League Rookie Pitcher of the Year in 1973
- Led American League in strikeouts in 1975 (269); in shutouts in 1977 (7)
- Named to All-Star team three times
- Has recorded more than 2,600 strikeouts

WARMING UP

A couple of clouds loomed on the Frank Tanana horizon as he pitched for the Angels in the late '70s. First, despite his youth and his amazing stats, he felt his career was in jeopardy. "I was struggling health-wise," he says, explaining problem number one. "My shoulder was messed up, and I was pitching through pain."

The second problem was one that had been building during the glory days in Anaheim. It was something that resulted from a way of living that Tanana is none too proud of today.

Frank Tanana

Lyman Bostock wasn't the first major league baseball player to die during a big league season when he was gunned down while riding through Gary, Indiana, on September 23, 1978. During the 1903 season, between games, Ed Delahanty mysteriously ended up at the bottom of the Niagara River. And during the 1920 season Ray Chapman took a Carl Mays fastball on the temple and didn't live to bat again.

But Bostock's death might have been the first one that helped straighten out a struggling teammate's life.

When 27-year-old Lyman Bostock, a fine-hitting outfielder for the California Angels, took that fateful car ride in the summer of '78, he had no plans to die. He was just visiting friends while the team was in Chicago to play the White Sox. But a bullet meant for someone else hit Bostock, snuffing out the talented hitter's life. With a .311 career batting average in his four big league seasons, Bostock's future looked bright. But in one second, his future was gone.

The teammate who was perhaps most affected by Bostock's shocking death at such a young age was the Angels' lefty hurler Frank Tanana. At age 25, Tanana had already won 80 games and struck out more than 1,000 batters for the Angels. But he was starting to feel mortal.

The death started him asking questions. *What if it was me?* Team chaplain John Werhas had already shared the gospel with him, and Tanana told himself, *If what John told me was true, boom, if I would have died—.* "It began my spiritual journey to the cross," Tanana says.

In his first few years with the Angels, Frank Tanana had it all. A blazing fastball. A swinging Southern California lifestyle. Tons of money. Adoring fans. He and Nolan Ryan teamed up to become the most feared mound duo in the game. Wall-to-wall heat was what the Tanana-Ryan express offered when the visitors dared show up at the Big A (Anaheim Stadium).

No one who saw Tanana pitch would begrudge him his youthful goals, which rightfully included making it to the Hall of Fame as well as "being the best pitcher in the game, and making the All-Star team year after year."

But a couple of clouds loomed on the horizon for Frank Tanana as he pitched for the Angels in 1978. First, despite his youth and his amazing stats, he felt his career was in jeopardy. "I was struggling health-wise," he says, explaining problem number one. "My shoulder was messed up, and I was pitching through pain." The previous year he had hurt his elbow and left the Angels' rotation with three weeks remaining in the season. He resumed light throwing in the winter, but soon the pitching shoulder began to bother him. He pitched all of 1978 with a hurt arm. Even with the bad shoulder, he was effective, winning 18 games and working 239 innings.

"But I knew something was wrong with my shoulder," he recalls. "I didn't have the velocity, and I didn't have the numbers. I wasn't striking out that many people [137, compared with 205 the year before]. My ERA went up a whole point [from 2.54 to 3.65]."

Frank Tanana's second problem in those late years of the '70s was one that had been building during the glory days in Anaheim. It was something that resulted from a way of living that Tanana is none too proud of today.

Almost reluctantly, he reveals now that he simply got bored with the life that he thought would be so much fun. "For four or five years I had really used people. I was very selfish. I got real tired of that. That wasn't really satisfying in the long run. It was getting very old."

By this time, Frank had done something that helped to calm his wild lifestyle. He had married Cathy Mull, a young woman he had met on one of his evenings out. The beginning of their relationship on the dance floor at a popular West Coast disco had seemed to be a chance meeting of two people who shared a superficial attraction to each other.

"I saw this lovely girl dressed in black," Frank remembers. "And I've always been partial to black clothing." For her part, Cathy didn't know the name *Frank Tanana*, major league pitcher, from the name of the capital city of Mongolia. "I really wasn't impressed with [the name] 'Frank Tanana.' But by him, by the person, I was."

Yet even marriage couldn't help him control his roller-coaster emotions. "If I was doing well, I was a great guy," he explains. "But if you didn't have anything for me, well, then, I'll just go on."

As Tanana observed the people around him, though, he saw someone who wasn't like that—someone who was even keeled and consistent. It was team chaplain Werhas, a former utility player who had hit less than .200 in a three-year career during the '60s. Werhas, Tanana recalls, "showed me by his lifestyle, his mannerism, by just the kind of guy he was that he had something going for him."

What he had going for him, as Frank later found out, was that he had a personal relationship with Jesus Christ. He was a Christian. The once-wild pitcher's free-wheeling lifestyle had become old hat, and now a new person had suggested a possible solution to Tanana's continued unsettled feeling.

Then the Angels took that trip to Chicago—leaving with Lyman Bostock and coming home without him. The impact hit a searching Frank Tanana hard; the "spiritual journey to the cross" had begun. And his marriage was not the same anymore; the beautiful young dance major and the playboy baseball player were both searching. Even before Frank had decided to consider seriously this gospel that John Werhas was talking about, Cathy had surrendered her life to Jesus Christ.

There was a definite turnaround in Frank's life after this summer of discovery. His marriage began to take on a quality that no
one would have predicted. Yet, as he looks back on that time, he
is not satisfied that he made a total commitment to God. He describes it now as something he did because "all I wanted was a
free ticket to heaven in the event I died." The Lyman Bostock tragedy was fresh on his mind, and he had asked himself, "What if
some idiot shot me?" His answer was to respond, as he puts it,
"kind of like you would take out fire insurance."

In the next five years Frank realized that "fire insurance"
against hell wasn't enough. He needed a relationship, and he recognized that he was not who people thought he had become. Finally he attended a Pro Athletes Outreach conference in Carefree,
Arizona, in 1983. Just as he had seen something appealing in the
lifestyle and demeanor of John Werhas in 1978, he saw something at this PAO conference that challenged him.

"It was really the spirit of the people that were there. I saw in
them a difference. I saw a love that I knew was missing in my life.
The whole atmosphere and the people in general forced me to
think clearly. It allowed God to convict me in my heart that although I professed to be a Christian, in reality I didn't know the
biblical Christ.

"I was very troubled at the time," Tanana says honestly about
those days. "I had professed being a Christian since 1978.
Through reading the Bible and going to some Bible studies, and
through some personal things that were going on in my life, I
came to the startling conclusion that I was a phoney. I was a hyp-
ocrite. I really had made up my own brand of Christianity. I had
absolutely no desire to follow Christ and to obey Him."

Tanana looked in his Bible and felt confronted with Scriptures about insincere belief by demons (James 2:19) and those
wanting to escape judgment (Matthew 7:21). Tanana realized he
had not given his life to Christ. So on November 6, 1983, he knelt
by his bed to pray.

"For the first time I humbled myself and honestly realized my
sin, my sinfulness, my depravity, and just poured out my heart and
asked God to forgive me and to come into my life and to take con-

trol of it, and save me. I had a dramatic experience with the Lord. Soon my tears of sadness turned to tears of joy at finding Christ.

"This was really what I had been searching my whole life for—significance and meaning and security. Boy, just having God come into my life was an awesome experience. From there it has had a dramatic effect, a real transformation in all of my life."

A journey that had started with arm troubles and a murdered teammate, and that had begun with a profession of faith, took five years to reach its final destination.

In between, Tanana experienced more arm troubles, made a complete change in pitching styles, and moved on to a new team. The days of Frank Tanana, fire-balling southpaw, were over. Perhaps he should have been accustomed to changes. He had been a swinging bachelor, but now he was married. He had been a devil-may-care alcoholic who would stay up all night partying and then pitch the next day, but now he was a family man. He had been one of the hardest throwing lefties in the game, but now he would have to change that too.

"In 1979, I really just blew out my shoulder. I was scared. I thought my career was over. This was my second serious arm injury, although I have never had it operated on. I knew that this was pretty serious stuff.

"It scared me as a baseball player, which was how I derived my identity. I knew that I would work hard and I wanted to continue to play, but I knew that I would have to change my style from a flame-thrower to more of a finesse pitcher." And he did.

By 1984, he was again a 15-game winner for the Texas Rangers, winning with the same consistency he had shown in 1977. And inwardly he had the steadying influence of his God and a loving wife. That supported him through some tough early days with the Texas Rangers.

"I was pitching for the Rangers. I should say I had the uniform on. I wasn't pitching at the time. They hadn't put me in a ballgame yet. Just in case the ballgame went extra innings and they might need me, I had to wait until the game was over to do my throwing.

"As all the people are leaving the stadium, I'm out there in the bullpen getting a little work in. The ushers are cleaning the seats and the people are going, and all of a sudden I hear this voice. It says, 'Hey, uh, hey, Tanana, what are you doing? The ballgame's over, we don't have a doubleheader tonight.'

"Well, I wasn't that happy to begin with, having to do my throwing at the end of a ballgame, and it was a pretty good blow to the ego to say the least. My pride wasn't doing too good. So I whipped around to see who had spoken those words.

"It was Cathy, my wife. She, of course, knew the pain and struggle I was going through. And she was laughing, so we shared a really good, laughable time."

It seems that Frank and Cathy have the kind of relationship that many men and women would desire in their marriage. Yet it wasn't always that way. According to Frank, he began to truly understand how to be the right kind of husband only after he committed his life to God. "Our relationship took on a whole new meaning as I saw Cathy as a gift from God—one that I could nourish and cherish and spend time with. She literally has become my best friend, when really I couldn't have said that before I came to Christ.

"I had only known how to treat a woman by role models that I had growing up. There really wasn't much of a biblical role model for parenting. My dad did a great job with what he knew, but he didn't know Christ. I got to know Christ and His Word and all that He said about relationships and how much He values them.

"According to the Lord, life is a relationship with Him and others. And He puts prime importance on the marriage relationship. I saw as my first priority, outside of my relationship with the Lord, that with my wife."

That Frank Tanana grew up to be a loving, devoted husband who is concerned about his relationship with God would probably surprise a lot of people who knew him as a youth. But the fact that he made it to the top in baseball would surprise perhaps no one. He was born to play baseball.

His father, a Detroit policeman, had been an athlete who loved to play baseball himself. He started little Frank early on the field, and Frank loved watching his dad play ball. He played catch with Dad at age three, and loved to play ball with the neighbors. Still, he doesn't consider himself a natural athlete.

"I think everybody works at it," he contends. "Nobody gets to the big leagues because he's a natural. Nobody climbs out of bed and goes out and makes it to the big leagues. Even with those people who look so good and so smooth, it's just from honing their skills and practicing and playing so much."

Which is exactly what he did. "I played in every league that was possible—from Little League to Pony League to Babe Ruth. Every chance I got to play, I would play. I remember, as a kid I would play in three or four leagues at a time, if I could. They had different scheduled game days, and I would take my bike and ride from park to park to play. There were plenty of opportunities for a young guy to play baseball if that's what he wanted to do."

And because that's what he wanted to do, Frank Tanana honed and practiced and played enough to attract major league scouts during his senior year at Detroit Catholic Central High School. Not only that, he also attracted the attention of college basketball coaches. In fact, he was given a full basketball scholarship to attend Duke University.

The only bump in the road at this point in his journey was a sore arm he had picked up in high school while throwing a junk pitch. The team Tanana dreamed of pitching for, the Detroit Tigers, knew about the problem and passed on the would-be hometown hero. The lefty teenager signed instead with the California Angels.

During his first year with the organization, they probably wished he hadn't. He was assigned to Idaho Falls in the Pioneer League—a summer Class A circuit. "I had that bad arm at the time," Tanana explains about that summer that went nowhere. "I didn't pitch at all that summer. We played 75 games, and I pinch-ran one time. It was a very difficult summer for me personally. I really was a troubled young man. I figured, here my career might be over, even before it began. And I also just had given up my basketball scholarship because you could not play collegiate if you had turned pro in any other sport, like you can today."

But if the summer of '71 was a worrisome year that seemed to indicate that maybe the road to the majors had washed out, the next two summers were a four-lane expressway to Anaheim. His arm strengthened while with the Quad Cities Single A club, where he pitched 129 innings, throwing 134 strikeouts and posting a 7-2 record. By the end of the following season, Tanana had swept through Double A El Paso, and Triple A Salt Lake City, and ended the year at the Big A as a member of the Angels.

There, through the mid '70s, he compiled his sterling stats as part of the Tanana-Ryan fastball express. But when the arm blew again from the stress and strain of 90 MPH fastballs, a despondent Tanana told a writer for *Sports Illustrated*, "My contract goes through 1981. I'll be lucky to be alive then. Let alone pitching."

Today, however, Frank Tanana is more alive than ever. His spiritual life is on track, his marriage is a true friendship, his family is his joy, and he has even had enough post-arm-injury success to keep the competitive fires burning. In 1992, with more than 220 wins under his belt, and with his old teammate Nolan Ryan still pitching at 45, Tanana was even doing some tentative thinking about what it would mean to win 300 games, if he can keep the body—and arm—healthy.

What extended his pitching career more than anything perhaps was his move to Detroit in 1985. At the time, the Tananas were happily established in Texas, and the move to Motown meant leaving a good church and good friends. But they felt it was the direction God wanted them to go, so they went willingly. "We were really committed to the Lord," Frank remembers about the move. "We knew that everything goes through Him first, and we just felt that He had some mighty things for us to do in Detroit."

One of the mightiest things Frank Tanana did in Detroit occurred on October 4, 1987. In his greatest thrill in baseball, Frank held off the powerful Toronto Blue Jays in the final game of the season, clinching the division title for the Tigers. The Blue Jays had come into Detroit on the previous Friday with a two-game lead over the Tigers. All they needed was one win to go on to face the Twins in the playoffs. But Detroit won both Friday and Saturday, making the Sunday game the equivalent of a playoff. Winner takes all.

Tanana had been there before. In 1979 he was on the mound when the California Angels clinched their first divisional championship. But now, eight years later, it was a different pitcher who silenced the Jays. No longer the kind of pitcher who could blaze fastballs past people like George Bell, he got them out with what he told the *Los Angeles Times* was "a little slop here, a little slop there. Once in a while, I got one in the '80s." And in the process he got the biggest win of his career.

But every day for a major league baseball player is not going to result in celebrations on the field and headlines off it. Sometimes, things are going to go wrong. How can a person respond properly? Tanana turns to a favorite book of his.

"I think one great thing about the Bible is that it doesn't pull any punches. I've tried to spend daily time in it for the past eight years. I think it gives wisdom, it shows you what reality is all about. That life is tough because of the sin involved. It's a fallen world. Because of man's sin and man's selfishness, it's not at all like what God designed it to be.

"Consequently, things are not going to be perfect. There are going to be highs. There are going to be successes. There are going to be failures. As long as I walk with the Lord and as long as I continue to follow Him and keep His commandments, it's phenomenal how the peace that the Bible talks about has been mine. That includes times when I couldn't get anybody out on the ball diamond, when I've been sent to the bullpen.

"Life is not a bed of roses, and faith is not a walk down the primrose lane. The beautiful thing is that in my heart I've experienced joy and heaven right here on this earth. But boy, circumstances don't always work the way I want them to."

And then there are those circumstances that come with the territory of major league baseball. The atmosphere is not always conducive to lofty thoughts. "The words I hear people say in the clubhouse," he begins, describing a part of baseball life he wishes he could bypass. "The Lord's name is used in vain. It's very hard to take. It hurts me deeply. The magazines, the garbage that people involve themselves in. You cringe at it. You know the damage they're doing to themselves. What I've tried to do is to stay strong in the Word and know my God and know whom I serve. I surround myself with men of like mind, men who also desire to follow Christ.

"Yet I don't shut myself out from the guys. I enjoy traveling with them, being their friend, playing golf with them, all the things that I have the freedom to do as long they don't go against the commands of the Lord. I'm all for that. I think being built up by the Word, knowing the God I serve, knowing His will for my life, having a reverent fear, a genuine fear for God has given me the strength to walk in His ways and serve Him and not fall."

Baseball fans sometimes forget that the players need privacy off the field. The attention they receive outside the stadium, is often artificial and insincere. "People walk up to me and act like they know me real well and call me by my first name and ask for autographs and stuff. My kids see through that. They say, 'Daddy, they don't even know you.'

"And all the attention sometimes takes away from our time as a family. How do we overcome it? By talking to the kids and explaining to them that sometimes people get a feeling of self-worth out of being around other people who have accomplished something, that it makes them feel good about themselves.

"We try to tell them [that the fans] are simply doing what other people are doing. They are just going with the crowd, getting those autographs. Being followers. We tell them how they incorrectly place their daddy on a pedestal, or really kind of idolize Daddy, and how that's not good for them to do, nor is it good for Daddy to think he is better than other people.

"There's a lot of teachable moments involved in all this. We've had some fun with it. We've had some good discussions, and it's also important for me that I build up Cathy, that I honor her when we're around people. I make sure she is introduced and questions are directed toward her and that I honor her in front of others."

Though Tanana's life-changing story is inspiring, few sports writers report it. "You really don't get a lot of press [talking about faith] because they really do not understand," Tanana says. "They'd rather give the press to those who are caught with cocaine or caught sexually harassing or raping women, or [they want to talk about] the money that the guys make. It's unbelievable how the press puts that as news, yet a man who will go out and be an upstanding citizen will give up his time and his money helping—

and there are many athletes out there doing that—and they ignore that and do not consider that as news."

But if the press did report it, they would have quite a story to tell about this hometown boy who returned as a changed man, one who can win you a few ballgames, but is most concerned that he be remembered as "a friend of God. One who is devoted to Christ, devoted to his family. . . who played the game to the best of his ability. One who had time for people. One who loved his children." And one who is a real class act.

Q & A WITH FRANK TANANA

Q: *What has been your secret to success in baseball?*
Frank: Perseverance. Keeping on keeping on, through the wins, through the losses, through the injuries. Never quitting. Always bouncing back. Always having a strong desire and a real strong love for the game.

Q: *When the press asks you a question and you respond with a witness, often they won't let you go on, will they?*
Frank: Yes, that's the case. They don't know what you're talking about. They see the scandals in the religious community, and they are hardened even more—the leaders and the ones they concentrate on, ignoring the hundreds of thousands that are living for Christ. Yeah, I think just out of ignorance and certainly out of willfully not wanting to touch that subject because they don't know what you're talking about. So they don't pursue it. I can understand that. How can you pursue something you know nothing about? I'm just thankful for the opportunity.

Q: *What image do you try to convey?*
Frank: I try to stay away from an image. An image is usually something that you are portraying that you are not. I try to simply allow the Holy Spirit to live through me and hopefully His fruit of love, joy, peace, and patience are exhibited in Frank Tanana's life. It's not an image, it's what I'm really all about. Up front, if He's in control, what people will see is a kind man, a gentle man, one

who loves his God, one who loves his family. One who is a very hard worker, a diligent worker, who never quits.

Q: *What do you think about the salaries in sports?*
Frank: As we know, it's the love of money that is the root of evil. There are many wealthy men in the Bible—godly men. I think it is knowing who the owner is. God is the owner. I am the steward. I am simply blessed far beyond what I deserve by the Lord, certainly by His grace, and also, of course, monetarily.

 I don't feel that I own it. It is God's. I think that perspective . . . helps me keep greed in check. God has certainly met all my needs, and I'm excited about what I'm able to make, because it allows me to share more, to give more to God's work. I think through Scripture, through some study, we've been able to set up some things for our kids and for our future that we feel God would have us do. Getting out of debt has freed us up to have more to share. More to give.

Q: *Do you think that once a player is under contract he should initiate discussions to renegotiate that contract?*
Frank: That's something that a Christian isn't at liberty to do. You signed a contract in good faith. Your job is to live up to that contract. Your job also is to be content in all things. And it doesn't matter what anybody else is making. If you've signed your contract, if you've given your word, to me it's a grievous, tragic sin. It's a major sin. It's not something that honors the Lord at all.

MAJOR LEAGUE CAREER PATH

June 8, 1971:	Selected by Angels in 1st round (13th player selected) of free-agent draft
January 23, 1981:	Traded to the Red Sox, along with Jim Dorsey and Joe Rudi, for Fred Lynn and Steve Renko
January 6, 1982:	Signed by the Rangers as free agent
June 20, 1985:	Traded to the Tigers for Duane James
November 20, 1989:	Re-signed by Tigers as free agent
November 1991:	Re-signed by Tigers as free agent

Year	Team	G	IP	W	L	H	SO	BB	ERA
1971	Id. Falls	Sore arm, appeared in one game as runner							
1972	Quad Cit.	19	129	7	2	111	134	57	2.79
1973	El Paso	26	206	16	6	170	197	63	2.71
1973	Salt Lake	2	14	1	0	11	15	2	2.57
1973	Angels	4	26	2	2	20	22	8	3.12
1974	Angels	39	269	14	19	262	180	77	3.11
1975	Angels	34	257	16	9	211	269	73	2.63
1976	Angels	34	288	19	10	212	261	73	2.44
1977	Angels	31	241	15	9	201	205	61	2.54
1978	Angels	33	239	18	12	239	137	60	3.65
1979	Angels	18	90	7	5	93	46	25	3.90
1980	Angels	32	204	11	12	223	113	45	4.15
1981	Red Sox	24	141	4	10	142	78	43	4.02
1982	Rangers	30	194	7	18	199	87	55	4.21
1983	Rangers	29	159	7	9	144	108	49	3.16
1984	Rangers	35	246	5	15	234	141	81	3.25
1985	Rangers/Tigers	33	215	12	14	220	159	57	4.27
1986	Tigers	32	188	12	9	196	119	65	4.16
1987	Tigers	34	219	15	10	216	146	56	3.91
1988	Tigers	32	203	14	11	213	127	64	4.21
1989	Tigers	33	224	10	14	227	147	74	3.58
1990	Tigers	34	176	9	8	190	114	66	5.31
1991	Tigers	33	217	13	12	217	107	78	3.77
1992	Tigers	32	187	13	11	188	91	90	4.39
Major League Career (20 years)		606	3984	233	219	3847	2657	1200	**3.63**

Bill Wegman
A Pitcher with a Purpose

VITAL STATISTICS

Born on December 16, 1962, in Cincinnati, Ohio
6 feet 5, 220 pounds
Current Team: Milwaukee Brewers
Position: Pitcher (right-handed)

CAREER HIGHLIGHTS

- Hurled seven complete games for Milwaukee in 1991
- Finished third in American League in ERA in 1991 with a 2.84 mark
- Won the Hutch Award in 1991 as Major League Baseball player who overcame great physical adversity

WARMING UP

If anybody wants to preach that becoming a Christian will solve all of your problems and make everything easier, they should talk with Bill Wegman first. He knows better.

Six months after becoming a believer, "My shoulder blew out," Wegman recalls. "Before that, I had some small injuries, but nothing major. After becoming a believer, while a baby Christian, this happens.

"I said, 'How can God let this happen? I accept Him and this happens. This ain't the way it's supposed to be.'"

Yet it really is, Wegman can testify now. "Through my injury, through that adversity, through that low point in my career, God showed me what He had for me to do. I would say it was the high point.

Bill Wegman

When Bill Wegman was born in 1962 in Cincinnati, the hometown Reds were led by a feisty manager named Fred Hutchinson. He had led the residents of Crosley Field to a 1961 meeting with the New York Yankees in the World Series and had coaxed them through a 98-win season in the year Wegman was born.

But if Bill Wegman ever made the trip to Crosley Field to see Fred Hutchinson in action, he wouldn't remember it. Hutchinson died on November 12, 1964, of cancer.

His memory, however, lives on in the form of the Hutch Award, which is given to the major league baseball player who overcomes a physical adversity to prolong or restore his career while best exemplifying the spirit of Fred Hutchinson.

Winners of the award have included Johnny Bench, Willie Stargell, Sandy Koufax, Paul Molitor, and Mickey Mantle. And Bill Wegman.

As a pitcher for the Milwaukee Brewers, Bill Wegman used the type of character, dedication, and competitive drive that marked Hutch's life to overcome almost two years of arm and shoulder problems in 1989 and 1990 to put together one of the top performances in baseball in 1991.

That Bill Wegman made it to the top in baseball is probably no surprise to those who knew him as a kid at Oak Hill High School in the Queen City. But that he did it as a pitcher might not be what they expected.

Instead the people of Oak Hill and all of Ohio probably figured Wegman would be battling it out for supremacy at shortstop with still another Cincinnatian. Across town at Moeller High School was a can't-miss prospect, a kid named Barry Larkin. Larkin and Wegman, who was primarily a shortstop in high school, finished one-two in the race for All-American at the number six position. Yet while Larkin would take his shortstop skills north to the University of Michigan, Wegman was surprised to discover that he had been drafted by the Milwaukee Brewers as a pitcher.

"I had pitched a little bit," Wegman explains, "but we had four other guys that were drafted also off our high school baseball team that played a little bit of minor league baseball for a while." Thus, as a pitcher Wegman faced those nearly devastating two years of surgery, rehabilitation, setbacks, and struggles.

But by 1989, when the seriousness of his arm troubles was made clear, he had discovered an asset that helped carry him through those months of pain and doubt. This discovery began during the off-season after the 1988 season. Wegman had become a successful major league pitcher and was near his goal of "getting all the money I could get."

Though Wegman "thought I had everything I needed," he finally let an unexpected visitor into his life. His wife had signed a visitor's card while attending a church, someone had called requesting to come and talk with the Wegmans, and Bill tried to avoid the visitor. "I kept blowing the guy off, saying that I had no desires and that he had nothing for me. I just couldn't find a good reason for me wanting to meet him."

Finally, though, Wegman relented.

"The pastor came to the house and just shared some things, and asked me where I thought I would spend eternity. At the time, I thought I had the answers to everything. I had never gone to church as a kid. I didn't know anything about the Bible, and I didn't know anything about religion. He just kind of turned my world upside down. He talked about things I had heard through the Christmas story and the Easter story—things like that and never really understood. He just turned my world upside down with questions that I didn't have answers to, and I asked the Lord to come into my life that night. I accepted the Lord in November of 1988."

If anybody wants to preach that becoming a Christian will solve all of your problems and make everything easier, they should talk with Bill Wegman first. He knows better. Six months after becoming a believer, "My shoulder blew out," Wegman recalls. "Before that, I had some small injuries, but nothing major. After becoming a believer, while a baby Christian, this happens.

"I said, 'How can God let this happen? I accept Him and this happens. This ain't the way it's supposed to be.'"

Yet it really is, Wegman can testify now. It was all part of the plan for Bill Wegman to have a new purpose to his pitching. "Through my injury, through that adversity, through that low point in my career, God showed me what He had for me to do. I would say it was the high point.

"My injuries helped me to put my life, and everything else, into perspective. I learned how important my family was and how I had rejected them because of the game. It taught me about my relationship with God and how I had neglected that, totally because of the game. It showed me how temporary the game is. And it also showed me how much I enjoyed playing the game, how much I missed it while I was away, but it was not the most important thing in my life."

Most important or not, playing the game was still a desire that burned in Wegman's heart. But that's not the only thing that spurred him on to the kind of commitment that the Hutch Award speaks of. "After I became a believer, I was under the firm belief that God put me into baseball, and if He wants me out of it, He'll take me out of it. I've kind of carried that same code through everything. If I'm supposed to be here, I'll be here, whether [baseball] people want me or not. I have work to do, I have to do my part. I've got to go out there and glorify the Lord in everything I do." If a successful year on the field can be a testimony to God,

Wegman's 1991 campaign, the one that earned him the Hutch Award, is certainly a good example.

To see how far Wegman had to come to regain his status as a top-notch starting pitcher and win the Hutch Award, we must return to his 1989 season. During the season after his November salvation, he went to the mound only 11 times. On June 1 he went on the 15-day disabled list with tendinitis in his right shoulder. On June 23, he moved up to the 21-day DL. On July 7, he underwent surgery to fix a torn tendon in his shoulder. He ended the year in the Instructional League.

The next season began for Wegman in Denver in the Triple A American Association. On April 28, nearly 11 months after going on the disabled list, he was back in a Brewers' uniform. He beat the Twins, shut out the A's, and seemed to be hitting his stride.

But the arm problems persisted. He visited the 15-day DL on June 4 because of tendinitis in his elbow, and then just as he had done the year before, moved up to the 21-day list. It was déjà vu for Wegman as he again underwent summer surgery, this time on August 14, and this time to remove bone chips in his elbow and to repair a ligament.

It had not even been two years yet since his decision to put his life in God's hands, and he had spent almost two entire seasons as a disabled spectator.

The next year didn't start off with much more promise than the previous two. Wegman opened the 1991 season on the 15-day DL, still recovering from the surgery. Then it was off to Beloit in the Midwest League, the second minor league team Wegman had played for while he was still a teenager. Then back to Denver for a short stint. Finally, on May 3, Wegman joined the Brewers again. Not until May 16 did he pick up his first victory of 1991. That gave him 5 wins since 1988.

Then good things started to happen. Despite starting late, Wegman picked up 15 wins on the year. He was voted the Brewers' Most Valuable Pitcher, and he finished in the top five in several categories in the American League. Finally he was back. He was a new pitcher with a new message. And with his return to success on the hill, a new platform from which to tell others of his love for Jesus Christ.

That's good news for Bill Wegman, for he is not shy about his faith. He knows what it has done for him, and he wants it to help others too. He wants them to know how it has helped his family.

"Our faith in Jesus Christ has brought us closer together. It has really showed me how screwed up my priorities were before. My family came second to baseball. Through my faith, God has shown me what I have and how thankful I should be for my family. They've just helped me to grow. They're my biggest fans. They're with me wherever I go. I don't go anywhere without them. They're a big part of me. They keep me strong. God has let me see that's my responsibility now. I'm accountable for my kids and my wife. If I'm going to call myself a Christian and live the Christian life, I've got to make sure things are in order at home."

Wegman also knows what his faith has done to straighten out other areas of his life, and he wants to tell people about that too. He presents his testimony of God's goodness several times each year, speaking in baseball chapels, church services, and sometimes doing "even a little bit of preaching."

"Last year we had an event where about 25 family members showed up. That was the first time I had witnessed face to face to my family—to show them that Christ was working through me. And it gave them a chance to decide whether they thought I was crazy or not.

"A lot of people knew me before, and I was living the baseball life. A drinker, a partier, a run-arounder. I played the game hard on the field, and I played the game off the field. People had seen the 180-degree change. I tell them it wasn't anything I had done. It was God working through me, because I didn't want to give those things up. It was God strengthening me and pulling me through these things and showing me how unimportant they were. And that He was to be glorified."

One person Wegman especially wanted to tell about his faith was an old drinking buddy who had seen the new Bill Wegman and was curious about him.

"One of my best friends in Milwaukee is a self-made millionaire. He started out as a low-level employee with a fast-food corporation. And he's worked his way up. He now owns three restaurants, and he's got the big house on the hill. He's got everything. Yet happiness or total joy is not there. He's got all the pleasures of his heart, but there's no joy.

"When I made this commitment to Jesus Christ, I stopped drinking and partying and hanging out with this friend—not to separate from him but to separate myself from the sin. He couldn't understand why, and he called me one night."

"If you're a Christian, I don't want to be like you," the friend said bluntly.

"Praise God!"

"What are you talking about?" he asked.

"Look," Wegman answered, "if you're looking for an excuse not to accept the Lord, you're going to find it in me. When you go to the cross, you look at Jesus Christ. And when you find a flaw in Him, you give me a call. I'll go drink with you. Until you give me that call and find a flaw, I'm right here, man. I'm going to stand firm in my faith."

Their friendship continued, however, and they still talked and visited. Then one day Wegman returned to Milwaukee during the off-season for a banquet. He decided to visit his friend's house and spend the night with his family.

"On the way home, we sat in the front seat of his truck, and he said, 'You know, I think I can be like you. I really respect where you're coming from. I didn't understand it at first, but I really think I can be like you.'

"This was the same guy who had said he didn't want to be like me, and now he was telling me he wanted to be like me. I told him, 'Here's what you have to do. I can't do anything for you. I can only witness to you. But it's got to be a personal commitment between you and God, sitting down face to face. Your accepting Jesus Christ into your heart. You know what you gotta do, now go do it. You want to change, you can't do it, only God can do it through you.'

"It was awesome. It was kind of like God showing me that I don't have to be constantly witnessing verbally. I can show a testimony through my actions, through my silent testimony."

This pitcher with a purpose is also open and willing to discuss his faith with the men he plays baseball with. Yet he always does it in a nonthreatening, almost inviting, way.

"I have a chance to fellowship on every team flight. I set up shop in the back of the plane. It's part of my calling. I'll set up shop on the charter flight, and I'll have three or four guys coming back—a couple of believers, a couple of nonbelievers—and they'll ask me questions. I'll open up my Bible. I have a little laptop computer I carry with all my studies and all my reference guides and my notes. I'll read a book until somebody comes back, and normally on every flight somebody will come back and ask questions.

"We've got some real good questions coming about evolution. I've been searching the Bible to try to help one of our guys who works with our team understand that God is the creator of the universe [and] the creator of man. It's funny. I'll set up shop, and I'll pray to the Lord, and I'll say, 'Lord, just give me opportunities and guide my words,' and sure enough, He just seems to do it. He brings these people to me. It's not only for their benefit, but it also helps me to grow. I've been searching out things about the creation that I really never scarched out before. It's got me hanging out in Christian bookstores, finding books, reference manuals, you name it. Just to try to get an answer."

Wegman's purpose is not to batter anybody over the head with a Bible and try to drag him into the kingdom. "I won't shove it down anybody's throat, because they're going to be standing before God.

"I tell them, 'You're going to die. I'm not going to be there. All your friends are not going to be there. It's going to be you and God. And God's going to ask you some simple questions. . . . And you're either going to be welcomed into heaven, or you're not.'

"That's why it's a personal relationship with Jesus Christ. I always take them to a verse of Scripture in Matthew, in the Beatitudes, where it says that many people will come to Him on that day and will say, 'Lord, Lord, did I not prophesy in your name? Did I not drive out demons, did I not perform many miracles in your name?' And Jesus will say to them plainly, 'I never knew you, depart from me you evil doers.' To me, that says it's a personal relationship."

This is the relationship that has given the pitcher his purpose, and it is the reason he cares enough for all those people—

family, friends, teammates—to make himself available for spiritual help. And it is the reason his biggest thrill in baseball is perhaps a bit unlike most. It is not a shutout over the Oakland A's or a 10-strikeout performance. It has to do with music and Milwaukee's County Stadium.

"Each pitcher gets to pick his own music for our home games. Some guys will play Hammer—something that motivates the crowd. The sound people called down and asked what kind of music I like, and I said, 'Well, I like Christian music.' And they said, 'You want us to play some?' I said, 'Are you serious?' They said they were, and I told them I would look around and find some stuff. The more I thought about it, the more I thought, that's kind of weird, I don't need to do that.

"When they called down the day of the game, I said, 'Look, if you've got some kind of Christian music, play it.' They said, 'We'll take care of you.'

"I walked out on the mound, and I was going through my warm-up tosses. I was into the game, and I wasn't even thinking about the music. Jim Gantner, who's a believer also, came over and said, 'Hey, nice music!' And then it clicked. I heard the words of one of Amy Grant's songs, I think it was 'Bringing Down the Walls,' and it was being played in the loudspeaker on the stadium in front of 11,000 people. It was nice, instead of hearing Hammer bang away at whatever he bangs away at."

It's all part of the purpose in Bill Wegman's thinking. He's struggled through career-threatening injuries to become a top Brewer pitcher, but not for his own glory. The purpose is as clear as the song over the loudspeaker. Wegman is there to help break down the walls that are stopping so many people—baseball players and fans alike—from realizing what he knows so well. That the real purpose in life is to serve God.

Q & A WITH BILL WEGMAN

Q: *Who were some people who played a big part in helping you make it to the majors?*

Bill: There were quite a few guys. Terry Bevington, the third base coach for the White Sox, played a big part. My best minor league season was at Stockton under Bevington, and he just gave me the ball and let me make or break myself. Whenever I had questions or something to work on, he helped me. He was the pitching coach, the manager, everything. His being a catcher helped out quite a bit. Former Brewers' manager Tom Trebelhorn was with me at Triple A too, and he was very helpful.

Q: *What do you think is your secret to success in the big leagues?*
Bill: Probably my health. During my first five years I had the injuries that I had fixed two or three years ago. Just the fact that I've been able to get back to health is a blessing. Also my faith—being a born-again Christian. That God put me in baseball, it's obvious to me. I'm just trying to do my part. So the keys are my faith, my beliefs, and the fact that I've been healthy.

Q: *How do you handle those things about baseball that go against you?*
Bill: The one thing I keep telling myself is that this is temporary. God has put me in this to glorify Himself. My actions, whether I win or lose, are how I glorify the Lord. I put a lot into this. I work hard. I work 100 percent. I do my part. But the glory goes to the Lord.

But all this is temporary. So when things didn't go my way, I didn't have to go in the locker room and beat things up and swear, go out and get drunk and forget about my problems. I just go to the Book and I look at Job and see how he suffered. All in one day. I didn't have to go through that.

Q: *What are the biggest problems with being a major league baseball player?*
Bill: Being away from my wife and facing the temptations the world throws at you are the big problems. I've eliminated putting myself in dangerous situations—like the temptations of going in the bars. You go in a bar, you make yourself vulnerable.

I stay in my room, I'll open up a book, or I'll invite a believer in and we'll sit around and talk about Scriptures or do a Bible study. I just try to deal with it by not putting myself in that situation.

Being away from your wife, you have a lot of temptations thrown at you. I think all men struggle with lust, and so I just eliminate the situation. When a tough situation comes up, I just try to glorify God through it. But there are times when you don't, when you laugh at the wrong joke or you give a second look—and the spirit of conviction is there stabbing you.

Q: *Besides the time the sound crew played Christian music for you at County Stadium, what is your greatest thrill in baseball?*
Bill: On Easter Sunday in 1987. It was April 19 when we beat the Rangers for our 13th straight win. We won the first 13 games of the season. We were on some kind of a roll. When Dale Sveum and Rob Deer hit the home runs against Texas to win it, it was an incredible high as far as baseball goes. But there's nothing more important for me than going out there and doing my best for the Lord, win or lose.

Q: *Can you recall a funny incident in baseball?*
Bill: A few years ago we were in Detroit for a Sunday day game, and I had pitched the night before. I was lying on one of the trunks in the clubhouse reading the newspaper, and I fell asleep during a rain delay. Well, one of the guys set my shoes on fire.

Usually they'll confess who did it, but nobody would fess up. About three weeks later, it's the middle of July, and it's about a hundred and twenty degrees in Milwaukee. I'm sitting in the dugout, and I get a phone call from the bullpen. It's Danny Plesac. I look down there, and he's jumping around blowing on his shoes, and waving on his shoe. He was showing me that he was the guilty party, but he had let it go on for three weeks.

Then a little later, Mike Birkbeck and I—in the middle of July—put parkas on and hats and grabbed sticks, and we acted like we had weiners on [the sticks]. We took out Dan's best pair of shoes, we drenched them in rubbing alcohol, and we set them on fire right on top of the dugout, and we had a weiner roast. Danny thought he had pulled something over on us, but he didn't.

Q: *What are your goals for your career?*
Bill: I want to stay in the game as long as God wants me to. I want to improve on each start, yet not put pressure on myself. If I won a Cy Young award, praise God. It's His award. My award is in heaven. I'm trying to walk with the Lord in every phase of my life. On the field and off the field. I want my walk on the field to be strong. God's will is sovereign in my life. If I'm meant to be a 25-game winner, then I'll be a 25-game winner. I have a responsibility to do my part.

Q: *Since baseball has made you very wealthy, how do you view money?*
Bill: God has given me an awesome responsibility with money. He's given everyone who is in this game an awesome responsibility. What I choose to do with it will either glorify God or deny Him. God thinks I can handle the money I am making, so He has given me the responsibility of handling it. He can take it away as quick as He gave it to me. I understand that.

He keeps giving it to me, I keep giving it back. He'll tell me when to stop giving—when I don't have it to give anymore. Until that time comes, I have that responsibility.

Four or five years ago, I wanted money. All the money I could get, but it wasn't God's time. Now that I've got it, it's not quite what I thought it was going to be. It's not like the high I thought it was going to be. Joy and happiness are through Christ.

MAJOR LEAGUE CAREER PATH

June 8, 1981: Selected by the Brewers in 5th round of free-agent draft

THE WEGMAN FILE

Year	Team	G	IP	W	L	H	SO	BB	ERA
1981	Butte	14	82	6	5	94	47	44	4.17
1982	Beloit	25	179	12	6	176	77	38	2.81
1983	Stockton	24	186	16	5	149	135	45	1.30
1984	El Paso	10	64	4	5	62	42	15	2.67
1984	Vancouver	6	27	0	3	30	16	8	1.95
1985	Vancouver	28	188	10	11	187	113	52	4.02
1985	Brewers	3	17	2	0	17	6	3	3.57
1986	Brewers	35	198	5	12	217	82	43	5.13
1987	Brewers	34	225	12	11	229	102	53	4.24
1988	Brewers	32	199	13	13	207	84	50	4.12
1989	Brewers	11	51	2	6	69	27	21	6.71
1990	Denver	3	13	1	0	10	14	7	3.29
1990	Brewers	8	30	2	2	37	20	6	4.85
1990	Beloit	1	2	0	0	1	2	1	0.00
1991	Beloit	3	11	0	2	11	12	1	1.64
1991	Denver	1	7	0	0	6	1	1	2.57
1991	Brewers	28	193	15	7	176	89	40	2.84
1992	Brewers	35	262	13	14	251	127	55	3.20
Major League Career (8 years)		**186**	**1175**	**64**	**65**	**1203**	**537**	**271**	**4.02**

Part Two
OFF THE FIELD

Sal Bando
Still Slugging Away

VITAL STATISTICS

Born February 13, 1944, in Cleveland, Ohio
6 feet, 195 pounds
Career Teams: Oakland A's (9 years); Milwaukee Brewers (5 years)
Position: Third Base. Now Brewers' general manager
Attended Arizona State University

CAREER HIGHLIGHTS

- Led American League in doubles in 1973 (32)
- Named to the All-Star team four times
- Batted .500 in 1975 playoffs against Boston (6-for-12)
- Named to the Baseball Chapel Hall of Fame in 1990

WARMING UP

In most cases, the impact people of the great Oakland A's teams of the mid-1970s, players who battled Cincinnati's famed Big Red Machine for supremacy in baseball, have gone on to other pursuits. Yet Sal Bando, one of the talented, powerful young men who came up through the A's farm system to bring glory to the Bay, has not set aside his baseball dreams.

As general manager for the Milwaukee Brewers, there are still World Series games and world championship rings to be won. It is just the latest step in a 40-year baseball journey for Sal Bando.

Sal Bando

Many of Sal Bando's teammates and managers during his playing days, men who accomplished splendid things in baseball, have settled into lives and lifestyles that are not closely related to baseball.

There's the great Reggie Jackson, he of the monstrous home runs and the wondrous quotes. And Dick Williams, the man who engineered two world championships out of a group of talented but often disagreeable stars. Then there's Vida Blue, the Oakland A's superstar pitcher whose career had its very high moments (1971, when he was both the Most Valuable Player and the Cy Young Award winner in the American League) and its low moments (when he admitted that he had used drugs while pitching).

These impact people of the great Oakland A's of the mid-1970s, teams who battled Cincinnati's famed Big Red Machine for supremacy in baseball, have gone on to other pursuits. Yet Sal Bando, one of the talented, powerful young men who came up through the A's farm system to bring glory to the Bay, has not set aside his baseball dreams.

True, he is no longer hanging around third base or pounding out line drives as he did for the colorful Oakland teams, but he is still in the game, as general manager for the Milwaukee Brewers. And in his new position, there are still World Series and world championship rings to be won. It is just the latest step in a 40-year baseball journey for Sal Bando.

What began as a kid's passion for sports back in Cleveland in the early fifties eventually turned into a ticket out of town. In high school, Bando excelled in basketball, football, and baseball—so much so that he was offered college scholarships in all three.

He chose the baseball route, which took him to Arizona State University. That decision definitely put him on the right road. He played there for three years for legendary coach Bobby Winkles, and Bando was aboard the Sun Devils' baseball express when they captured the 1965 College World Series by beating Ohio State 2-1 in Omaha. For his efforts in helping the Sun Devils take home the trophy, Bando was named the Most Outstanding Player of the College World Series that year.

His College World Series performance led to the big prize for Bando. He caught the eye of Kansas City A's owner Charlie O. Finley, who was busy putting together a group of young men he would be taking with him from Kansas City to Oakland in 1968, players such as Joe Rudi, Bert Campaneris, Reggie Jackson, Rollie Fingers, Vida Blue, Jim "Catfish" Hunter, and John "Blue Moon" Odom. In return, these players and Bando would hand Charlie O. a series of World Series wins.

The championships began to accumulate in Oakland in 1972. The A's, after edging past the Detroit Tigers in the playoffs 3 games to 2, went up against a team that sported one of the best lineups ever to be written on a scorecard. The Cincinnati Reds furnished the competition for the upstarts from Oakland, and the Reds came stocked with a roster that sounded like a future Hall of Fame roll call. Pete Rose led off. Joe Morgan played second. Tony Perez stood poised to knock in runs. Johnny Bench was there collecting superlatives from anyone who saw him hit, catch, or throw. And the "bottom" of the lineup featured Hal McRae, Davey Concepcion, and Cesar Geronimo.

Besides such a potent lineup to shut down, the A's had to overcome a feeling in the baseball community that they had rung up 93 wins against an inferior league. No less an expert on baseball and overstatement as Reds' manager Sparky Anderson told *Sports Illustrated* before the Series began, "If I said the American

League was as good as the National League, I'd be lying. Yes, Oakland could come over and play in our league and maybe Boston. But they're the only ones."

What Sparky apparently forgot was that his team wasn't playing the whole league—just what proved for the next three years to be the best team in the whole world. And in the 1972 Series, what Sparky and his gang failed to foresee was the amazing performance that would come from a fellow southern Ohioan. Gene Tenace, who grew up about 90 miles up the Ohio River from Cincinnati in Lucasville, dismantled the Reds' pitching staff single-handedly with four home runs, including two in his first two World Series at bats—both at Riverfront Stadium before a record crowd of fellow Buckeyes. Sal Bando and his mustachioed teammates went on to win the Series 4 games to 3.

So how did this fledgling bunch from out West shut down the Big Red Machine? It might have had something to do with attitude. Bando, who hit .267 for the A's while playing the entire Series at third, felt that after the battle they had against the Tigers, the Fall Classic was a relief. "After Detroit," he told *Sports Illustrated,* "this just seems like the regular season. I came in here [Cincinnati] feeling as if a 5,000 pound weight had been taken off my back."

With that weight gone, the A's bore down on the Reds and claimed the world championship. That first World Series title is the event that Sal Bando still calls his most thrilling moment in baseball.

In 1973, of course, the A's were back in the Series, this time on a different kind of mission. As Bando stated before the A's took on the National League champion New York Mets, "I don't believe people think of us as legitimate world champions. We are out to prove that we are."

The A's did just that by beating the New York Mets 4 games to 3. The only surprise came after the Series when Oakland manager Dick Williams announced that he was calling it quits. Someone else would have to lead the team in their pursuit of three in a row.

Someone else did. In 1974, in an ending to the baseball season that was beginning to become monontonous, the A's trounced the Los Angeles Dodgers in five games. This was to be the final ring for the Oakland A's in the era of Jackson, Rudi, Bando, and Fingers. Yet to Bando there was something—make that someone—special about this team. The special person was Dick Williams's replacement, a man who led Bando to make a life-changing decision.

Williams's resignation had opened the door for a man who was familiar to many of the A's—Alvin Dark—to step back in and take the helm. Dark had been the skipper of the Kansas City A's when some of the players of the championship teams were first coming up to the majors. And then, in February of 1974, Charlie O. made him manager again, even though he had fired him during the 1967 season when the team was on its way to a last-place finish.

Alvin Dark was a Christian who didn't shrink from letting people know about that. He certainly wasn't perfect, however, and he knew that. He had made a few enemies during his managing career because of some of his methods, but he sincerely wanted to present a good testimony. In fact, after one unfortunate incident that occurred while he was spending a few frustrating years in Cleveland as manager and general manager, he wrote to every person he had offended while on the job, simply because he thought his duty as a Christian was to apologize.

This was the man who took over the A's in 1974, and he was grateful for the opportunity, despite the no-win situation it put him in. Having inherited a World Series champ, he was expected to repeat Dick Williams's success. Amazingly, he did so, leading the players to their third straight title. Early on, he downplayed any role he might have in the A's success that year when he said in spring training that "players make a manager look good. A manager does not make players look good." But there was one player on his team he did help. While he may not have made Sal Bando "look good," he did help Bando be good—and even today do good.

Bando did not need to be introduced to Jesus Christ by Alvin Dark. He had grown up in a home where Jesus was worshiped. But there was still something missing for Bando, and Dark helped him find out what it was. "Under the influence of Alvin Dark during my years in Oakland," Bando recalls, "I finally made a commitment to Jesus. I knew who Christ was, but there wasn't a dedication to Him in all areas of my life. It wasn't until August of 1975 that I got on my knees and made that dedication to Him."

Those championship years in Oakland were also turbulent years, for the team members were often perceived to be at each other's throats and were sometimes viewed as unruly. It would stand to reason that Bando would have struggled during this time, since they were, he says, his "precommitment years." Yet that is not the case. Because of his upbringing in a church-going home, he "still knew morally right and wrong." He continues: "I think that because of having a foundation, that helped me through those times. In those days, I think God gave me the balance I needed. But I probably would have been different if I had made a commitment to Christ earlier."

The third baseman stayed in Oakland just two more years. On November 16, 1976, he signed on as a free agent with Milwaukee. What the A's lost when Bando headed back East was their all-time leader in games played (1,410) and RBI (789), as well as the man who was second in hits, extra base hits, at-bats, and total bases. When spring training of 1977 rolled around for Oakland, "Captain Sal," as he was called, was gone.

While playing for Milwaukee, Bando had one more stellar playoff performance still in him. In 1981, the season of baseball's longest players' strike, the Brewers won the first half of the season (before the strike), and the Yankees won the second half. In a five-game divisional playoff to determine the American League East champ, the Yanks won three games to two. In his final series as a major league player, Bando hit .294 for the Brewers and banged out three doubles in the losing cause.

What had started with such promise in 1965 was over. And what a career it had been for Bando! A College World Series ring. Three Major League World Series rings. More than 1,700 hits while playing in more than 2,000 games.

And, oh yes, one appearance as a pitcher. In 1979, while playing for the Brewers, he was called on to take the mound. He worked three innings, giving up three hits and two runs. Besides ending his 16 years in the majors with a career slugging average of .408, Bando also ended with a career ERA of 6.00. Not bad for a third baseman.

When Sal and Sandy Bando moved to Milwaukee in 1976, they must have liked what they saw, because upon Sal's retirement from the game in 1981, the family stayed in the Wisconsin city. Perhaps one of the reasons for that was the fact that as soon as Bando stopped playing, he was snapped up by the team for a part-time front office position. He was named a special assistant to the general manager.

Bando always had an interest in business, inside baseball and out. His major at Arizona State was business, and he was just one semester away from graduating from ASU when the A's came calling. Without baseball, he says, "I probably would have been involved in some type of business. At one point I thought about being a stock broker." When the playing days were over, he began his own company. Along with Jon McGlocklin, formerly of the Milwaukee Bucks in the NBA, and a third partner, Bando organized Bando-McGlocklin Capital Corporation, a financial company that made real estate loans to businesses.

In the fall of 1991, the Brewers asked Bando to consider joining the team on a full-time basis as the team's senior vice president of baseball operations, or general manager. What sounds like a huge challenge and a heavy responsibility is not seen as too burdensome by Bando. Sounding as smooth and confident as he was when he was holding down third base, Bando speaks of how he handles the ups and downs that come with a job like his.

"The hectic pace of the position and all that goes with it is part of the job. You learn to accept it. As far as how do I deal with it, I recognize that it is just a part of my life—it is not my whole life. There are things that I can control and things that I can't. I don't really dwell on those things that I can't control. I pray for guidance. I pray for understanding and wisdom, but I hope that I've made a good decision. If I have, I hope it has been a decision that is right, even though it may not work out." Just as he knew the importance of the morally correct choice when he played for Oakland, he understands it even now as a front-office executive. And he says he now has the added advantage of understanding the importance of prayer.

Another thing Sal Bando understands very well is the importance of family. He works hard to be a good husband for his wife, Sandy, and a good dad for their boys, Sal, Jr., Sonny, and Stefano.

Sandy and Sal Bando met in a most unusual way long before the World Series rings and the Oakland limelight. Sal was in Puerto Rico, playing winter baseball, when Sandy and some of her friends showed up on the Caribbean island for a vacation from studies at Villanova University where she was earning her degree in nursing. The two met and have been vacationing together ever since.

"We've been married 23 years," Sal recounts. "We are very close. We are committed to each other. In everything that we do, we are very committed to Scripture as the guiding force in our life. I think we moved from a very narrow view as new Christians to one that lets God decide what's right, and we just know what we have to do."

Just as Sal has remained involved in the game he loves, so do Sal and Sandy get involved in interests and causes that are close to them. Sandy began a Bible study for women only, and it grew; now the Bandos lead a church Bible study for couples. They also give of their time to talk to people outside of that smaller group. "We've both been very involved in giving our testimonies and talking to people in the community. We've shared many times."

And he also knows the importance of expressing their faith one-to-one. "A friend and I were playing golf," Bando begins as he tells of one such incident. "He noticed my contentment—the peace I had, and I shared with him briefly why. Later, we got together and he told me, 'You know, you gave me a lot to think about, and I've made a commitment of faith, and it's because of what we talked about.' So I give the glory to God for that."

Besides telling others of their faith, the Bandos also put their faith into action through helping the less fortunate and the young people in their community. Sandy and Sal cochair a child abuse prevention fund in Milwaukee. In addition, he is a member of Boys and Girls Clubs and serves on the advisory board of the Wisconsin Fellowship of Christian Athletes.

All of those activities take a backseat, however, to Sandy and his three sons. "My family is my biggest interest," Bando declares. "Watching the kids play and be involved in their activities [consumes] the time that's left. I do enjoy golf, but that's really been set aside because when I do have time it will be spent with the family.

"We enjoy just being together. Having dinner together is always an excitement in our household. Everybody enjoys eating. My wife is a good cook. It's just a fun time together."

His commitment to God, his family, and ongoing ventures was recognized in 1990 when Baseball Chapel honored Bando with its annual Hall of Fame Award. The award recognizes a player who was an active Christian during his playing days and who has carried that commitment into his retirement from the sport into his new ventures. The acceptance speech Bando gave at that award luncheon in the Heisman Room of the Downtown Athletic Club in New York City lets us in on why they thought so much of the former third baseman.

"I don't feel worthy of this award," he told the gathering. "If anyone is worthy it is Baseball Chapel, because back in my playing days if it was not for Baseball Chapel I might not be standing here today. It was through the tremendous speakers' program with the different gentlemen that would come into the clubhouse and talk to me and show me where my faith wasn't.

"I had put the faith that I grew up with on the shelf and let my interests get so involved in the game of baseball and my own self-worth. Because of the program, I was able to dust off that Holy Spirit that was inside my heart and give Him some room to grow and burst forth and open my eyes as a Christian. I've been able to handle the disappointments that baseball had to offer, along with the success stories, and the move from that into business."

As a high executive in major league baseball, Sal Bando has a solid foundation. It is based on his faith, his commitment to his family, and his love for the game of baseball. And something else—desire and dedication. These are two traits that he thinks are his secret to success. "I think you have to have both desire and dedication. One thing I've learned is that desire comes from the mind and dedication comes from the heart. You need both to be successful." In his drive to succeed and his commitment to God he has shown sufficient amounts of each—enough to keep him slugging away at life and baseball.

Q & A WITH SAL BANDO

Q: *Could you tell us about a funny incident that happened to you as a player?*
Sal: One of the most humorous came after I failed to pick up an RBI. We had a runner on third base, and I didn't get the guy in. I was so angry that I took my helmet and kind of half-tossed it and half-jammed it in between the steps of the dugout in Milwaukee where we were playing. It bounced back up and hit me in the lip and cut my lip. It was bleeding unbelievably, and there was this big knot there. I look back now and it is humorous, but it wasn't too funny then. The guys on the bench were biting their lips and their tongues and everything else trying not to laugh.

Q: *What book or books are important to you?*
Sal: I think Chuck Colson's book *Born Again* was monumental. I don't have time to read books all the way through as much as I would like. I'll read when preparing Bible studies by looking at different commentaries on Scripture. Also, my wife will suggest I read different chapters in certain books, and I'll do that.

Q: *Who is the toughest pitcher you ever faced?*
Sal: There were a lot of them. But one of the ones that comes to mind was Sam McDowell in his prime. And Frank Tanana in his prime, and Jim Palmer. They were all very tough.

Q: *What is your opinion of the high salaries being paid today?*
Sal: My feeling has always been that there is nothing wrong with money—it's the love of money that's the problem. When that interferes with the way you are, what you are, and what you should be, then it is a problem. And I think greed has become a very big factor in all of sports. Greed is no different from lust; it's no different from any other sin. It's evil.

Q: *If you were commissioner, what would you change?*
Sal: The commissioner doesn't really have a whole lot of power, so he can't change too many things. But I think I would get the American League and National League to be consistent in umpiring and consistent in the designated hitter rule. I think there should be designated hitters.

Q: *Who are the top three players in baseball?*
Sal: Jose Canseco, Barry Bonds, and Barry Larkin are three players of tremendous ability.

I'm looking at guys that play every day. An everyday player to me of that caliber is much more valuable than a pitcher, because a good pitcher is only out there every fourth day.

MAJOR LEAGUE CAREER PATH

June 1965:	Drafted by the Athletics
November 16, 1976:	Traded to the Brewers for a free-agent the Athletics would choose later
October 1981:	Retired; became special assistant to GM for Brewers
October 8, 1991:	Named Senior Vice President of Baseball Operations for the Brewers

THE BANDO FILE

Year	Team	G	AB	R	H	2B	3B	HR	RBI	Avg.
1966	KC Athletics	11	24	1	7	1	1	0	1	.292
1967	KC Athletics	47	130	11	25	3	2	0	6	.192
1968	Oak. Athletics	162	605	67	152	25	5	9	67	.251
1969	Athletics	162	609	106	171	25	3	31	113	.281
1970	A's	155	502	93	132	20	2	20	75	.263
1971	A's	153	538	75	146	23	1	24	94	.271
1972	A's	152	535	64	126	20	3	15	77	.236
1973	A's	162	592	97	170	32	3	29	98	.287
1974	A's	146	498	84	121	21	2	22	103	.243
1975	A's	160	562	64	129	24	1	15	78	.230
1976	A's	158	550	75	132	18	2	27	84	.240
1977	Brewers	159	580	65	145	27	3	17	82	.250
1978	Brewers	152	540	85	154	20	6	17	78	.285
1979	Brewers	130	476	57	117	14	3	9	43	.246
1980	Brewers	78	254	28	50	12	1	5	31	.197
1981	Brewers	32	65	10	13	4	0	2	9	.200
Major League Career (16 years)		2019	7060	982	1790	289	38	242	1039	.254

Ernie Harwell
The Voice of Summer

VITAL STATISTICS

Born on January 25, 1918, in Washington, Georgia
Was baptized in the Jordan River

CAREER HIGHLIGHTS

- Announcer for Brooklyn Dodgers: 1948-49
- Announcer for New York Giants: 1950-53
- Announcer for Baltimore Orioles: 1954-59
- Announcer for Detroit Tigers: 1960-91
- Announcer for CBS radio: 1992
- Bestowed Ford Frick Award at the Baseball Hall of Fame in Cooperstown, New York, on August 2, 1981
- Holds U.S. patent for a bottle-can opener
- Has written nearly 50 songs that have been recorded

WARMING UP

A firestorm of protest flared around Tiger Stadium in 1991 when Ernie was dismissed after 30 years as the Tigers' radio voice. Harwell's response was simple and humble: "The main thing is that I know I've got God on my side, and this is just a small thing. I'm just a radio announcer. It's not life and death. I just can't understand why it's such a big story."

Ernie Harwell

You don't often hear Song of Solomon quoted on major league baseball games. But then, you don't often hear a man with the class and depth of play-by-play announcer Ernie Harwell anywhere in sports.

For anybody who loves baseball, his is a dream job. Great seats behind home plate, a chance to see every inning of 162 games plus spring training, the opportunity to hobnob with baseball's finest, and the joy of talking about baseball—and getting paid for it to boot.

That's been the basic scenario for Ernie Harwell since 1948. And every year he has introduced springtime by reading from Song of Solomon:

> Lo, the winter is past, the rain is over and gone; the flowers appear on the earth; the time of the singing of birds is come, and the voice of the turtle is heard in our land. (2:11-12; KJV*)

From that moment forward, baseball fans knew that an important friend had returned. The voice of summer was back.

* King James Version.

But don't spend time telling Ernie Harwell how great he is, how important his classy broadcasts are, and how lousy the Detroit Tigers were for dropping him like a hot mike after the 1991 season. He's not too interested in listening.

He may be a Hall-of-Fame broadcaster with admirers throughout the country, but Ernie Harwell doesn't take himself too seriously.

A firestorm of protest flared around Tiger Stadium in 1991 when Ernie was dismissed after 30 years as the Tigers' radio voice. Harwell's response was simple and humble: "The main thing is that I know I've got God on my side, and this is just a small thing. I'm just a radio announcer. It's not life and death. I just can't understand why it's such a big story."

It's such a big deal because Ernie Harwell has what many people yearn to see in their leaders today: respect, character, self-control, love for family, fairness, and honesty. There were boycotts organized, petitions signed, "Fire Bo [Schembechler, the team president]; Keep Ernie" T-shirts sold, sponsors canceling their support, and myriad stories written during the spring and summer of 1991. The *Detroit Free Press* had the Ernie story on the front page for almost a week. For many Tiger fans, it must have shattered at least one more area of stability in a world that already seemed to be reeling.

A link to the past had been severed. A friend had been shipped off. A member of the family had been locked out. One psychologist even noted during the spring of 1992 that patients coming to his office because of depression often said, "Ernie's gone," as one of the reasons they were feeling so blue.

That was what the big story was about—an institution being shut down. And there was nothing anyone could do about it.

The irony of the whole thing is that Ernie never set out to be one of the best play-by-play men in baseball. As a kid growing up in Georgia he wanted only to play baseball.

"I wanted to be a major league ballplayer. I tried, but I couldn't hack it," he says now about his attempt at the game. And then, with his usual self-effacing style, he recalls the levels at which he did compete. "I played American Legion ball and high school and college, but I really wasn't that talented."

That realistic assessment of his talent on the field led him to change his approach. "I knew that if I wanted to be around base-ball and sports, I'd have to do it either by writing or by being an announcer. I think my first broadcasting ambition was to broad-cast the minor league Atlanta Crackers. They were my hometown heroes. I thought those guys were great."

But before he could crack into the lineup behind the micro-phone for Atlanta, Harwell had to establish himself in the world of baseball journalism.

Whether he was brave or foolhardy at age 16 is not clear, but as a teen he landed a job in a most unheard of way. "I wrote to the editor of *The Sporting News* in St. Louis and suggested that I could be the Atlanta correspondent. I thought that I could cover the Atlanta Crackers. I had no experience. I didn't have sense enough to know that I probably didn't have a chance.

"I signed my name W. Ernest Harwell to sound a little more mature than Ernie. He didn't know I was 16, so he said, 'Send some stuff in,' and I did. They gave me the job."

Surprisingly, the situation worked. In 1934, without any for-mal training, Harwell performed admirably for *The Sporting News* and used that experience as a steppingstone to continue his climb. He stepped up to the *Atlanta Constitution* as he continued high school and college studies. He did rewriting in the sports department, but there were no openings for a sports writer, so he finally left with six years writing experience and a college degree.

So what does a writer who got his first writing job without any training do when he has to move on? How about auditioning for another job for which he has no training?

A classmate of Harwell's at Emory University had noticed his strong, melodious voice while attending a speech class with him. The classmate, who worked for a local radio station, talked Ernie into stopping by the station for a rip-and-read try-out. "So I took an audition at WSB in Atlanta, the NBC station, and got lucky. They hired me as their sports announcer."

In 1940, Harwell, still only 22, became the sports director at WSB radio. During the next few years, Harwell gained admirers as he worked his way from doing sports reports to fulfilling his "first broadcasting ambition" by doing the play-by-play for the Atlanta Crackers.

It is characteristic for any of us with ambition that when we reach one plateau in life and can see further ahead, we start to dream about reaching the higher hills in the distance. That describes Harwell's view of the future. "After I started to do minor league ball," he explains, "I set my sights on the major leagues—doing a team, doing a World Series, doing an All-Star game or a playoff game. And through the grace of God, I got to do all those things."

Harwell arrived in Brooklyn in the middle of the 1948 season to begin his major league broadcasting career. Characteristic of his previous debuts, all rather anonymous, Harwell arrived in Flatbush alone. He knew no one, and no one knew him. "I sort of went out there on my own. When I got to the stadium, I just sort of found my way around and finally got started."

His marvelous career, spanning six decades, began in an unassuming way. After spending two years with the Dodgers, Harwell moved across town in 1950 to the Polo Grounds to broadcast the New York Giants' games. It was in that famous baseball park that the man from Georgia had his biggest thrill behind the microphone.

October 3, 1951. The Giants and the Dodgers had been playing baseball since April, and they were still in a dead heat. Now it's game 3 of a best-of-3 playoff for the National League title. The winner will go on to face the Yankees in the World Series. In perhaps the most dramatic game in baseball history, Bobby Thomson of the Giants finally ends the battle with his "shot heard 'round the world," a ninth-inning, 3-run home run.

"I was broadcasting on NBC television when Bobby Thomson hit that famous home run," Harwell recalls. "My partner, Russ Hodges, was on the radio. He won the fame with his call. It just happened that on TV we didn't have any replays or anything, so nobody knows that I was there." So it is Russ Hodges screaming, "The Giants win the pennant! The Giants win the pennant!" that has kept alive memories of that incredible ending to the 1951 season. And Ernie Harwell is left with the knowledge that although his TV call of that home run is not remembered, his lasting contribution to the game as one of its finest announcers was firmly established.

From New York, Harwell moved on to Baltimore in 1954, where he was in the booth when this transplanted team first occupied Memorial Stadium. The Orioles had just moved east from St. Louis, where they had played in Sportsman's Park as the Browns. But now they were the Orioles, and Harwell was new to the American League. And it would be in the junior circuit that Harwell would remain—first for 6 years with the Birds, and then for a marvelous 32 years with the Detroit Tigers.

Ernie Harwell may have slipped into Brooklyn unnoticed and unappreciated in 1948 to call that first game for the Dodgers, but his final game as a day-to-day team announcer in 1991 was anything but inconspicuous.

For one thing, by virtue of a schedule maker's choice, the Detroit Tigers closed out their 1991 season at Baltimore. And the Orioles were saying good-bye to their old ballpark, preparing to move to a stadium in Camden Yards. Memorial Stadium's career had matched to a day the American League broadcasting career of Ernie Harwell. Amid the hoopla and hype of the closing of the stadium, the Orioles also said a classy so-long to Harwell.

The other thing that made Harwell's departure from the Tigers well-known was the way the Detroit ballclub brought it about. One day in the winter between the 1990 and 1991 seasons, the Tigers met with Harwell and informed him that as far as announcers were concerned, they were headed in a different direction. He could call the games for 1991, but that would be the end of it.

No reasons given. No explanation. Just a firm and unquestioned good-bye.

As always, Harwell handled himself with class, despite what he describes as "the worst thing that happened to me. I had worked there for 32 years, and we had a good relationship. When this thing happened, some of the Tiger front office was very bitter and very antagonistic toward me and I had to accept that. It was a business decision. Maybe they had a reason, but I didn't [delve] into that too much.

"It sort of hurt me, but I had to forgive them. It taught me that people were watching me, and I knew that the way I reacted would reflect on my Christian walk. And I just tried to do the very best I could on that. I think I learned a lesson that people really are people, and you just can't worry about what the world does. You've just got to keep your eyes on Jesus."

And then, of course, there was that strong reaction from the fans. "I didn't like the attention," he confides. "I don't think the announcer should deserve that much attention. It think the game is the main thing, and the announcers should be sublimated to the game. But it was gratifying to see the affection and love that was generated by the fans out this way and even all over the country, for that matter."

What attracts people to such a man? Why would his departure send such shock waves? He isn't flamboyant in his style. He rarely shows great excitement, and he never criticizes players or management. He simply tells you, in what he calls a "reportorial style," what is happening below on the baseball field. But those who listen to him very long or know anything about him realize that there is much more than just an encyclopedic memory for baseball stories and a comforting voice to Ernie Harwell.

For one thing, there is his faith. It is not something he shoves down anyone's throat, but neither is it something he is ashamed to talk about. And appropriately enough, the story of Ernie Harwell's faith includes the influence of another man who has accumulated great amounts of respect and admiration over the years —Billy Graham.

"I had always grown up in a so-called Christian home, but I was always seeking some kind of fulfillment," Harwell says about his days of searching. "I thought I could find it through writing or announcing, but I discovered that each plateau that I reached, which I thought would give me that fulfillment, failed to do it.

"So I kept searching. One year in spring training down at Lakeland—it was the only year my family wasn't with me—I read that Billy Graham was to have an Easter service over in Bartow, Florida, right near Lakeland. Something told me to go over there, and I did. When Billy Graham issued the invitation, I walked down the aisle and right there I dedicated my life to Christ. I made Him my Lord and my Savior, just completely turned my life over to Him. I had never done that before.

"I just had been a fellow who went to Sunday school and thought that if I did a few good deeds I'd get to heaven, and that if

I didn't hurt anybody's feelings, it would be OK. That was about the extent of my 'religion.' I really didn't have a personal relationship with Jesus until that Easter Sunday in 1961."

Over the years, he has taken many opportunities to share his faith with others. For instance, he has been a popular speaker for Baseball Chapel services in the clubhouse. In Toronto he addressed the players at the 1991 All-Star game, along with All-Stars Joe Carter, Brett Butler, Howard Johnson, and Paul Molitor. And there have been times when he has talked about his faith in one-to-one situations.

"There was a sportswriter over in Canada who covered the Tigers. I took him out to dinner one time and led him to Christ. It's a great thrill!"

Without beating on drums and putting people down, Ernie Harwell has quietly presented himself as a man of faith, and he has earned respect in the process.

Another thing about Ernie Harwell makes it almost impossible to dislike him—his consistency. No matter when you tune in or what is happening on the field, you know that this famous Southern voice will give it to you straight, with sincerity and honesty, every time. When the mike is on, Ernie's always the same. And even though you know that anyone who does something for nearly a half a century must have faced many difficulties, Harwell assesses life by saying, "I don't think I've had any real tough times. It's a matter of showing up and trying to keep your health and doing the job day by day. The thing about baseball broadcasting [is its] continuity . . . it's such a day-by-day endeavor.

"Sometimes when you're working and you're not feeling well, you have to go ahead and do the same kind of job as if you were feeling well. That's not too easy. God has given me good health. In the major leagues I've worked 44 years, and I've missed only two games. Neither one of those was due to health problems.

"My brother died in 1968, and I left the team and went to his funeral down in Georgia. The only other time was when I was named to the Hall of Fame. The Tigers got me a plane to be there on Monday night, and I came back and broadcast the game on Tuesday."

To compile such a wondrous record takes some help. Besides recognizing that God has blessed him with good health, Harwell also knows someone else who made it possible for him to conquer the difficulties that are a part of any such astounding success.

"I overcome those problems by having a fine wife, Lulu." "She's a lady who has been very supportive and who was not only a mother but also a father when I was on the road. There's an old saying in sports announcing that all the crises happen when you're on the road. And she has to sort of take over in the role as both parents."

Lulu came into Ernie's life while both were in college. She had come to Georgia from Hazzard, Kentucky, to attend Brenau College in Gainesville, and Ernie was at Emory. As a student in a German class, she and her classmates attended a German breakfast given by the students from Emory. She met a fraternity brother of Ernie's and began dating him. But it was Ernie who eventually won her heart.

"She knew when we married back in 1941 what she was getting into, and she's been very good about it. She's accepted it and adapted to it. She's been loving and supportive, and she's my best friend. I think that's why it has worked for me. I think that if you had somebody who didn't understand her role or your role and didn't cooperate and didn't give that love and support, it would be a very tough job."

Along the way, the Harwells added four children to their family, including twin girls. And after 50-plus years of marriage they also have seven grandchildren. "Three grandchildren live within a couple of blocks of me, and the others live in Georgia," Grandpa Harwell explains. "We have a good time. We sort of like to relax when I'm home. I have so much hustle and bustle on the road with the crowds, I just like to take things easy when I'm home."

Faith. Consistency. Family. All traits of people we like.

But there's another characteristic that endears Ernie to his listeners—his ability not to take baseball or himself too seriously. Consider just two stories from this Hall of Famer's announcing career. First, a story that shows that this man who has captivated millions with his rhetorical splendor over the years can laugh at himself.

"The biggest blooper I pulled was more than just saying a word or two on the air. We had a game with California back in the early '70s at Tiger Stadium, and it was raining. My wife had come to the ballgame to be with me.

"We got a phone call from the press box saying that the game would probably be called. 'But don't announce it until we announce it on the intercom,' they said. They told us there would be a doubleheader on Saturday—this was a Friday night game. Then I heard the intercom voice say, 'Game called, doubleheader Saturday.' Thinking it was the official word, I put it on the air.

"My wife and I left the ballpark, but some people weren't leaving. I thought a lot of them weren't leaving because they didn't want to get wet. It was still raining.

"We got out on the expressway, and I turned on the radio. My partner Ray Lane was doing the scoreboard show. He was giving the other scores when all of a sudden he said, 'Now, wait a minute, folks, that announcement that Ernie put on the air about the game being called is not true. It was an erroneous announcement—the game is still on! Ernie, Ernie, wherever you are, come on back.'

"We were listening, so we got off the expressway, made a U-turn, and came back to the ballpark. Sure enough [the umpires and Tigers] had changed their minds, and the game was played. The Tigers won it, but the management got mad because they had to give their money back to a lot of people who had heard my announcement and had headed home to Grand Rapids or Battle Creek or Saginaw, wherever they were going, and didn't want to come back. It didn't make them too happy in the front office."

Baseball is supposed to be fun, but some people take it too seriously. Harwell obviously realizes that life is too short to get all excited about someone who pulls a trick during a baseball game. He calls the following story one of the funniest he's seen in all baseball.

"Well, we've had a fellow in Detroit by the name of Norm Cash. His nickname was Stormin' Norman. He had a great personality. One time at first base he had a pair of glasses on that had windshield wipers on them. When Nolan Ryan was pitching his second no-hitter in 1973, Norman came in to bat in about the eighth inning. The no-hitter was intact. Ryan was mowing the Tigers down. They were literally lucky to get a foul ball off him, and Norman was sent back to the dugout because his bat was illegal.

"Later on I asked him what was so illegal about the bat. He said, 'Well, Ernie, I wasn't going to hit Nolan Ryan anyway, so I got a table leg off a table in the dugout, and I was going to bat with it.'"

Perhaps the Tigers showed some insensitivity and lack of appreciation in 1991 when they showed Ernie the door, but new owner Mike Ilitch atoned for the error in the middle of 1992 when he came calling on Ernie. Within one month of acquiring the Tigers, Ilitch had signed Harwell to return for one final year. Harwell agreed to do three innings a game in 1993, and then to retire. And after that final tour of the American League, Harwell will continue to represent the Tigers as a team spokesman.

Tiger fans and their new owner were not alone in their recognition of Harwell's importance to baseball. In 1981 Major League Baseball presented Ernie Harwell the Ford C. Frick Award for his contribution to the game. Among all his experiences as a Major League baseball announcer, Harwell describes "being up on the platform with those great players and participating in the ceremony and making the speech of acceptance" as "the greatest thing that happened to me."

The "greatest thing" that ever happened to baseball fans in the Midwest was being able to turn on the radio and listen to the unassuming man who began as W. Ernest Harwell and ended up as just plain Ernie, a man whose secret to success is simple: "I just try to be myself, I think. God made me the way I am, and He gave me the talent to broadcast, and I just tried to be whatever I was and not try to fool anybody."

We're not fooled. Ernie Harwell, the man behind the voice of summer, is for real.

Q & A WITH ERNIE HARWELL

Q: *Being a professional broadcaster, you're exposed to athletes who are sometimes known as a rowdy bunch. A lot of things hap-*

pen that go against your beliefs. How do you deal with the bad language and other things that go on?
Ernie: I ignore it. I don't pay any attention to it. Sometimes fellows are reluctant to use that kind of language in front of me. Sometimes it doesn't make any difference. I'm not judgmental about it. I understand that it's part of the worldly scene, and I'm not going to change things by correcting people or any other way than just being an example. I don't use that kind of language myself, and when I hear other people use it, I don't jump on them. I don't try to tell them it's not the thing to do. If I do have any influence, I try to [influence others] by my actions.

Q: *What's the most important thing to Ernie Harwell?*
Ernie: Well, the most important thing is the way I walk with God. Then my family is second, and my job is third. I know that I can't please men all the time, but I do know that Jesus is my companion. I can always count on Him.

Q: *If you hadn't become an announcer, what do you think you would have become?*
Ernie: I think sooner or later I probably would have been a sportswriter. I probably would have toughed it out until I found a job as a sportswriter. Also, later on, I began to write songs. That was sort of a fail-safe situation for me. I felt like if I went to that full-time I could exist or make somewhat of a living. So I had some other irons in the fire.

Q: *How do you feel about being a role model?*
Ernie: I just try to be myself. I try to be as kind and nice to people as I can. I think that people in the situation I'm in can really be a testimony for Jesus. People are looking at you, and they want to know what your reaction is going to be—how you handle various situations. As has been said many times, they don't have to believe what you say, but they have to believe what you do.

Q: *When you are on the road, how do you pass the time?*
Ernie: I've been a pretty good traveler. I've traveled for so many years—I've traveled since 1948 in the big leagues—I've got into

pretty much a routine. Unlike a lot of people, I don't dislike good traveling. I've got friends in each town. I just try to take a positive outlook, that somebody's paying my way to stay in a nice hotel, eat good food, go to a ballgame, and see my friends in each city.

Here's my routine on the road. I would get up early, eat an early breakfast, read the papers, get on the phone a little bit, then go out for a walk and meet somebody I knew in that town for lunch. I'd come back, have a little nap, read some more, get on the bus, and go to the ballpark, come back, go straight to bed. I tried not to stay out late after the game. I didn't like to eat after the game—I knew I would eat too much. I just tried to watch my diet and pretty much do everything in moderation.

When I was with the Tigers, the last seven years, Sparky Anderson and I always went for a walk in the morning. We'd go out about 10 o'clock. We'd get our exercise. We'd walk an hour. And then by the time we got back, it was time to go out for lunch.

Q: *How do you want people to remember you?*
Ernie: I want people to remember me as a man who tried to walk with his God and tried to do the very best he could.

Q: *What's your philosophy on calling a no-hitter?*
Ernie: By the seventh inning I would certainly mention that it's a no-hitter. Number one, I don't believe that any announcer can control the game or jinx the pitcher. And number two, I think a lot of people listening to the radio only half listen. If you say it in positive terms, they realize what's happening, instead of trying to be coy and hint around about it.

Q: *If you could change one thing about baseball today, what would you change?*
Ernie: I would try to do something about the salaries. I don't know what the solution is, because every time the owners try to do something, it's collusion. I would try to work out a salary cap.

If they keep paying these salaries and the TV money begins to shrink, as it might, they're going to have some problems with finance. Something's got to give.

Part Three
EXTRA INNINGS

Besides the 20 baseball personalities profiled in parts one and two, many other men of faith play professional baseball today. On the following pages you'll take a brief look at nine other major league players who know and love the Lord Jesus Christ.

Glenn Davis

VITAL STATISTICS

Born March 28, 1961, in Jacksonville, Florida
6 feet 3, 210 pounds
Current Team: Baltimore Orioles
Position: First Base
Attended Manatee Junior College, Bradenton, Florida
Attended University of Georgia, Athens, Georgia

CAREER HIGHLIGHTS

- Hit three home runs in a game twice: September 10, 1987, and June 1, 1990
- Named to All-Star team twice
- Led National League in fielding average for first basemen in 1988 at .996

Early in his high school days, Glenn Davis did not seem headed for stardom. He seemed destined for an early grave. Although he was a fine athlete, his life was miserable. His dad, a former minor league baseball player, shoved off one day and left Glenn and his mom to fend for themselves.

It was not a happy combination. For one thing, Glenn firmly rejected his mother's Christian faith. Things were so bad that this big, strapping kid, who was a lethal weapon on the baseball diamond, almost let a small-caliber pistol become a fatal weapon in his life. Feeling his life at home was going nowhere, Glenn often thought his only way out was suicide. Sometimes he even sat in his room with that handgun, toying with the idea of killing himself. Perhaps the best way to get back at his absentee father and his too-strict mother, he felt, was to blow his brains out.

One of the arguments he used to talk himself out of pulling the trigger was that he was not sure what eternity held for him. He just was not willing to send himself out into the unknown. And the other thing that kept that bullet in the chamber was baseball.

He loved the game, and he realized he would be missing the enjoyment of the baseball diamond if he were dead.

At his mother's insistence, Glenn transferred to University Christian High School, where he met Storm Davis, a highly touted athlete. At first their only similarity was the last name. Glenn regarded Storm as only a rival for athletic supremacy at University Christian. But they worked together, and both would lead the school to two state championships in baseball. Eventually they ended in the same household, after the relationship between Glenn and his mother became so tense that Storm's parents invited Glenn in.

He was drafted on January 13, 1981, by the Houston Astros. But the battle within was still raging. He had become the hottest player in the Florida State League in 1982, but his ungodly lifestyle now had stretched Storm's mom, Norma, to the limit. She told Glenn that if he didn't end his ungodly lifestyle, he would have to move out of their house, where he was living. His .315 batting average and league-leading 19 home runs were not as important as his well-being.

For Glenn Davis, Norma's clear proclamation that "going out and partying and sleeping with girls" would not be permitted for anybody living under her roof was the right warning at the right time. He finally got the message that he was not equipped to run his own life. Finally turning to the God he had rejected for so long, Glenn Davis became a Christian.

Today, as a slugging first baseman, he gives much of his time and money to help young people, especially through a children's home he and his wife have started in Columbus, Georgia.

Storm Davis

VITAL STATISTICS

Born December 26, 1961, in Dallas, Texas
6 feet 4, 200 pounds
Current Team: Baltimore Orioles
Position: Pitcher (right-handed)

CAREER HIGHLIGHTS

- Named American League Comeback Player of the Year in 1988
- Pitched in two World Series (1983 and 1988)

It's the summer of 1987. The San Diego Padres are in Houston to take on the Astros. On the mound for the visitors is Storm Davis—a pitcher the Padres had given up catcher Terry Kennedy to get.

It was not turning out to be an easy year for Davis. Padres' manager Larry Bowa was on his case for not pitching well. People who expected big numbers from Storm Davis were not happy that his big numbers represented his ERA.

It was a time for a visit from a friend. When you're up to your belt buckle in troubles, it's good to have someone you know and care for to be nearby. So, here's Storm, looking in from his perch on the mound, and who should saunter toward the batter's box but his bosom buddy, Astros' first baseman Glenn Davis.

The lives of Storm Davis and Glenn Davis are forever intertwined. Not because, as the name might imply, they are brothers; but they did share the same home, as noted in Glenn's story.

First it was Storm who enjoyed the home of George and Norma Davis as the son born to them. Davis was a standout in both baseball and football in high school. On the gridiron he led his University Christian team as the quarterback, and on the diamond he won 42 games and lost only 3 as he compiled a 0.45 ERA by striking out 496 batters in 278 innings.

Glenn Davis showed up at University Christian after a troubled past at his previous school and a home life far different from

Storm's. After they graduated, Storm moved on to pro baseball and Glenn moved in. Thus for a season, the Davis boys shared households.

Now, five years later, times are tough for Storm Davis. He isn't pitching well. And here comes Glenn, who shares with Storm a mutual admiration and a strong Christian faith. The slugging part of the Davis duo was putting together another great season to follow his 101 RBIs and 31 home runs in 1986.

Storm walked Glenn. But then it got worse. He plunked Glenn with a pitch the next time he was up. Here was probably the only person in Houston who really cared that his good buddy was struggling to survive this summer of his discontent in San Diego, and Storm nails him with a pitch.

Life, like a bad baseball season and like plunking your best friend with a pitch, can take dips and turns that are seemingly out of control. For Storm, the ups and downs never seem to stop. The amazing high school years. The successful early years at Baltimore. The unsuccessful trade to San Diego. His parents' divorce. The trip back to the minor leagues in 1987. The three good years in Oakland, which included the 1988 Comeback Player of the Year Award. Two forgettable years in Kansas City. The culmination of a dream in playing on the same team with Glenn in 1992, when he joined Glenn as an Oriole at the new Camden Yards stadium.

But one thing has been constant for Storm through it all. His faith. It was his mother who was the catalyst for his interest in salvation. When he was seven years old, he attended a Thursday night choir practice with his mom. As they sang, he stood outside in the foyer, listening.

One the way home, Storm picked up the songbook and began singing "Blessed Assurance." "As I began to sing," he recalls, "my mom began to sing it with me. And the Holy Spirit used the song to touch my life as a seven-year-old boy." When he got home, he knew that he needed Jesus Christ in his life, and he told his mom that. They read Scripture together from Romans and John. That night, he recalls, "I got down on my knees and accepted Jesus into my life."

It's that faith—the faith of a child grown up—that guides Davis and helps him when even his best friend, standing 60 feet 6 inches away, can't.

Bryan Harvey

VITAL STATISTICS

Born June 2, 1963, in Chattanooga, Tennessee
6 feet 2, 212 pounds
Team: California Angels
Position: Relief Pitcher (right-handed)
Attended University of North Carolina

CAREER HIGHLIGHTS

- Named *The Sporting News* American League Rookie Pitcher of the Year, 1988
- Led the American League in saves in 1991 (46)
- Selected to American League All-Star team one time

Bryan Harvey is an Angel. His daughter Whitney suffers from Angelman's Syndrome. Those two facts make Harvey's being a Christian doubly important.

The fact that a major league pitcher has a daughter with a rare form of mental retardation makes him, in a sense, a spokesman. In the same way that his teammate Jim Abbott, the Angels' one-handed ace pitcher, is a symbol for the disabled, so Harvey is a symbol for parents whose children suffer from Angelman's.

In 1991, Harvey set the standard for saves in the American League with 47. In just five seasons he has racked up more than 100 of them. His skill at saving baseball games gets tested almost every day, and he can handle the pressure. Former major league infielder John Werhas says about him, "On the mound he's not afraid to challenge the hitter."

Of the bigger challenge that lies ahead at home, he doesn't seem to be afraid, either. He and his wife, Lisa, "thank the Lord for His blessings," Harvey says. And one of those blessings is coming home and having Whitney run up to him and hug him after a hard day in the bullpen.

Off the field, the Harveys are doing what they can to help the few hundred other families whose children have the same syndrome as Whitney. They know the difficulties that come to a family when one of their own has what is sometimes referred to as the "happy puppet" syndrome, a chromosomal imbalance that causes the child to be severely retarded mentally and to laugh and smile uncontrollably without reason.

Once ESPN reporter Roy Firestone asked Harvey the key question, "Did you blame God?" Harvey's reply was honest and revealing. "At first just a little bit. Right now we aren't angry at anything. Lisa and I try not to look on anything negative. We thank the Lord for His blessings. I'm able to play baseball and handle medical bills."

Who better to be the symbol of hope for children with Angelman's Syndrome than a California Angel who knows, loves, and trusts God.

Orel Hershiser

VITAL STATISTICS

Born September 16, 1958, in Buffalo, New York
6 feet 3, 190 pounds
Team: Los Angeles Dodgers
Position: Pitcher (right-handed)
Attended Bowling Green State University, Bowling Green, Ohio

CAREER HIGHLIGHTS

- Holds major league record for pitching most consecutive scoreless innings (59) August 20 through September 28, 1988
- Won Cy Young Award, 1988
- Named MVP of both playoffs and World Series, 1988
- Named to All-Star team three times

For about two months in 1988 Orel Hershiser was perhaps the best pitcher who ever threw a baseball. From the last part of August through the World Series, he had an ERA of 0.60 and led the Dodgers to an improbable world championship.

But the whole time it was happening, Hershiser knew it could stop at any point, and he knew that he needed to place the glory where it really belonged. Despite the fact that he had been a Christian for only a few years, he became a symbol of boldness in witnessing as he spoke of his Savior in interviews. He put a grand exclamation point on his performances by kneeling on the mound in thanks after one World Series victory and by singing the doxology on "The Tonight Show" the night after winning the Series's final game.

This stretch of phenomenal pitching wasn't the first time Hershiser had thrown so well. But the first time he did, it didn't end quite so triumphantly. It ended in his learning a valuable lesson that would help him keep his perspective during that fantastic pennant drive and World Series of 1988.

While pitching in the minor leagues at San Antonio a few years earlier, he also had fashioned a 0.60 ERA going into June. This first time he became untouchable, though, it changed him.

"I got caught up in the scouting reports, what I read in the papers, and the phone calls from the Dodgers. I stopped praying. And I stopped listening to God. I started going out with the guys and not really having a focus on what I was supposed to be doing. I stopped doing the things that got me that 0.60 ERA."

By the time he was done with his next three pitching assignments, Hershiser's ERA had ballooned to 8.6.

"It was like God had come down from heaven and hit me over the head and said, 'You dummy. Remember who got you here. Remember what's going on here. Remember where your abilities came from.'"

It was a lesson that not only helped him in 1988 but also in 1990 and 1991 when career-threatening surgery kept him out of action for nearly a year. But he came back, still throwing hard and still depending on God.

Jeff Huson

VITAL STATISTICS

Born August 15, 1964, in Scottsdale, Arizona
6 feet 3, 180 pounds
Current Team: Texas Rangers
Position: Shortstop
Attended Glendale Community College, Glendale, Arizona
Attended University of Wyoming, Laramie, Wyoming

CAREER HIGHLIGHTS

- Hit .310 in first major league season with Montreal (1988)
- Led Rangers in stolen bases in 1992

Someday, his family tells him in jest, Jeff Huson will get a real job. Coming as he does as the last of five children, Huson takes a little heat from his older siblings since as he says, "The rest of them are either CPAs or teachers. They have 'real' jobs."

If Huson, who has played infield for both the Expos and the Rangers, is understandably reluctant to throw away his glove to follow his family into accounting, no one would question his wisdom. When it came to following his family in their faith, though, even he might wonder today what took him so long.

After growing up in a Christian home, he had not made a decision to trust Jesus Christ by the time he had made it to pro baseball. Perhaps his family felt he was casting aside everything in the family heritage. First, he didn't have a "real job." Second, he seemed to be rejecting their faith.

That all changed, though, when he met Tim Burke, Andy McGaffigan, and Tom Foley when he played for the Expos. They took him to a Pro Athletes Outreach conference where he saw the examples of the Christian players there. Finally he joined hands spiritually with his teammates and with his family, and he put his trust in Jesus Christ.

After a laid-back start at letting his new faith be known, Huson became a spiritual leader, especially after joining the Rangers. And now, besides his family back home, he has a family throughout baseball he can depend on. "There's somebody on every team that you can rely on," he says of his fellow believers.

And, of course, they'll never tell him to go get a real job.

Doug Jones

Born June 24, 1957, in Covina, California
6 feet 2, 195 pounds
Team: Houston Astros
Position: Relief Pitcher (right-handed)
Attended Central Arizona College, Coolidge, Arizona
Attended Butler University, Indianapolis, Indiana

CAREER HIGHLIGHTS

- Selected to the All-Star team twice
- Named National League Comeback Player of the Year in 1992
- Has ERA of 0.00 in two All-Star games
- Has more than 150 career saves

Baseball has not made life easy for Doug Jones. For the first four years of minor league ball, he had a difficult time just continuing to play. He felt as if he had no friends, and at the end of every year he felt like a defeated Christian.

After being drafted in the third round of the 1978 free agent draft, Jones traveled a zig-zag minor league road that had more stops than a New York subway car. He played in Newark, Burlington, Stockton, Vancouver, Holyoke, El Paso, and back to Vancouver before getting his first cup of coffee with Milwaukee in 1982.

Even when he got married and rededicated his life to God in 1982, things didn't get much better. Doug Jones still had to keep the road map handy. Back to Vancouver. Off to revisit El Paso. Then to Waterbury and then to a team in Maine.

Finally, the Doug Jones tour stopped in Cleveland for some outstanding years as the Indians' relief ace. Still, though, there was one detour to Buffalo, a surprise demotion to Colorado in 1991, and eventually a startling release from the Cleveland club.

In 1992 Doug Jones blossomed as a pitcher in Houston's Astrodome. Playing for a team that was going nowhere, he put together an earned run average of 1.85, won 11 games, and recorded 36 saves. He pitched more than 100 innings, yet he walked fewer than 20 batters. After Milwaukee, after Cleveland, and a dozen minor league stops in between, Doug's baseball life began anew in Houston.

So what kept Doug Jones going when everything signaled the end in 1991? He has learned that his "Christian life isn't based on circumstances. It's not based on today only." He can look back now and see that God had led him all the way—through all those stops in baseball. And he doesn't complain, for no matter what baseball throws his way, he and his wife have learned to "use it to our advantage and to improve our relationship with Him."

Doug Jones has learned that a life of faith beats a life of ease any day.

Paul Molitor

VITAL STATISTICS

Born August 22, 1956, in St. Paul, Minnesota
6 feet, 185 pounds
Current Team: Milwaukee Brewers
Position: First Base/Designated Hitter
Attended University of Minnesota

CAREER HIGHLIGHTS

- Stole three bases in one inning, a major league record (July 26, 1987)
- Holds World Series records for most hits (5) and most singles (5) in a game (October 12, 1982)
- Hit safely in 39 straight games in July and August 1987
- Batted .320 in 1992, fourth highest average in American League
- Named to All-Star team five times

If you're a pessimist, you'll look at Paul Molitor's list of major league accomplishments and notice that he has spent more time on the disabled list than many players spend in the majors. You might even wonder how a person who gets injured so often and so badly has spent part of three decades in the majors.

But if you're an optimist, you'll look at a different part of Paul Molitor's stat sheet. You'll notice some of the things it tells you, such as his 2,000-plus hits, his 150-plus home runs, his nearly 400 doubles, his 1,200-plus runs scored, his .300-plus batting average. You'll see that Paul Molitor's career stats put him near the top in just about every hitting category you can find among active players. And in 1992 he remained an offensive force; his .320 batting average was fourth highest in the American League.

So how does a player who spent parts of 1980, 1981, and 1984-90 on the disabled list accomplish so much? He has a solid foundation in his faith in Jesus Christ.

"The Lord means everything to me," Molitor says. "I don't know how anyone can face each day not having that foundation."

And since he himself became a Christian while in college, he has discovered several ways to share the life-changing faith he has experienced. Through his work with Fellowship of Christian Athletes, Molitor has spoken in schools and even at County Stadium about how Christ can change lives.

He knows people are looking at him, and he knows it is in his hands to "choose which way people perceive me." Through his testimony and his willingness to speak out, he hopes people look at him as an optimist—a person who can overcome those injury obstacles and build a remarkable career.

Only a pessimist would look at Paul Molitor any other way.

John Smoltz

VITAL STATISTICS

Born May 15, 1967, in Detroit, Michigan
6 feet 3, 185 pounds
Current Team: Atlanta Braves
Position: Pitcher (right-handed)

CAREER HIGHLIGHTS

- Went 2-0 with 1.76 ERA in League Championship Series in 1991
- Led National League in strikeouts in 1992 with 215
- Named MVP of 1992 National League Championship Series
- Named to All-Star team two times

The first half of 1991 was a disaster for John Smoltz. His ERA stood at 5.16. His won-lost was a miserable 2 and 11. After 18 starts, Smoltz had lasted through the eighth inning only two times. It would have been logical to write off that year as a total failure and start saying, "Wait till next year."

Who would have thought—who would even dream—that when the 1991 season had ended, John Smoltz's record would look like this: 14 wins, 13 losses; an ERA of 3.80; 148 strikeouts?

And who could have foreseen that this 24-year-old from Lansing, Michigan, would be handed the ball to start the seventh game of the dramatic 1991 World Series? The Atlanta Braves had risen from last to first place in one year, and now the outcome of their drama was left in the hands of a pitcher who had been struggling on the mound only three months earlier.

Yet there he was, pitching against his boyhood idol, the Twins' gritty hurler Jack Morris. For eight innings the youngster and the veteran battled—keeping the Series outcome in limbo. By the time the Braves' skipper, Bobby Cox, replaced Smoltz in the eighth inning, neither team had scored. "All I needed was one run," Smoltz would lament after the game, aware that he had nearly become a World Series hero.

Only when Gene Larkin singled in Dan Gladden in the 10th were the Twins able to capture what some baseball experts have described as the greatest World Series ever played.

For John Smoltz, this was a prime-time turnaround that wouldn't be expected of anybody, but can be understood of John Smoltz. Two factors, which he calls the secret to his success, contributed to such a reversal of fortune. First, he credits his hard work and never doubting his ability to pitch. And second, he credits his faith.

His faith in Jesus Christ, which has been nurtured by other players, such as teammate Sid Bream, has helped Smoltz develop patience. And patience in the face of what might have been a forgettable season was just what Smoltz needed in 1991 to salvage the year and turn it into something incredible.

And just as incredible was Smoltz's return engagement in 1992. Not only did the Braves' hurler continue to win, but he also outdid his 1991 playoff performance. Again leading the way for the Braves against the Pirates, Smoltz was named the Most Valuable Player of the series. The outcome of the playoffs was in question until the last batter, when Sid Bream slid home safely under the tag. However, concerning the pitching of John Smoltz, the Braves' fans agreed—there was never any doubt.

Andy Van Slyke

VITAL STATISTICS

Born December 21, 1960, in Utica, New York
6 feet 2, 195 pounds
Current Team: Pittsburgh Pirates
Position: Center Field

CAREER HIGHLIGHTS

- Led National League in sacrifice flies in 1988 (13)
- Led National League in doubles in 1992 with 45; was second in batting with a .324 average
- Named to All-Star team two times
- Named *The Sporting News* National League Player of the Year in 1988

I f baseball were politics, Andy Van Slyke would be the sound bite champion. Van Slyke's verbal gems run the gamut from current events to his teammates to his team. On the 1992 newspaper strike in Pittsburgh: "I must say I've enjoyed it. I mean, it's bad for readers and reporters. But it's the environmentally correct thing to do." On teammate Doug Drabek's career record of 54-26 before the All-Star break and his less than stellar record after the midsummer break: "Maybe we should put a fake calendar in his locker at the beginning of the season and make him think it's June."

During the 1992 season, reporters asked him to describe Pittsburgh's even-keel style of play. Van Slyke replied: "The key is to play like Nebraska. Just as flat as you can."

One of the great ironies of baseball reporting is that Van Slyke, who is the master of the intelligent, colorful, humorous quote, has been seen as somewhat unusual by the press. They, of all people, should be able to recognize intelligence, color, and humor. They have a master quote-maker in Andy Van Slyke, and they sometimes don't appreciate it. One writer surmised that perhaps it is because they have not achieved Van Slyke's level of intelligence.

Of course, Van Slyke doesn't get paid for his articulate quotes. He gets paid to help lead his team to the World Series.

Through the 1992 season, that had been a frustration for Van Slyke, as four times his teams have been in the playoffs. First it was the Cardinals in 1985, then the Pirates in 1990, 1991, and 1992. Despite Van Slyke's considerable contributions, he has seen the dream die each time. And in October 1992 it seemed to die hardest, as he watched helplessly while Sid Bream motored home with the winning run. After Atlanta's Bream was called safe at home, Van Slyke sat stunned in the outfield grass for a long, long time.

Even though he has missed that Series dream, Van Slyke has found both baseball and life to be rewarding and fulfilling. He credits his salvation in 1981 with being a "starting point in my career." While playing minor league ball in Florida, Van Slyke heard a chapel speaker who "was more excited over Jesus than anyone I had ever seen. I started to hear God's Word and His promises for the first time." A short time later Van Slyke responded by walking out to home plate at the small ballpark in St. Petersburg and asking God to enter his life. "I wanted what He offered," Van Slyke says. "I asked Him to make Himself real and to help me put baseball where it should be—a vocation, not a life."

More than 10 years later, that faith is the basis for his career and his family.

It is a faith that was tested during spring training of 1992 when one of the Van Slyke children fell into a hot tub and almost drowned before his brother pulled him out. Jared, only three, had turned blue and was rushed to the hospital; yet after a one-night stay he returned home and now is fully recovered.

Andy's wife, Lauri, not as noted as is her baseball husband for her quotes, told *Sports Illustrated,* "I hate to use the word *miracle*, but both Andy and I definitely feel like the Lord wasn't ready to let Jared go." Andy himself noted, "This is February 29, which is Leap Day. Jared almost leaped into another world." When the recovery was complete, the Van Slykes knelt in praise to God.

Listen to what Andy Van Slyke has to say to the reporters who gather around his locker, scribbling notes. It will be intelligent, quotable, and, most likely, a testimony to his faith in God.

Moody Press, a ministry of the Moody Bible Institute,
is designed for education, evangelization, and edification.
If we may assist you in knowing more about Christ
and the Christian life, please write us without obligation:
Moody Press, c/o MLM, Chicago, Illinois 60610.

For my parents, Al and Dena Hutchens,
who instilled in me a love of sports.

For my wife, Susan, who brought me to Indiana.

For my boys, Bryan and Kevin,
who make me proud to say that I'm their dad.

So You Think You Know

Indiana University

Basketball

(We'll see about that)

TERRY HUTCHENS

Terry Hutchens Publications

Indianapolis, IN

So You Think You Know Indiana University Basketball © 2015
Terry Hutchens
EAN-ISBN-13: 9781935628545

Cover designed by Phil Velikan

All interior and cover photos in this book appear courtesy of
either the Indiana University Archives, Indiana University
Athletics or Indiana University athletics photographer Mike
Dickbernd.

The Indiana University Archives photos on the cover include
Steve Downing (P0020193), George McGinnis P0020284),
Everett Dean (P0044208) and Bob Knight/Steve Alford
(P0044991).

Packaged by Wish Publishing

Printed in the United States of America
10 9 8 7 6 5 4 3 2 1

Distributed in the United States by Cardinal Publishers Group.
www.cardinalpub.com

TABLE OF CONTENTS

ACKNOWLEDGEMENTS

This is my sixth book and one of the things I realize every time is that these are not projects you can accomplish by yourself. With this book, I've tried something new which is self-publishing the book but I still have Tom Doherty and Cardinal Publishing handling the distribution. I've had a good relationship with Tom and the Cardinal Publishing family over the years as they have had a role in each of my last five books.

I want to thank my book handler, Holly Kondras at Wish Publishing, for helping me get through the self-publishing process smoothly the first time. We've worked together on all of my previous projects and it's a connection I try not to take for granted. Thanks again Holly for your expertise.

I wish to thank the IU Archives for giving me permission to use the photographs in this book. Brad Cook was extremely helpful in getting me the images we were able to use for this project.

I want to thank the authors of the various resources I used for this book. Jason Hiner, who wrote the first edition of the *IU Basketball Encyclopedia* (I actually penned the updated edition) in 2004. The book has always been my go-to tool when it comes to confirming Indiana basketball information from the past. Another source is the IU Basketball Media Guide, most recently edited by J.D. Campbell and his staff. A third resource was Stan Sutton's book *100 Things Hoosiers Fans Should Know and Do Before They Die* that was published in 2012. I've always had a great deal of respect for Stan as a writer and reporter and a resource like that one was very useful. The final book I leaned on was *Branch*, the interesting biography of Branch McCracken that was written by Bill Murphy and published in 2013. Again, there was just a lot of good information there.

When you need Indiana basketball information, it's good to have sources like those at your fingertips.

Finally, I'd like to thank Ken Bikoff, a long time IU basketball writer and historian. Ken had written a several-part series in Inside Indiana magazine in early 2010 about IU's various athletic venues and the history behind them. He was able to come through with some great anecdotes that I was able to use in the venue section. Thanks Ken for the past research that came in handy when I was looking for a few more good questions.

I also would like to thank a few other people on a personal level. I would like to thank Steve Demas for his inspiration and motivation. Keep fighting the good fight my friend. I would like to thank Jason Eadie, founder of btownbanners.com, for providing me with an outlet to continue to do what I love which is writing about Indiana University athletics (see the ad in the back of this book for more info on btownbanners.com). I'd like to thank the IU Alumni Association and particularly CEO J.T. Forbes and four members of his staff, Michael Mann, Bryan Bradford, Wes Erwin and Mallory Evans for providing me with opportunities to speak to IU Alumni chapters and tell my stories of 18 seasons covering IU athletics.

Finally, I want to thank my wife, Susan, and my boys, Bryan and Kevin, for their constant support. Whenever I hit that writing wall, Susan is always there to get me pointed in the right direction again.

INTRODUCTION —
HOW THE BOOK WORKS

As I've traversed the country covering Indiana University basketball for three publications for nearly two decades, the one constant is the passionate IU basketball fan. IU fans love their traditions, worship their players and coaches and are connected through many events that have occurred in the course of IU basketball history. Whether it's Keith Smart's baseline jumper that gave IU the 1987 national championship over Syracuse, the 1976 unbeaten IU national champions led by national player of the year Scott May, the smooth shooting stroke of all-time IU and Big Ten leading scorer Calbert Cheaney or the 3-pointer from the left wing by Christian Watford that beat No. 1 Kentucky, IU fans rejoice in the past and embrace the future.

At one level, this could be considered a highly challenging book of Indiana University basketball trivia that even the biggest of IU basketball experts might have a difficult time with the wide variety of questions. On the other hand, you may just be up for the challenge, too. The book is broken up into nine different chapters with various categories of trivia.

At another level, more than just a trivia challenge, this book could serve as a tremendous educational tool that takes you on a trip down memory lane, helping you to relieve some of the great memories from all of IU's greatest players. If you think you know the five national championship teams for example, then there's a chapter just for you to test your skills. Have a good feel for IU coaching greats? There's a coaches trivia chapter, too. Are you one of those IU fans who prides themselves on knowing the uniform numbers worn by various IU standouts over the years? There's a chapter that deals just with player numbers. Are you one of those people who if given a clue about the identity of a certain person can show off your recall and remember that individual? Then the Who Am I? chapter is the one for you. There are 50 biographies there with five clues in each. The challenge is to see how many clues it takes you to guess the identity of the player.

The book begins with a 50-question warm up chapter that deals with several topics and gives you the opportunity to gain some early confidence. Next comes player, coach and venue trivia followed by trivia questions focused on the national championship teams. Next up is something called Fun Facts which again is a hodgepodge of stories and anecdotes from IU basketball. You couldn't have a true IU basketball trivia book without at least one chapter dedicated just to Bob Knight trivia. There is some Knight trivia sprinkled through the rest of the book, too, but that one chapter is all Knight, all the time. The trivia challenge wraps up with the player number section and then the 50 biographies which will jog your memory on countless Hoosier greats. All of the answers can be found at the end of the book so that you don't find the urge to glance down to the end of the page for an answer.

If you want to take the Trivia Challenge, each question in the first eight chapters is worth two points for a total of 800 points. Chapter nine, which is the 50 Who Am I? biographies, is worth four points each. If you guess the person on the first clue you get four points, the second clue three points and on and on. If you get it on either the fourth or the fifth clue you receive one point.

For the die-hard IU basketball fan who wants to take the trivia challenge, here are a couple of charts to help you grade your performance. Let's say you just want to take one of the individual challenges and test your knowledge in one of the nine chapters. This would be like if you were playing Trivial Pursuit and were just good in Geography. In this case, perhaps it's national championship trivia or venue trivia or uniform number trivia that you want to test your skills with.

INDIVIDUAL CHAPTER SCORECARD	
(First eight chapters)	
100-88 points	IU National Champion
87-80 points	IU All-American
79-70 points	IU All-Big Ten
69-60 points	Honorable Mention All-Big Ten
59-50 points	Part-time Starter
49-40 points	Bench player
39 points and below	Better luck next time

OVERALL TRIVIA CHALLENGE SCORECARD	
1000-880 points	Player of the Year
879-800 points	Hoosier All-American
799-700 points	IU All-Big Ten
699-600 points	Honorable Mention All-Big Ten
599-500 points	Part-time Starter
499-400 points	Bench player
399 points and below	Are you a Purdue Grad?

Whether you use the book as a trivia challenge or an IU basketball resource guide, I hope you find it to be an enjoyable trip through more than 100 years of Indiana University Basketball.

IU junior guard Keith Smart puts up a jump shot in the second half of Indiana's 74-73 victory over Syracuse in the national championship game in New Orleans. (Indiana University Archives, P0047791)

1

THE WARM UP

1. **What player holds the Indiana University school record for most points in a career?**

   A. Steve Alford

   B. Don Schlundt

   C. A.J. Guyton

   D. Calbert Cheaney

   E. Damon Bailey

2. **What player hit 'The Shot' to beat Syracuse in the 1987 national championship game?**

   A. Steve Alford

   B. Keith Smart

   C. Dean Garrett

   D. Daryl Thomas

   E. Ricky Calloway

3. **When Indiana beat Duke in 2002 in the Sweet Sixteen, where was that game played?**

   A. Rupp Arena, University of Kentucky

   B. RCA Dome, Indianapolis

   C. Freedom Hall, Louisville

   D. Georgia Dome, Atlanta

   E. Mackey Arena, Purdue

4. **Who is IU's career leader in rebounds?**

   A. Archie Dees

   B. Kent Benson

   C. Walt Bellamy

   D. Alan Henderson

   E. Steve Downing

5. **The IU school record for points in a game is 56 and it was done twice by the same player. Who was that player?**

   A. Don Schlundt

   B. Jimmy Rayl

   C. George McGinnis

   D. Steve Alford

   E. Mike Woodson

6. **What is the largest winning point spread for an IU basketball team in one game? Hint: It was against Notre Dame in 1971.**

   A. 55

   B. 58

   C. 62

   D. 65

   E. 68

7. **One player has made more than 100 3-point field goals in a single season and holds the IU school record in that category. Name him.**

   A. Jordan Hulls

   B. Jay Edwards

   C. Steve Alford

   D. Bracey Wright

   E. A.J. Guyton

8. **Who holds the IU record for consecutive free throws made in a season?**

   A. Jordan Hulls

   B. Pat Graham

   C. Steve Alford

   D. Jimmy Rayl

   E. Christian Watford

9. **The IU school record for most free throws made in a game is 26. Who holds that record?**

   A. Ted Kitchel

   B. Luke Recker

   C. Greg Graham

   D. Pat Graham

   E. Steve Alford

10. **What IU player holds the school record for most points scored in a season by a freshman?**

    A. Cody Zeller

    B. Eric Gordon

    C. George McGinnis

    D. Steve Alford

    E. Mike Woodson

11. **In Indiana basketball history, there has only been one triple double. Who has it?**

    A. Earl Calloway

    B. Yogi Ferrell

    C. Scott May

    D. Calbert Cheaney

    E. Steve Downing

12. **What was the makeup of the lone triple double in IU history?**

   A. Points/Rebounds/Assists

   B. Points/Rebounds/Steals

   C. Points/Rebounds/Blocks

   D. Rebounds/Assists/Steals

   E. None of the above

13. **What is the IU school record for consecutive wins at home?**

   A. 34

   B. 40

   C. 48

   D. 56

   E. 64

14. **Indiana's school record made 3-pointers in a game was 18 in the 2014-15 season. What team did IU do that against?**

   A. SMU

   B. Georgetown

   C. Ohio State

   D. Maryland

   E. Rutgers

15. How many times has Indiana been a No. 1 seed in the NCAA Tournament?

   A. 8

   B. 6

   C. 5

   D. 3

   E. 2

16. When was the most recent time that IU was a No. 1 seed in the NCAA Tournament?

   A. 1987

   B. 1993

   C. 2013

   D. 2002

   E. 1991

17. How many times has Indiana won the Big Ten Conference Tournament title since the tournament began in 1998?

   A. 3

   B. 2

   C. 1

   D. IU has never won the Big Ten Tournament

18. How many IU players have been selected as the No. 1 player overall in the NBA Draft?

    A. 4

    B. 3

    C. 2

    D. 1

    E. IU has never had the overall No. 1 player selected

19. Four IU players have been selected with the No. 2 pick overall in the NBA Draft. Which of the following players WAS NOT selected No. 2 overall?

    A. Isiah Thomas

    B. Calbert Cheaney

    C. Scott May

    D. Victor Oladipo

    E. Archie Dees

20. How many IU players who played on the 1976 national championship team were later drafted in the NBA Draft?

A. 3

B. 4

C. 5

D. 6

E. 7

21. What IU player in 1975 broke his arm which turned out to be a devastating blow to that teams' national title chances?

A. Steve Green

B. Scott May

C. Kent Benson

D. Quinn Buckner

E. Bobby Wilkerson

22. What IU player tore his ACL during the 1993 Big Ten season, a year where the Hoosiers would go 17-1 in conference?

A. Alan Henderson

B. Calbert Cheaney

C. Greg Graham

D. Matt Nover

E. Damon Bailey

23. Who was the first team that Indiana ever beat in a basketball game in the inaugural season in 1901?

A. Butler

B. Purdue

C. Wabash

D. DePauw

E. Indianapolis YMCA

24. Who was Indiana's interim head coach in the 2007-08 season after Kelvin Sampson was let go?

A. Ray McCallum

B. Dan Dakich

C. Jeff Meyer

D. Rob Senderoff

E. Kerry Rupp

25. When Christian Watford hit 'The Shot' on Dec. 10, 2011 to knock off No. 1 Kentucky, who threw him the pass?

A. Victor Oladipo

B. Jordan Hulls

C. Verdell Jones III

D. Remy Abell

E. Cody Zeller

26. This player holds the school record for the highest scoring average in Big Ten play. The average was an impressive 32.4 points per game. Name the player?

A. Don Schlundt

B. Jimmy Rayl

C. George McGinnis

D. Archie Dees

E. Steve Alford

27. What are the most games Indiana has ever won consecutively in Big Ten play over multiple seasons? Hint: It involved the 1976 national championship season.

A. 36

B. 37

C. 38

D. 39

E. 40

28. What is the largest losing point spread for an IU basketball team in one game? Hint: Bob Knight was the coach and the year was 1994.

A. 36

B. 38

C. 41

D. 43

E. 50

29. Indiana's school record for most points in a game came against both Ohio State in 1959 and Notre Dame in 1962. How many points did Indiana score?

A. 115

B. 118

C. 120

D. 122

E. 127

30. What is the longest winning streak in Indiana history? Hint: It could be over multiple seasons.

A. 32

B. 34

C. 36

D. 38

E. 43

31. Which IU player holds the school record for most points in a season by a sophomore? The total was 734 points.

A. George McGinnis

B. Don Schlundt

C. Calbert Cheaney

D. A.J. Guyton

E. Steve Alford

32. Two IU players scored 714 points in their junior year alone which is a school record. Who are the two players?

A. Jay Edwards

B. Jimmy Rayl

C. Don Schlundt

D. Archie Dees

E. Steve Alford

33. This player holds the school record for most rebounds in a season by a freshman. Who is it?

A. Walt Bellamy

B. George McGinnis

C. D.J. White

D. Noah Vonleh

E. Ivan Renko

34. **What was significant about Nov. 11, 2010 in IU basketball history?**

    A. Indiana opened Tom Crean's second season with a win over Howard

    B. Calbert Cheaney joined IU's staff as the director of operations

    C. Cody Zeller signed with the Hoosiers

    D. Yogi Ferrell signed with the Hoosiers

    E. Victor Oladipo signed with the Hoosiers

35. **When Indiana reached the Sweet Sixteen in back-to-back seasons in 2012 and 2013, it was the first time IU had accomplished the feat since when?**

    A. 1993 and 1994

    B. 2001 and 2002

    C. 2007 and 2008

    D. 1980 and 1981

    E. 1975 and 1976

36. When Indiana failed to qualify for the NCAA Tournament in 2003-04 after posting a 14-15 record it snapped a streak of consecutive years that the Hoosiers had been to the NCAA Tournament. How many years had it been?

A. 10

B. 14

C. 17

D. 18

E. 21

37. The following season, IU made it back to postseason play but it was in the NIT not the NCAA. What team did IU host in a first round NIT game in the 2004-05 season?

A. Notre Dame

B. Vanderbilt

C. Ball State

D. Indiana State

E. Belmont

38. **What team beat Indiana in the regional finals of the 1975 NCAA Tournament?**

   A. Notre Dame

   B. Kentucky

   C. Purdue

   D. North Carolina

   E. Duke

39. **What was IU's record going into that game?**

   A. 28-0

   B. 29-0

   C. 30-0

   D. 31-0

   E. None of the above

40. **Following the 1975 season, two IU players, Steve Green and John Laskowski, were both drafted in the second round of the NBA Draft by the same team. What team drafted the pair?**

   A. Chicago

   B. Indiana

   C. Detroit

   D. New York

   E. Los Angeles

41. True or False, Indiana has had the Big Ten MVP every year it has won the national championship?

A. True

B. False

42. How many times has Indiana played in the championship game of the Big Ten Tournament since it began in 1998?

A. Four

B. Three

C. Two

D. One

E. Zero

43. Who holds the Assembly Hall record for most points in a game by an IU player? He scored 42 points in a game against Michigan State.

A. Mike Woodson

B. Steve Alford

C. George McGinnis

D. Eric Gordon

E. Alan Henderson

44. Only one player has ever won the Big Ten's Sixth Man of the Year award since it came about following the 2006 season. Who was IU's winner of the award?

A. Rod Wilmont

B. Lance Stemler

C. Will Sheehey

D. Matt Roth

E. None of the above

45. The player who holds the Assembly Hall record for assists only had one game in his career with 10 or more assists. In this game, in 1985 against Marquette, he had 14 assists.

A. Keith Smart

B. Steve Alford

C. Ricky Calloway

D. Stew Robinson

E. Todd Jadlow

46. Which of the following players were two-time Academic All-Americans at Indiana?

A. Dick Van Arsdale

B. Steve Green

C. Kent Benson

D. Randy Wittman

E. All of the above

47. What IU player, who played for Bob Knight, holds the school record for playing in the most NCAA Tournament victories?

A. Quinn Buckner

B. Kent Benson

C. Scott May

D. Steve Alford

E. Damon Bailey

48. How many NCAA Tournament wins was that player a part of at IU?

A. 13

B. 11

C. 10

D. 9

E. 8

49. Todd Leary became a late addition to the 1989 recruiting class because what transpired?

A. An IU player was declared academically ineligible

B. An IU player transferred

C. An IU player was dismissed from the team

D. An IU player declared for the NBA Draft

E. None of the above

50. George McGinnis is IU's all-time leader in games where he scored 30 points or more. How many times did he do it in his lone IU season which spanned 24 games?

A. 6

B. 8

C. 10

D. 12

E. 13

Answers are on page 215

Steve Alford had one of the sweetest shots in Indiana basketball history. Here he shoots a free throw in his sophomore year in December of 1984. (Indiana University Archives, P0044801)

2

PLAYER TRIVIA

1. **Who was the first IU basketball player to earn All-American honors?**

   A. Vern Huffman

   B. Everett Dean

   C. Jim Strickland

   D. Branch McCracken

   E. Ken Gunning

2. **Which of the following IU basketball players is not in the Basketball Hall of Fame?**

   A. Walt Bellamy

   B. Calbert Cheaney

   C. Branch McCracken

   D. Isiah Thomas

   E. None of the above

3. **Only one IU basketball player has ever won the Wooden Award, given annually to the best college basketball player in the country. Who won it?**

   A. Calbert Cheaney

   B. Steve Alford

   C. Cody Zeller

   D. Scott May

   E. Isiah Thomas

4. **TWO of the following IU players earned Big Ten MVP honors twice in their careers. Which of the following players took home the award twice?**

   A. Don Schlundt

   B. Archie Dees

   C. Scott May

   D. Steve Alford

   E. Calbert Cheaney

5. **IU's school record for assists in a game is 15. Two players have done it. Name them.**

   A. Tom Coverdale

   B. Michael Lewis

   C. Bobby Wilkerson

   D. Isiah Thomas

   E. Keith Smart

6. **Who is IU's single season career rebounding leader? Hint: He had 51 more than the No. 2 person on the list.**

   A. George McGinnis

   B. Walt Bellamy

   C. Kent Benson

   D. Alan Henderson

   E. Archie Dees

7. **What IU player has the most career points in Big Ten games only?**

   A. Calbert Cheaney

   B. Don Schlundt

   C. A.J. Guyton

   D. Steve Alford

   E. Mike Woodson

8. In terms of average points per game, IU's all-time single season scorer averaged 29.9 points per game. Can you name him?

A. George McGinnis

B. Don Schlundt

C. Archie Dees

D. Jimmy Rayl

E. Calbert Cheaney

9. One of the following players never scored more than 40 points in a game in his IU career. Can you name him?

A. Alan Henderson

B. Ted Kitchel

C. George McGinnis

D. Dick Van Arsdale

E. Calbert Cheaney

10. One of the following players never scored more than 35 points in a game in his IU career. Can you name him?

A. Tom Bolyard

B. Damon Bailey

C. A.J. Guyton

D. Brian Evans

E. Steve Green

11. One of the following players, who was selected in the first round of the NBA Draft, never scored more than 20 points in a game in his IU career?

A. Ray Tolbert

B. Victor Oladipo

C. Noah Vonleh

D. Kirk Haston

E. D.J. White

12. **Who holds the IU record for most rebounds in a game with 33?**

A. George McGinnis

B. Walt Bellamy

C. Alan Henderson

D. Archie Dees

E. D.J. White

13. **Eight times in IU history, Indiana players have pulled down 25 or more rebounds in a game. Which of the following players NEVER had more than 25 rebounds in a game?**

A. Dick Neal

B. Dick Van Arsdale

C. Steve Downing

D. Archie Dees

E. George McGinnis

14. Who holds the IU record for steals in one game?

A. Earl Calloway

B. Scott May

C. Victor Oladipo

D. Michael Lewis

E. Steve Alford

15. What IU player holds the record for blocks in one game?

A. George Leach

B. D.J. White

C. Steve Downing

D. Dean Garrett

E. Jeff Newton

16. This player holds the IU school record for blocks in one season. In fact, he occupies the top two seasons with the most blocks in IU history. Who is it?

A. George Leach

B. D.J. White

C. Steve Downing

D. Dean Garrett

E. Jeff Newton

17. **TWO IU players hold the school record for most 3-pointers made in one game with nine. Can you name them?**

A. Robert Vaden

B. Matt Roth

C. Rod Wilmont

D. Jordan Hulls

E. Steve Alford

18. **This player attempted 30 free throws in one game (he made 25 of them). Who was that player?**

A. Greg Graham

B. Don Schlundt

C. Luke Recker

D. Wally Choice

E. Steve Alford

19. This player attempted 1,076 free throws in his IU career. Second on the career list had 692 attempts. Who attempted more than 1,000 free throws in his four-year IU career?

A. Greg Graham

B. Don Schlundt

C. Alan Henderson

D. Jordan Hulls

E. Steve Alford

20. Who holds the IU school record for most double-doubles in one season with 23?

A. Walt Bellamy

B. Jimmy Rayl

C. George McGinnis

D. D.J. White

E. Alan Henderson

F. Archie Dees

21. This player holds the IU school record with 59 career double-doubles. Who is it?

A. Walt Bellamy

B. Jimmy Rayl

C. George McGinnis

D. D.J. White

E. Alan Henderson

22. This player holds the IU school record for most games with at least 20 points and at least 10 rebounds in one game. Can you name him?

A. Walt Bellamy

B. Jimmy Rayl

C. George McGinnis

D. Archie Dees

E. Alan Henderson

23. TWO players had at least 30 points and at least 10 rebounds in a game 12 times. Who are the two players?

A. Walt Bellamy

B. Don Schlundt

C. Archie Dees

D. George McGinnis

E. Steve Downing

24. What IU player holds the school record for most games played in their career with 135?

A. Calbert Cheaney

B. Jordan Hulls

C. Greg Graham

D. Matt Nover

E. Randy Wittman

25. This player holds the record for most games started in one season. Can you name him?

A. Cody Zeller

B. Calbert Cheaney

C. Jordan Hulls

D. Dane Fife

E. Tom Coverdale

26. On Nov. 29, 1996, Indiana beat Duke 85-69 to win the preseason NIT in Madison Square Garden. Indiana had a player erupt for a career-high 39 points that night. Who was that player?

A. A.J. Guyton

B. Andrae Patterson

C. Neil Reed

D. Charlie Miller

E. Jason Collier

27. Four players have scored a total of 47 points or more in a game in Indiana history a total of six times. Which of the following players HAS NOT scored 47 points or more in a game in his IU career?

A. George McGinnis

B. Don Schlundt

C. Jimmy Rayl

D. Steve Downing

E. Mike Woodson

28. This player scored 35 points or more in a game 10 times in his Indiana career, which is a school record. Who is the player?

A. George McGinnis

B. Don Schlundt

C. Jimmy Rayl

D. Steve Downing

E. Mike Woodson

29. **This player was the quickest in Indiana basketball history to eclipse the 1,000-point scoring mark. He did it in 43 games. Who was that player?**

A. George McGinnis

B. Don Schlundt

C. Jimmy Rayl

D. Archie Dees

E. Steve Alford

30. **Second on that list is a player that did it in 47 games. And he accomplished the feat four years after the No. 1 person on the list did so. Who was that player?**

A. George McGinnis

B. Don Schlundt

C. Jimmy Rayl

D. Archie Dees

E. Scott May

31. **True or False, Will Sheehey is a member of Indiana's 1,000-point scoring club for his career?**

A. True

B. False

32. True or False, Isiah Thomas is a member of Indiana's 1,000-point scoring club for his career?

A. True

B. False

33. True or False, Verdell Jones III is a member of Indiana's 1,000-point scoring club for his career?

A. True

B. False

34. What player came the closest to getting to 1,000 points but just fell short. He finished with 978 points and played at IU in the mid-1990's?

A. Michael Lewis

B. Neil Reed

C. Pat Graham

D. Matt Nover

E. Charlie Miller

35. Since 2001, five Indiana players have been named Big Ten freshman of the year? Which of these players WAS NOT the Big Ten freshman of the year.

A. Jared Jeffries

B. Eric Gordon

C. Noah Vonleh

D. Bracey Wright

E. Cody Zeller

36. Who was the most recent IU player to earn first team all-Big Ten honors three times?

A. D.J. White

B. Tom Coverdale

C. Calbert Cheaney

D. Steve Alford

E. Mike Woodson

37. Prior to that who had been the last three-time first team all-Big Ten selection?

A. Calbert Cheaney

B. Steve Alford

C. Mike Woodson

D. Kent Benson

E. Scott May

38. In 2006, IU had a pair of Auburn transfers that sat out one year and then played their senior seasons only at Indiana. One of them was Marco Killingsworth. Who was the other?

A. Robert Vaden

B. Ben Allen

C. Cem Dinc

D. Lewis Monroe

E. Rod Wilmont

39. **What was Dan Dakich best known for as a player at Indiana?**

    A. Scoring more than 1,000 points in his career

    B. Earning All-American status

    C. Shutting down Michael Jordan in the Sweet Sixteen in 1984

    D. Hitting a game winning shot against Kentucky

    E. None of the above

    F. All of the above

40. **Don Schlundt was one of the most highly recruited players in the country before deciding to play for Branch McCracken and IU in 1951. He narrowed his final decision down to two schools, the other being a big IU rival. What was the other school?**

    A. Kentucky

    B. Notre Dame

    C. Purdue

    D. Ohio State

    E. Duke

41. True or False, Don Schlundt played a full four years at Indiana while most players in that era only got to play three?

A. True

B. False

42. How many former state of Indiana Mr. Basketball players have played at Indiana?

A. 15

B. 18

C. 24

D. 26

E. 29

43. Who was the first Mr. Basketball from Indiana to play at IU?

A. Ed Scheinbein, Southport

B. Tom Schwartz, Kokomo

C. Bill Garrett, Shelbyville

D. Bill Masters, Lafayette

E. Hallie Bryant, Crispus Attucks

44. Six different high schools have had two Indiana Mr. Basketball's play at IU. Which of the following schools IS NOT one of them?

A. Indianapolis Washington

B. Indianapolis Manual

C. Indianapolis Crispus Attucks

D. Indianapolis North Central

E. Kokomo

F. Marion

G. New Castle

45. When Jimmy Rayl tied his school record with 56 points against Michigan State in February of 1963, how many shots did he need in order to get that point total?

A. 28

B. 32

C. 36

D. 42

E. 48

46. When Rayl was IU's high-scoring long distance shooter in the early 1960's there was no 3-point line. In later years, someone found a shot chart of Rayl's 56-point game against Michigan State and determined that this many of his 23 made field goals in that game would have been 3-pointers had Rayl played in the future. How many of the shots would have been from beyond the arc?

A. 5

B. 7

C. 10

D. 13

E. 17

47. Which of the following IU combos were brothers? Hint: It could be more than one.

A. Tom and Dick Van Arsdale

B. Lou and Burke Scott

C. Greg and Pat Graham

D. Vern and Marv Huffman

E. Jim and Isiah Thomas

48. Don Ritter, a 5-10 guard from Aurora, Ind., was a two-year starter and captain for IU from 1947-49. In '48, he led IU with a 13.8 point scoring average. But Ritter was an All-American in another sport at IU. What was the sport?

A. Football

B. Baseball

C. Wrestling

D. Tennis

E. Swimming

49. Who is the player that played for Kelvin Sampson and had de-committed from another Big Ten school before choosing to play at IU? The night he played at that school on the road his freshman season was a memorable one in terms of intensity.

A. Jamarcus Ellis

B. DeAndre Thomas

C. Eric Gordon

D. Jordan Crawford

E. Kyle Taber

50. What IU player, who was recruited by Bob Knight, once had a quote where he used the names Charles Manson, Jeffrey Dahmer and Gandhi all within in a two-sentence span? The question was how do you think Indiana is going to do this season?

A. Todd Leary

B. Dane Fife

C. Jason Collier

D. Antwaan Randle El

E. A.J. Moye

Answers on page 218

Dane Fife came to Indiana to play for Bob Knight but he went to the national championship game with Mike Davis. Fife was always willing to do whatever it took to gain an edge. (Indiana University Archives, P0041209)

They say a picture is worth a thousand words? This one is that and much, much more. Bob Knight is pictured in a state of bewilderment in this November, 1989 photo. (Indiana University Archives, P0028867)

3

COACHING TRIVIA

1. Bob Knight is IU's winningest coach of all-time with 662 wins at Indiana. Branch McCracken is second with 364 wins. Who is the third winningest coach of all-time at Indiana?

   A. Lou Watson

   B. Mike Davis

   C. Everett Dean

   D. Tom Crean

   E. Harry C. Good

2. Who was the Indiana basketball coach prior to Bob Knight?

   A. Lou Watson

   B. Harry C. Good

   C. Jerry Oliver

   D. Branch McCracken

   E. Everett Dean

3. In 29 seasons at Indiana, how many years did Bob Knight take the Hoosiers to a postseason tournament?

A. 29

B. 28

C. 27

D. 26

E. 25

4. What was the percentage of Bob Knight's four-year players who graduated at Indiana?

A. 100 percent

B. 99 percent

C. 98 percent

D. 96 percent

E. 94 percent

5. In 24 seasons at Indiana, how many times did Branch McCracken finish either first or second in the Big Ten?

A. 8

B. 10

C. 12

D. 13

E. 14

6. **What school did Bob Knight coach at prior to being hired at Indiana?**

    A. Army

    B. Navy

    C. Penn

    D. Ohio State

    E. It was his first job

7. **After spending 29 seasons at Indiana, how many seasons did Bob Knight coach at Texas Tech?**

    A. 3

    B. 4

    C. 5

    D. 6

    E. None of the above

8. Branch McCracken had four seasons where his teams won 20 games or more at Indiana. Prior to McCracken coming to IU how many 20 win seasons had the Hoosiers garnered in school history?

    A. 4

    B. 3

    C. 2

    D. 1

    E. 0

9. Indiana has had 28 coaches all time in the school's history. How many of those coaches had winning records?

    A. 19

    B. 17

    C. 15

    D. 13

    E. 11

10. **What school did Mike Davis coach at before becoming Indiana's head coach in 2000?**

A. Alabama

B. Indiana

C. Butler

D. South Alabama

E. UAB

11. **What school did Kelvin Sampson coach at before becoming Indiana's head coach in 2006?**

A. Kansas

B. Oklahoma State

C. Oklahoma

D. Washington State

E. Washington

12. **What school did Tom Crean coach at before becoming Indiana's head coach in 2008?**

    A. Marquette

    B. Wisconsin

    C. Notre Dame

    D. Central Michigan

    E. Villanova

13. **In what year of his IU coaching career did Branch McCracken lead the Hoosiers to their first national championship in 1940?**

    A. 4

    B. 3

    C. 2

    D. 1

    E. None of the above

14. In what year of his IU coaching career did Bob Knight lead the Hoosiers to a national championship in 1976?

A. 4

B. 3

C. 2

D. 1

E. None of the above

15. In what year of his IU coaching career did Mike Davis lead the Hoosiers to the national championship game in 2002?

A. 4

B. 3

C. 2

D. 1

E. None of the above

16. Since 1970, how many head basketball coaches has Indiana had?

A. 8

B. 7

C. 6

D. 5

E. 4

17. Branch McCracken was IU's head coach for the '53 national championship team. One of his assistants was a former IU All-American basketball player himself. Name the player.

A. Marv Huffman

B. Bill Menke

C. Ernie Andres

D. Ralph Hamilton

E. Lou Watson

18. **Bob Knight was named Big Ten coach of the year five times including two of his three national championship seasons. Which title year did he not get the Big Ten coach of the year honor?**

A. 1976

B. 1981

C. 1987

19. **In November of 1922, IU basketball coach George Levis announced he would resign his position on Dec. 1 to take another job? What was that job?**

A. Head coach at Kansas

B. Head coach at DePauw

C. He was going to become the new athletic director

D. He was taking a job in a furniture factory

E. He was going to become an insurance salesman

20. Who was the Indiana basketball coach prior to Branch McCracken?

A. Leslie Mann

B. George Levis

C. Everett Dean

D. Ewald D. Stiehm

E. Dana M. Evans

21. Branch McCracken took a three-year hiatus as the IU basketball coach and served as a lieutenant in the United States Army in World War II. Who coached the Hoosiers from 1944-46?

A. Ralph Graham

B. Bill Johnson

C. Harry Good

D. Lawrence McCreary

E. Ernie Andres

22. The grandfather of what future Indiana player came to Indiana from Army with Bob Knight in 1971?

A. Errek Suhr

B. Jordan Hulls

C. Cody Zeller

D. Will Sheehey

E. Lance Stemler

23. Which of the following assistant coaches was NOT on Bob Knight's final coaching staff in the 1999-2000 season?

A. Pat Knight

B. Ron Felling

C. Mike Davis

D. John Treloar

24. This former Indiana player spent six seasons on Lou Watson's staff as an assistant coach. Can you name him?

A. Jerry Oliver

B. Jimmy Rayl

C. Tom Bolyard

D. Jon McGlocklin

E. Bobby Leonard

25. What was Leslie Mann's side profession while the head coach at Indiana in 1923 and 1924?

A. He was the athletic director

B. He was a car salesman

C. He played professional baseball

D. He was an elementary school teacher

E. He was a circus performer

26. How many Big Ten titles did Bob Knight win at Indiana? The number is tied with Purdue's Ward Lambert for the most in Big Ten history.

A. 14

B. 12

C. 11

D. 10

E. 9

27. **How many NCAA Tournament victories did Bob Knight amass at Indiana? He is one of only eight coaches to have at least this many NCAA Tournament victories.**

A. 50

B. 45

C. 40

D. 39

E. 38

28. **In his final six seasons at Indiana, how many times did Bob Knight's teams advance to the Sweet Sixteen or beyond?**

A. 4

B. 3

C. 2

D. 1

E. They did not advance past the Sweet Sixteen

29. True or False, when Tom Crean was introduced as the new IU head basketball coach he predicted IU would win the national championship within the next 10 years?

A. True

B. False

30. In IU's 2002 run to the national championship game, IU coach Mike Davis faced how many past or future head IU coaches in the regular season or the tournament?

A. Zero

B. One

C. Two

D. Three

E. Four or more

31. Since the award became official in 1974, how many different Indiana basketball coaches have been named Big Ten coach of the year?

A. 3

B. 2

C. 1

D. 0

E. None of the Above

32. In Indiana's magical 2002 run to the national championship game, IU coach Mike Davis faced off against how many of the following big name college coaches in the NCAA Tournament alone?

A. Tom Izzo

B. Mike Krzyzewski

C. Rick Majerus

D. Kelvin Sampson

E. All of the above

33. Who was the first head basketball coach in Indiana University History?

A. Phelps Darby

B. J.H. Horne

C. Zora Clevenger

D. Branch McCracken

E. James Sheldon

34. Before Everett Dean was the head coach of the Hoosiers for 14 seasons from 1925-38, what was the longest a coach had lasted in number of seasons at IU?

A. 6

B. 5

C. 4

D. 3

E. 2

35. In 1970, IU basketball coach Lou Watson was forced to take a leave of absence and miss the 1970 season. What prevented Watson from coaching that season?

A. Heart attack

B. High Blood Pressure

C. Surgery to remove cancer from his back

D. Open heart surgery

E. He tore his ACL and had to rehab it for several months

36. Who coached Indiana on an interim basis in the 1970 season?

A. Tom Bolyard

B. Jerry Oliver

C. Don Luft

D. Gene Ring

E. Phil Buck

37. How many times did Bob Knight earn national coach of the year honors at Indiana?

A. 6

B. 5

C. 4

D. 3

E. 2

38. True or False, Mike Davis was the first coach in Indiana basketball history to win 20 games or more in each of his first three seasons at IU?

A. True

B. False

39. What was Indiana's record through 26 games in the 2007-08 season when Kelvin Sampson was forced to resign after the NCAA announced that possible major violations had occurred during his tenure?

A. 25-1

B. 23-3

C. 22-4

D. 20-6

E. 19-7

40. When Tom Crean's first team in the
2008-09 season took the floor, how many
players from the season before were still
on the team?

A. 7

B. 6

C. 5

D. 2

E. 1

41. How many of those players had
originally been scholarship players
when they arrived at IU?

A. 5

B. 4

C. 3

D. 2

E. 1

F. Zero

42. True or False, while the interim coach at
IU in 2008, Dan Dakich kicked Jamarcus
Ellis and DeAndre Thomas off of the
team?

A. True

B. False

43. In the early rebuilding years that faced Indiana under Tom Crean, which team or teams were able to come into Assembly Hall and beat IU in non-conference play?

A. Elon

B. Eastern Kentucky

C. Loyola (Md.)

D. Stony Brook

E. South Alabama

44. Prior to coaching at his alma mater and after playing at Indiana, Branch McCracken was the head coach for this in-state school for eight seasons. He left there with an 86-57 record. Name the school.

A. Indiana State

B. Ball State

C. Evansville

D. Valparaiso

E. Purdue

45. Along with coaching the national champion IU basketball team in 1940, what other team did McCracken coach at IU as well in the 1939-1940 season?

A. He was the baseball coach

B. He coached freshman football

C. He was the tennis coach

D. He was the swimming coach

E. He was the wrestling coach

46. How many times in IU history has a coach taken over for the coach he played for at Indiana?

A. Three

B. Two

C. One

D. It has never happened

47. In 1948, Branch McCracken was offered the head coaching job at the following school. After IU chancellor Herman B. Wells told him that Indiana would match any offer to keep McCracken in Bloomington, he opted to stay.

A. Notre Dame

B. UCLA

C. Kansas

D. Purdue

E. Arizona

48. True or False, when Bill Orwig was hired as the IU athletic director at IU in 1961, he and his basketball coach Branch McCracken became instant friends and were almost inseparable socially?

A. True

B. False

49. Who was the coach that said before a key game against a No. 1 opponent that "We're going to shock the world."?

A. Branch McCracken

B. Lou Watson

C. Bob Knight

D. Mike Davis

E. Kelvin Sampson

50. True or False, when Indiana hired Bob Knight it was the first time since the 1923 season that the Hoosiers had hired a coach who hadn't played at IU, a span of nearly 50 years?

A. True

B. False

Answers on page 221

The original IU Fieldhouse, later renamed the Wildermuth Fieldhouse, housed IU basketball from 1928-60 including Indiana's first two national championship teams. Today it's the Wildermuth Intramural Center but most people just call it the HPER (pronounced HYPER). (Indiana University Archives, P0026774)

4

VENUE TRIVIA

1. **What was the first season that basketball was played in the current Assembly Hall?**

   A. 1973-74

   B. 1967-68

   C. 1970-71

   D. 1969-70

   E. 1971-72

2. **What was the first event held at the current Assembly Hall?**

   A. A rock concert

   B. A graduation ceremony

   C. A variety show

   D. A basketball game

   E. A volleyball game

3. **Which of these rock n' roll luminaries have not played at Assembly Hall at least once?**

A. The Rolling Stones

B. Elvis Presley

C. Bob Dylan

D. Led Zeppelin

E. Elton John

4. **What kind of circus animal once roamed loose in the bowels of the current Assembly Hall?**

A. Lion

B. Tiger

C. Bear

D. Horse

E. Camel

5. **The first game played in the current Assembly Hall was played against which in-state opponent?**

A. Ball State

B. Indiana State

C. Valparaiso

D. Notre Dame

E. Purdue

6. **In the first game ever played in Assembly Hall, an arena record was set that still stands today. What was that record?**

A. Most points by an IU player

B. Most rebounds by an IU player

C. Most points by an opposing player

D. Most rebounds by an opposing player

E. Most points by an IU team

7. The name of the playing surface in Assembly Hall today is what?

A. The Old Fieldhouse Floor

B. Robert Montgomery Knight Court

C. Branch McCracken Court

D. Hoosier Memorial Court

E. The surface does not have an official name

8. Before the current Assembly Hall was built IU played its games in a facility that was expected to be just an interim solution but housed the Hoosiers for 11 years. What is the name of that facility today?

A. Mellencamp Pavilion

B. The Hyper

C. Gladstein Fieldhouse

D. Men's Gymnasium

E. The original Assembly Hall

9. **The basketball floor IU played on from 1928-60 and hosted two national champions later spent more than a quarter century serving what purpose?**

A. A cafeteria

B. Paneling the wall of a horse barn

C. Paneling the interior great room of a wealthy IU donor

D. Used as the surface for an indoor track and field stadium

E. Used by a local gymnasium in the Bloomington area

10. **What key part of the Gladstein Fieldhouse made its home in Assembly Hall for 24 years before being replaced in 1995?**

A. The basketball playing surface

B. The scorer's table

C. The scoreboard

D. The bleachers

E. The railings on the balcony

11. **What baseball team used the IU Fieldhouse (now Wildermuth Fieldhouse) as an indoor practice facility for Spring Training during World War II?**

    A. Bloomington High School

    B. Indiana University

    C. Cincinnati Reds

    D. St. Louis Cardinals

    E. Indianapolis Indians

12. **What was the cost of a student season ticket for the first season in the New IU Fieldhouse built in 1960?**

    A. $20

    B. $15

    C. $12.50

    D. $10

    E. $5.50

13. The Assembly Hall design is based off of what other type of structure?

    A. A cattle auction house

    B. A state fair pavilion

    C. A cathedral

    D. A circus tent

    E. None of the above

14. The IU basketball program in the winter of 1900 held its first tryouts in what kind of building?

    A. A high school gymnasium

    B. A barn

    C. A carpenter's shop

    D. A dance hall

    E. A factory in Bloomington

15. The first Assembly Hall was built in 1896 and housed the Hoosiers from 1901-1917. How much did it cost to build?

    A. $20,000

    B. $16,000

    C. $12,000

    D. $10,000

    E. $8,000

16. **What was the seating capacity of that first basketball arena on campus?**

    A. 2,200

    B. 1,500

    C. 1,200

    D. 800

    E. 600

17. **The Original Assembly Hall not only featured IU basketball games, but what other piece of sporting equipment?**

    A. Gymnastics equipment

    B. Swimming pool

    C. Portable Blocking Sled

    D. Indoor batting cage

    E. Early model treadmills

18. **The Men's Gymnasium built in 1917 and home to IU basketball until 1928, featured the first version of what fan-friendly item?**

    A. Luxury Box

    B. Hot dog vendors

    C. Glass backboards

    D. Replay Equipment

    E. Game programs

19. When the Men's Gymnasium made its debut in 1917, IU beat Iowa in a game where the Hoosiers set a school record that still stands today for the fewest points scored in a victory. Iowa scored 7 points. How many points did IU score?

A. 8

B. 10

C. 11

D. 12

E. 16

20. The Fieldhouse played host to IU basketball from 1928-1960. What IU player scored the first points in the Fieldhouse in the inaugural game on Dec. 8, 1928?

A. James Strickland

B. Branch McCracken

C. Dale Wells

D. Lucian Ashby

E. Robert Correll

21. The IU Fieldhouse, now the Wildermuth Fieldhouse, saw its floor surrounded by what safety feature?

   A. Armed security guards

   B. Padding

   C. Pillows

   D. Netting to keep players from sliding off the floor

   E. Pools of water

22. How much did it cost to build IU's current venue Assembly Hall?

   A. $12.2 million

   B. $8.6 million

   C. $17.5 million

   D. $20.4 million

   E. $38 million

23. In the original plans for Assembly Hall, what was the seating capacity supposed to be?

   A. 16,555

   B. 17,343

   C. 18,200

   D. 21,455

   E. 25,000

24. True or False, Assembly Hall has been used in the past for games with the Indiana Pacers?

A. True

B. False

25. The current Assembly Hall, as well as Gladstein Fieldhouse, two venues that have housed IU basketball, were constructed on land that was once used as what?

A. A farm

B. A furniture factory

C. A dirt racing track

D. A church

E. The land was undeveloped

26. What happened in February of 2014 at Assembly Hall that caused the university to postpone that night's Big Ten home game against Iowa?

A. Leaky roof

B. Power outage

C. Earthquake caused floor to crack

D. Metal beam fell from the ceiling damaging some of the seating

E. The floor was flooded

27. **What milestone event in IU basketball history occurred while the Hoosiers played in the Gladstein Fieldhouse from 1960-71?**

A. Jimmy Rayl scored 56 points – twice

B. Walt Bellamy had 33 rebounds in one game.

C. George McGinnis had his magical season at IU averaging nearly 30 points per game.

D. All of the above

E. None of the above

28. **True or False, the area to the end of the court at Gladstein Fieldhouse was made up of sawdust and dirt and the playing floor was elevated 18 inches off the ground?**

A. True

B. False

29. **What kind of fruit grew on the land later occupied by the Men's Gymnasium built in 1915 and the Wildermuth Fieldhouse?**

A. Cherries

B. Apples

C. Peaches

D. Oranges

E. None of the above

30. **What was one of the reasons cited by IU when discussing the need for the construction of the Men's Gymnasium in 1915?**

A. Old facility was unsafe

B. IU was falling behind in recruiting

C. It would improve the campus

D. Old facility was embarrassing

E. There were no luxury boxes

31. **What famous tournament got its start in IU's original Assembly Hall?**

A. NIT

B. NCAA Tournament

C. Big Ten Tournament

D. Indiana State High School Basketball Tournament

32. **What athletics superstar was on hand to help clear ground for construction of the Men's Gymnasium in 1915?**

    A. Ty Cobb

    B. Babe Ruth

    C. Jim Thorpe

    D. Don Fischer

    E. George Montgomery

33. **IU's basketball floor at the Men's Gymnasium built in 1915 featured what unusual feature in the corners just outside the playing area?**

    A. Banking for joggers

    B. Nets

    C. Folding chairs

    D. National championship banners

    E. All of the above

34. The chairs along the sideline at Assembly Hall feature what security feature? This has been in place since the mid-1980s.

A. Collapsible backs

B. Cushions that can be used as a flotation device

C. They're secured to the floor

D. Laser guns

E. None of the above

35. What sort of record did the bleachers used for IU's first basketball game in Wildermuth Fieldhouse break?

A. Largest bleachers in the United States

B. Railroad speed record being shipped from Seattle to Bloomington

C. Steepest seating in the Big Ten

D. All of the above

E. None of the above

36. **Approximately how high was the basketball floor used at Wildermuth Fieldhouse raised above the floor of the facility?**

A. Six inches

B. 18 inches

C. Two feet

D. Six feet

E. None of the above

37. **What issue did the basketball floor used at Wildermuth Fieldhouse suffer during its first official game?**

A. Too bumpy

B. Dangerously slick

C. Too small

D. Sharp edges

E. Gaping sink holes

38. The Gust K. Newberg Construction Company that built Gladstein Fieldhouse was also involved in what other major sports construction project?

A. Wrigley Field

B. U.S. Cellular Field in Chicago

C. New Yankee Stadium

D. The New Orleans Superdome

E. Hoosier Dome

39. The current Assembly Hall once showed evidence that it hosted what unwanted guest?

A. Family of Beavers

B. An unnamed person

C. A large hornet's nest

D. A Mountain Lion

E. None of the above

40. True or False, the Wildermuth Fieldhouse was lit by 47 electric lights hanging from the ceiling from 500-1500 watts?

A. True

B. False

41. The final game in the Wildermuth Fieldhouse in 1960, also the final game in the building's history, was played between Indiana and Ohio State. Which future IU head or assistant coach was in uniform that day?

A. Lou Watson

B. Bob Knight

C. Tom Bolyard

D. Dave Bliss

E. John Hulls

42. One year after the original Assembly Hall wasn't being used for basketball anymore, how was the arena used in the fall of 1918?

A. A church

B. A factory

C. A hospital

D. A library

E. None of the above

43. The Indiana high school state championship game was played in the Assembly Hall in 1911? How much was admission to get into the game?

A. $1

B. 75 cents

C. 50 cents

D. 25 cents

E. Free

44. If fans wanted to come back for the Indiana-Northwestern that followed the high school championship, they had to leave, come back and pay how much?

A. $2

B. $1

C. 75 cents

D. 50 cents

E. Free

45. The current Assembly Hall opened in the early 1970's but when did bids go out to find an outfit to build it?

A. 1968

B. 1966

C. 1964

D. 1960

E. 1957

46. What was the main delay in Assembly Hall not being built right away?

A. It was decided that a new football stadium presented the best chance for increased revenue.

B. The price tag was close to double what university officials wanted to spend.

C. Instead of building things as a package deal, the decision was made to do the projects separately.

D. All of the above

E. None of the above

47. True or False, the dedication of the new Assembly Hall was 75 years to the day that the original Assembly Hall had been dedicated, Dec. 18, 1896?

A. True

B. False

48. When were the final plans approved and the bids awarded for construction for the current Assembly Hall to finally begin?

A. The fall of 1967

B. The summer of 1968

C. The fall of 1968

D. The spring of 1969

49. True or False, Branch McCracken got to enjoy games in the new Assembly Hall and see young coach Bob Knight in his first year at IU a few months before McCracken died?

A. True

B. False

50. True or False, on the night of the Assembly Hall dedication Indiana beat Notre Dame and its own first year coach Digger Phelps, 94-29?

A. True

B. False

Answers on page 224

Todd Meier, Daryl Thomas and Steve Alford hoist the 1987 national championship trophy at the podium in New Orleans following IU's 74-73 win over Syracuse. (Indiana University Archives, P0023290)

5

NATIONAL CHAMPIONSHIP TRIVIA

1. On the 1987 national championship team, Steve Alford led that team in scoring with a 22.0 points per game average. Who was the second leading scorer at 15.7 points per game?

   A. Dean Garrett

   B. Daryl Thomas

   C. Keith Smart

   D. Ricky Calloway

   E. None of the above

2. Not surprisingly Isiah Thomas was the leading scorer on the '81 national championship team with a 16 points per game average. Who was the second leading scorer on that team with a 12.2 average?

A. Ray Tolbert

B. Randy Wittman

C. Landon Turner

D. Ted Kitchel

E. None of the above

3. In the unbeaten 1976 national championship year, Scott May was the leading scorer and the national player of the year with a 23.5 points per game average. Who was second on that team in scoring at 17.3 points per game?

A. Quinn Buckner

B. Kent Benson

C. Bobby Wilkerson

D. Tom Abernethy

E. None of the above

4. **Don Schlundt was the leading scorer on the 1953 national championship team with an impressive 25.4 points per game average. Who was the second leading scorer on that team at 16.3?**

A. Dick Farley

B. Burke Scott

C. Lou Scott

D. Charlie Kraak

E. None of the above

5. **The leading scorer on the 1940 national championship team was Paul "Curly" Armstrong who averaged 8.9 points per game. One other player was right behind him. This will test even the biggest IU trivia buff but who was that player?**

A. Herm Schaefer

B. William Menke

C. Bob Dro

D. Marv Huffman

E. Jay McCreary

6. In the 1987 national championship game everyone knows that Keith Smart hit the baseline jumper in the final seconds that gave IU a 74-73 victory over Syracuse. But the Orange led 73-70 before this player hit a leaning 10-footer to make it a one-point game with 30 seconds to play. Who was the player that hit the shot that cut the lead to 73-72?

A. Ricky Calloway

B. Keith Smart

C. Steve Alford

D. Daryl Thomas

E. Dean Garrett

7. What current member of the IU athletic administration was a manager on the 1987 IU national championship team?

A. Fred Glass

B. Scott Dolson

C. Mark Deal

D. Chuck Crabb

E. Jeremy Gray

8. There were three seniors on the '87 national championship team. Two of them were Steve Alford and Daryl Thomas. Who was the third senior on that team?

A. Brian Sloan

B. Keith Smart

C. Steve Eyl

D. Todd Meier

E. Kreigh Smith

9. Everyone remembers that Indiana beat Syracuse to win the '87 national championship. But who did IU beat in the first Final Four semifinal game to get to the title game?

A. Providence

B. North Carolina

C. UNLV

D. LSU

E. Duke

10. **What city was the 1987 national championship game played in?**

   A. New Orleans

   B. Houston

   C. Denver

   D. Los Angeles

   E. Seattle

11. **Where was the 1981 Mideast Regional played that IU advanced out of, beating UAB and St. Joseph's to reach the Final Four?**

   A. Rupp Arena

   B. Freedom Hall

   C. Hoosier Dome

   D. Crisler Arena

   E. Assembly Hall

12. IU beat North Carolina to win the NCAA title in 1981. What team did IU beat in the national semifinals that year?

   A. Virginia

   B. St. Josephs

   C. LSU

   D. Kansas

   E. BYU

13. What Indiana player scored a game-high 23 points in the 1981 national championship victory over North Carolina? He had 19 of those points in the second half.

   A. Isiah Thomas

   B. Randy Wittman

   C. Ray Tolbert

   D. Landon Turner

   E. Steve Risley

14. **What city was the 1981 national championship played in?**

   A. Boston

   B. Philadelphia

   C. New York City

   D. Washington D.C.

   E. Providence

15. **How many games did the unbeaten 1976 national champion Indiana Hoosiers win?**

   A. 30

   B. 32

   C. 34

   D. 35

   E. 36

16. **How many ranked opponents did Indiana beat in 1976 to win the national championship?**

   A. 2

   B. 4

   C. 6

   D. 8

   E. 10

17. **What city was the 1976 national championship game played in?**

    A. Boston

    B. Philadelphia

    C. New York City

    D. Washington D.C.

    E. Providence

18. **Two IU players combined to score 51 points in the national championship game victory over Michigan in 1976. Scott May led the Hoosiers with 26. Who scored 25?**

    A. Quinn Buckner

    B. Kent Benson

    C. Bobby Wilkerson

    D. Tom Abernethy

    E. Wayne Radford

19. The most points ever scored by an IU player in a national championship game came in 1953 when this player scored 30 points in IU's 69-68 win over Kansas. Name the player.

A. Charley Kraak

B. Bobby Leonard

C. Don Schlundt

D. Dick Farley

E. Burke Scott

20. What city was the 1953 national championship game played in?

A. Chicago

B. St. Louis

C. Louisville

D. Kansas City

E. Omaha

21. **What IU player hit the game-winning free throw in the 1953 national championship game with 30 seconds to play?**

A. Dick Farley

B. Bobby Leonard

C. Don Schlundt

D. Charlie Kraak

E. Burke Scott

22. **Indiana beat Kansas in the national championship game in 1953. Which team did it beat the day before to get there?**

A. Notre Dame

B. DePaul

C. LSU

D. UCLA

E. Washington

23. **What team did Indiana beat to win the 1940 national championship?**

A. North Carolina

B. Ohio State

C. Duquesne

D. Villanova

E. Kansas

24. **How many postseason games did the 1940 team have to win to capture the NCAA championship?**

A. 6

B. 5

C. 4

D. 3

E. 2

25. **What city was the 1940 national championship game played in?**

    A. Chicago

    B. St. Louis

    C. Kansas City

    D. Louisville

    E. Indianapolis

26. **Of Indiana's five national championships, how many times did IU win the Big Ten title outright in those championship seasons?**

    A. 1

    B. 2

    C. 3

    D. 4

    E. 5

27. In Indiana's 1976 national championship run, how many times did the Hoosiers beat the Michigan Wolverines that season?

A. They didn't beat Michigan that season

B. Once

C. Twice

D. Three times

E. They didn't play Michigan that season

28. Later Branch McCracken teams were known at IU as the Hurryin Hoosiers. But what were two of the nicknames for Indiana basketball when IU won the 1940 national championship?

A. The Rockets

B. The Crimsons

C. The Spectaculars

D. The MacMen

E. Branch's Boys

29. **What place did the 1940 national championship team finish in the Big Ten?**

A. First

B. Second

C. Third

D. Fourth

E. Fifth

30. **Andy Zimmer was the tallest Indiana player on the 1940 national championship team. How tall was he?**

A. 6-foot-7

B. 6-foot-5

C. 6-foot-4

D. 6-foot-2

E. 5-foot-11

31. In the 1976 national championship game, one of IU's starters was knocked cold less than 3 minutes into the game by an inadvertent elbow. He was taken to the hospital and didn't return to the game. Who was the player?

A. Quinn Buckner

B. Bobby Wilkerson

C. Scott May

D. Kent Benson

E. Ted Abernethy

32. By finishing 32-0, Indiana tied one other former NCAA champion for the most victories by an undefeated national champion. What was the other team?

A. UCLA

B. University of San Francisco

C. North Carolina

D. UTEP

E. Houston

33. Prior to Big Ten play in the 1953 national championship season, IU only played three non-conference games. They were against Valparaiso, Notre Dame and Kansas State. What was IU's record going into Big Ten play?

A. 3-0

B. 2-1

C. 1-2

D. 0-3

34. Once Big Ten play started in 1953 through the national championship victory over Kansas, Indiana would only lose one more game. It would win 22 of 23. What was the lone team that beat the Hoosiers on the road, 65-63?

A. Minnesota

B. Wisconsin

C. Ohio State

D. Purdue

E. Illinois

35. Indiana added a pair of junior college transfers prior to the 1986-87 national championship season that would be instrumental in IU's title season. One of them was Keith Smart who hit the game-winning shot to beat Syracuse for the national title. Who was the other player?

A. Joe Hillman

B. Dean Garrett

C. Steve Eyl

D. Magnus Pelkowsi

E. None of the above

36. Indiana shared the Big Ten title in 1987 with one other team, both with 15-3 records. In fact that other team, beat IU with three games to go and then got fortunate when the Hoosiers lost the next game, too, to Illinois. Who was the team that IU shared the '87 title with?

A. Ohio State

B. Michigan State

C. Michigan

D. Purdue

E. Wisconsin

37. What IU player had a key tip-in in the closing seconds that gave IU a 77-76 victory over LSU, a win that gave the Hoosiers a trip to the Final Four?

A. Steve Alford

B. Ricky Calloway

C. Daryl Thomas

D. Keith Smart

E. Dean Garrett

38. True or False, the 1987 national champs were cardiac kids. They were 4-0 in one-point games and 13-2 that season in games decided by five points or less?

A. True

B. False

39. What U.S. president was in office and hosted Indiana in a White House visit following the 1987 national championship?

A. Gerald Ford

B. Jimmy Carter

C. Ronald Reagan

D. George Bush

E. Bill Clinton

40. Prior to the 1981 national championship season, Indiana lost two players to graduation who had combined to average more than 30 points per game the year before. One of them was Mike Woodson. Who was the other, who was a co-captain with Woodson on that team?

A. Randy Wittman

B. Ray Tolbert

C. Steve Risley

D. Butch Carter

E. Landon Turner

41. True or false, when Indiana and Michigan met for the 1976 national championship it marked just the second time in NCAA history that two teams from the same conference had met for the title?

A. True

B. False

42. True or False, the 1987 IU-Syracuse national championship was one of the top five watched NCAA title games of all time with a 22.2 share?

A. True

B. False

43. At the time in 1987, the crowd that packed the Louisiana Superdome in New Orleans for IU-Syracuse was the largest crowd for a championship game in NCAA history. How many fans were at that game?

A. 66,121

B. 64,959

C. 62,809

D. 61,234

E. 70,004

44. True or false, Ricky Calloway picked up a technical foul in the NCAA title game in 1981?

A. True

B. False

45. In the five seasons when Indiana won the national championship, how many times were they ahead at halftime of the title games?

A. 5

B. 4

C. 3

D. 2

E. 1

Isiah Thomas and Bob Knight have a conversation in IU's game with Purdue in January of 1980, the season before IU would win the national title. (Indiana University Archives, P0035265)

46. **When Indiana won the 1953 national championship by a 69-68 decision over Kansas, what IU player or players received a technical foul in the game?**

A. Bobby Leonard

B. Charlie Kraak

C. Don Schlundt

D. All of the Above

E. None of the Above

47. **In the 1981 national championship game, Ray Tolbert had 11 rebounds but he wasn't nearly as effective on the other end. How many points did he get in the title game?**

A. 9

B. 7

C. 5

D. 3

E. 2

48. **Where was IU ranked in the nation going into the 1987 NCAA Tournament?**

A. No. 10

B. No. 6

C. No. 3

D. No. 2

E. No. 1

49. **How many weeks was the 1981 Indiana basketball team not ranked in the top 25?**

A. 1

B. 2

C. 3

D. 4

E. They were ranked all season

50. **After winning the 1981 Big Ten title outright with a 14-4 record going into the NCAA Tournament, where was IU ranked in the top 25?**

A. No. 5

B. No. 7

C. No. 9

D. No. 15

E. The Hoosiers weren't ranked going into the NCAA Tournament

Answers on page 227

Indiana coach Bob Knight talks with Scott May (left) and Quinn Buckner before a game in Assembly Hall in the fall of 1975. Indiana won the national championship that year. (Indiana University Archives, P0020272)

From 1978-88, opera singer Martha Webster entertained Indiana fans in television advertisements for Indiana Farm Bureau Insurance as a custodian who would walk the bowels of Assembly Hall singing the IU fight song as she worked. (Indiana University Archives, P0020988)

6

FUN FACTS

1. In 1982, this IU player at that time became the tallest player in school history. Who was the player?

   A. Steve Bouchie

   B. Mike LaFave

   C. Landon Turner

   D. Uwe Blab

   E. None of the above

2. How tall was he?

   A. 6-10

   B. 6-11

   C. 7-0

   D. 7-1

   E. 7-2

3. **When Luke Recker announced he was transferring from IU after his sophomore season, he waited until Bob Knight was where?**

A. On a hunting trip in Wisconsin

B. On a fishing trip in Canada

C. On an airplane headed toward Cuba

D. On a hunting trip in Colorado

E. Asleep in his home in Bloomington

4. **When Bob Knight threw the chair against Purdue in February of 1985, he was assessed how many technical fouls before later being suspended for one game by the Big Ten, too?**

A. 4

B. 3

C. 2

D. 1

E. None of the above

5. **Steve Reid was at the foul line for Purdue when Knight threw the chair. He ended up shooting the technical free throws, too. How many free throws did he end up attempting?**

   A. 2

   B. 4

   C. 6

   D. 8

   E. 10

6. **In a Big Ten game against Iowa in 1999, this Indiana player threw an inbounds pass off the face of Iowa's Jacob Jaacks. Bob Knight later said the Iowa players had been crossing the inbounds line the whole game and his player was just attempting an inbounds pass. Who was that player?**

   A. A.J. Guyton

   B. Michael Lewis

   C. Luke Jimenez

   D. Dane Fife

   E. Jeff Newton

7. This player, in a game against Iowa in 2000, was caught in a replay in a nationally televised game on ESPN biting Iowa player Duez Henderson in the arm during a scuffle when the two players had fallen to the floor. The player would later say of the incident, "He tasted like chicken." Who was the IU player?

A. A.J. Guyton

B. Larry Richardson

C. Dane Fife

D. Luke Recker

E. Lynn Washington

8. In the season opener in 1999-2000, Indiana was the first team to play in the new United Spirit Arena, home of the Texas Tech Red Raiders. Two years later, Bob Knight would be the new head coach at Texas Tech. What street is the United Spirit Arena appropriately located on in Lubbock, Texas?

A. Indiana Avenue

B. Hoosier Road

C. Purdue Boulevard

D. Brand Avenue

E. Bloomington Court

9. Which of the following IU players DID NOT play on the Olympic team?

A. Quinn Buckner

B. Scott May

C. Calbert Cheaney

D. Steve Alford

E. Kent Benson

10. What year did Indiana begin wearing its famed candy-striped warm up pants?

A. 1952-53

B. 1960-61

C. 1968-69

D. 1971-72

E. 1973-74

If you're a fan of any team other than Indiana and you think of Bob Knight, this is the picture that comes to mind. It was Feb. 23, 1985 and Indiana was playing Purdue at Assembly Hall. (Indiana University Archives, P0044977)

11. In a game against Kentucky in 2002, Mike Davis ran onto the court enraged that a foul wasn't called on a drive to the basket with 2.6 seconds remaining and his team trailing by one point. He was T'd up by official Bert Smith and ejected from the game, and Kentucky hit five free throws. Who was the IU player that Davis believed was fouled on the play?

A. Tom Coverdale

B. Marshall Strickland

C. Bracey Wright

D. A.J. Moye

E. Sean Kline

12. In the 1981 season, the two games with Purdue were very physical. IU coach Bob Knight was upset about some of the play and brought a donkey wearing a Purdue cap on to the set of his television show that week. He said the donkey was a substitute for Purdue athletic director George King, who declined to appear on the show. What was the donkey's name?

A. Wilbur

B. Jack

C. Gene

D. Pete

E. Donk

13. **What was the name of the IU manager in the 2008-09 season that actually suited up and played three games for the Hoosiers?**

A. Brandon Profitt

B. Patrick Cogan

C. Josh Lee

D. Jeremy Growe

E. Michael Santa

14. **When Bob Knight was fired in September of 2000, players threatened to boycott the season unless IU hired assistant coaches Mike Davis and John Treloar to coach the team. The university did just that. One player still opted not to return because of Knight's dismissal. Who was that player?**

A. Mike Roberts

B. Tom Geyer

C. Ryan Tapak

D. Mark Johnson

E. Andre Owens

15. Which of the following states have had at least one player in history play basketball at IU?

A. Alaska

B. Maine

C. Montana

D. North Dakota

E. South Dakota

16. How many players from the state of Kentucky have ever played basketball at IU?

A. 22

B. 16

C. 12

D. 8

E. 6

17. Which bordering state has had the most players play at IU?

A. Kentucky

B. Ohio

C. Illinois

D. Michigan

18. As of 2015, there had been 587 players who hailed from the state of Indiana that had played at IU. The most from one town was 61 from Indianapolis. Second was 35 from one town. Which town was that?

A. Fort Wayne

B. Bloomington

C. Terre Haute

D. South Bend

E. Kokomo

19. Prior to the NCAA Tournament run in 2002, Mike Davis told his players that if they won the national championship he would do what?

Λ. Let them get rid of the candy striped warmup pants

B. Let them put names on the back of their jerseys

C. Get them another Hawaii trip in the upcoming season

D. Shave his head

E. All of the above

20. **When Victor Oladipo came to Indiana what was his national rank in the top 150 by Rivals.com?**

A. 44

B. 64

C. 104

D. 124

E. 144

21. **What happened at the Sea Wolf Classic in November of 1978 that eventually resulted in three players being dismissed by Bob Knight from the IU basketball team?**

A. Players broke curfew

B. Players were arrested for shoplifting

C. Players had smoked marijuana on the trip

D. Players had been out drinking and missed curfew

E. Players missed the flight home

22. Indiana played the Indiana Classic in Bloomington from 1974-2000. What was IU's record in the Indiana Classic?

A. 54-0

B. 53-1

C. 52-2

D. 49-5

E. 48-6

23. What former IU basketball manager went on to be an NBA head coach?

A. Brad Stevens

B. Frank Vogel

C. Lawrence Frank

D. Rick Carlisle

E. Stan Van Gundy

24. Which year did Indiana basketball games first begin to be shown on television? The games were shown initially on Channel 10 in Bloomington.

A. 1951-52

B. 1956-57

C. 1962-63

D. 1966-67

E. 1968-69

25. How many different seasons has Indiana basketball been ranked No. 1 in the nation for at least one week?

A. 2

B. 4

C. 6

D. 8

E. 10 or more

26. When Indiana played Duke in the 1992 Final Four, who was the player that brought the Hoosiers back in the final minute by hitting three 3-pointers in a 24-second span to help nearly erase a 9-point Duke advantage?

A. Matt Nover

B. Chris Reynolds

C. Jamal Meeks

D. Todd Leary

E. Greg Graham

27. Indiana fans still talk about how it was criminal that the player above did not take IU's final shot of the game with the Hoosiers trailing 81-78. Instead, what player hoisted the final 3-point attempt for the tie?

A. Matt Nover

B. Chris Reynolds

C. Jamal Meeks

D. Todd Leary

E. Greg Graham

28. In 1963, Jimmy Rayl tied a school record by scoring 56 points against Michigan State. How many points did he score in the second game against the Spartans that season?

A. 10

B. 16

C. 55

D. 40

E. 44

29. Indiana won the NIT championship following the 1978-79 season. Who did the Hoosiers beat in the championship game in Madison Square Garden?

A. Utah

B. Washington

C. Valparaiso

D. Texas Tech

E. Purdue

30. When Bob Knight and Steve Alford helped the United States team win the gold medal in the 1984 Olympics, what other IU basketball player represented his country in the Olympics?

A. Haris Mujezinovic

B. Magnus Pelkowski

C. Uwe Blab

D. Tijan Jobe

E. Bawa Muniru

31. In the 2012-13 season, Indiana had how many players on its roster that would ultimately, in their IU careers, end up scoring 1,000 points or more?

A. 6

B. 5

C. 4

D. 3

E. 2

32. When Indiana named its 15-man All-Century team in 2000, there was one player not on the squad that was particularly conspicuous by his absence. In fact, he is one of IU's select number of 2,000 point scorers. Who is the player?

A. A.J. Guyton

B. Mike Woodson

C. Alan Henderson

D. Don Schlundt

E. Steve Alford

33. Since 1978, Indiana has had 28 McDonald's All-American's decide to play basketball at IU. How many of the 28 completed their eligibility at Indiana?

A. 24

B. 22

C. 17

D. 15

E. 10

34. From 1978-88, Indiana Farm Bureau Insurance used an advertising campaign featured a janitor walking the halls of Assembly Hall singing the IU fight song with it getting louder as she went. The commercial spot was resurrected by Tom Crean and is played before every IU home game on the big screen. What was the fictional name of the woman who has become an IU legend?

A. The Singing Custodian

B. The Singing Mop Lady

C. The Hoosier Mop Lady

D. Martha the Mop Lady

E. None of the Above

35. **What happened in the 2002 Big Ten opener at Northwestern that shook up the starting lineup for that team?**

   A. IU got wiped out and Mike Davis wasn't happy

   B. Jared Jeffries was benched

   C. Dane Fife was advised to stop flopping so much

   D. George Leach injured his ankle on the opening tip

   E. None of the above

36. **At Hoosier Hysteria prior to the 2001 season, Andre Owens did something that caught the ire of IU head coach Mike Davis. What did he do?**

   A. He was late arriving

   B. He grabbed the microphone and started speaking to the crowd

   C. He took off his shirt during the slam dunk contest trying to get the crowd riled up

   D. He got in scuffle with one of his players

   E. None of the above

37. How many times in IU history has a basketball head coach's son played for his father?

   A. 4

   B. 3

   C. 2

   D. 1

   E. It has never happened

38. True or false, Dane Fife proposed to his longtime girlfriend on the microphone during his Senior Night speech at IU?

   A. True

   B. False

39. What was the name of the movie that several IU basketball players had bit parts in, starred Nick Nolte and came out in 1994?

   A. *Space Jam*

   B. *Blue Chips*

   C. *Hoosiers*

   D. *He Got Game*

   E. *White Men Can't Jump*

40. True or False, the movie was filmed in three Indiana locations: Frankfort, French Lick and Bloomington?

A. True

B. False

41. In the 1985-86 season, Steve Alford's junior year, he was suspended by the NCAA for one game. What did he do?

A. Cheated on a test

B. Punched another player

C. Appeared in a sorority calendar that was done to raise money for handicapped kids.

D. Overslept and missed practice

E. He accepted a meal from an IU booster

42. Who was the opponent in the game he was suspended?

A. Purdue

B. Notre Dame

C. North Carolina

D. Duke

E. Kentucky

43. **What was the name of the fictional international player that Bob Knight announced on his television show in 1993 that Indiana was about to recruit?**

A. Antonio Boynton

B. Ivan Renko

C. Hoops McGee

D. Kevin Hunt

E. Bill Lorah

44. **What country was he supposed to have hailed from?**

A. Slovenia

B. South Africa

C. Yugoslavia

D. Sweden

E. Turkey

45. When Indiana knocked off Duke in the Sweet Sixteen in 2002, what Indiana media member stood on his chair as the celebration began and raised his arms into the air?

A. Don Fischer

B. Todd Leary

C. George Montgomery

D. Michael Grant

E. Terry Hutchens

46. Indiana led Duke by four with 11.1 seconds to play in the 2002 Sweet Sixteen game before this IU player fouled Jay Williams on a 3-point attempt – which he made. Who was the player?

A. Tom Coverdale

B. Dane Fife

C. Kyle Hornsby

D. Jared Jeffries

E. Jeff Newton

47. The news that Mike Davis would step down following the 2006 season leaked out during IU's Feb. 15 game at Penn State. How did the local media learn that night that it was happening?

A. Don Fischer let it slip on the radio

B. His wife mentioned it to a reporter at the game

C. The story broke at SI.com

D. A member of IU's administrative traveling party at the game told a reporter

E. Davis announced it in the postgame press conference

48. True or False, after Bob Knight was dismissed at Indiana in September of 2000, the university offered the head coaching position on an interim basis to both John Treloar and Mike Davis, but Treloar insisted Davis be the head coach?

A. True

B. False

49. What IU basketball player under Mike Davis was known for calling into Davis's weekly radio show, disguising his voice, and often asking questions about not only the team but himself?

A. Tom Coverdale

B. A.J. Moye

C. Jared Jeffries

D. Dane Fife

E. Bracey Wright

50. True or False, longtime IU radio play-by-play announcer Don Fischer has been on the call for all five of IU's national championship games?

A. True

B. False

Answers on page 229

This portrait photo of Bob Knight was taken in the fall of 1971 as he was about to begin his first year as the Indiana head coach. (Indiana University Archives, P0028521)

7

BOB KNIGHT TRIVIA

1. Bob Knight was born in Massillon, Ohio. What town in Ohio did Knight grow up in and play high school basketball?

   A. Wooster

   B. Orrville

   C. East Union

   D. Perry Heights

   E. Akron

2. After high school, Knight played college basketball and in fact, played on the 1960 national championship team. What college did he attend?

   A. Kansas

   B. Duke

   C. Ohio State

   D. UCLA

   E. Kentucky

3. In college basketball history, three men have both played on and coached national championship teams in college. Can you name the three?

   A. Dean Smith

   B. Mike Krzyzewski

   C. John Wooden

   D. Bob Knight

   E. Joe B. Hall

4. True or False, Bob Knight is the only coach in history to win the NCAA, the NIT, an Olympic gold medal and a Pan American Games gold medal?

   A. True

   B. False

Bob Knight pictured on the bench in a game in the 1990's in Assembly Hall. (Indiana University Archives, P0028808)

5. **In between his playing days in college and his first head coaching job at Army, Knight spent one year doing what?**

   A. He worked at a grocery store in his home town.

   B. He was a head varsity football coach.

   C. He worked in a construction job.

   D. He coached junior varsity basketball at Cuyahoga Falls, Ohio.

   E. He was an assistant varsity basketball coach in Wooster, Ohio.

6. **In 42 years as a college basketball head coach, Bob Knight had an overall record of 902-371. When he retired from coaching at Texas Tech after the 2007-08 season, where did Knight rank in terms of the most wins all time by a college coach?**

   A. He was ranked first all-time.

   B. He was ranked second all-time

   C. He was ranked third all-time

   D. He was barely in the top 10.

   E. He ranked No. 17 all-time.

7. **What were the staples of Bob Knight's coaching philosophy?**

   A. The motion offense

   B. Hard-nosed man-to-man defense

   C. Instilling mental toughness in his players

   D. All of the above

   E. None of the above

8. **Which of the following successful college and NBA coaches DID NOT play for Bob Knight?**

   A. Randy Wittman

   B. Mike Woodson

   C. Keith Smart

   D. Bill Self

   E. Steve Alford

   F. Marty Simmons

   G. Jim Crews

   H. Mike Krzyzewski

9. In 42 seasons as a head college basketball coach, how many winning seasons did Bob Knight have?

A. 42

B. 40

C. 38

D. 37

E. 35

10. Bob Knight is known as one who supports philanthropic causes, too. True or False, it is believed Knight, over the years, has raised nearly $5 million for the IU library system and also supports other library causes?

A. True

B. False

11. In 42 years as a college head coach, how many of Knight's four year players did not graduate from college?

A. 10

B. 8

C. 6

D. 4

E. 2

12. Knight's final year at Indiana was a difficult one beginning with a videotape that was aired for the first time – coincidentally? – the week of the NCAA Tournament where Indiana was playing Pepperdine in Buffalo, N.Y. A few months later the heat was turned up when three brothers claimed they had an altercation with Knight. What did IU student Kent Harvey claim that Bob Knight did to him outside of Assembly Hall on Sept. 7, 2000?

A. He said Knight slapped him and called him a name.

B. He said Knight grabbed him and admonished him after he yelled, "Hey Knight" at the IU coach.

C. He said Knight chased him into the parking lot.

D. None of the above.

E. All of the above.

13. **What happened three days later?**

   A. Knight was suspended by the university.

   B. Knight was cleared of all charges made by Harvey.

   C. Knight was fired by IU president Myles Brand for a "pattern of unacceptable behavior."

   D. Knight was fined $10,000 by the university.

   E. None of the above.

14. **It began getting tougher on the night when the CNN tape aired showing Knight allegedly choking former player Neil Reed during a practice in 1997. This led to the IU Board of Trustees putting an edict on Knight in May of 2000. What was it called?**

   A. The No Forgiveness Policy

   B. The Bob Knight Pattern of Behavior Policy

   C. Zero Tolerance

   D. Bob Knight's Rules to Live By

   E. None of the above

15. At the time that the policy was imposed, what other action did the university take against Knight?

    A. He was suspended for six games in the upcoming season

    B. He was fined $10,000

    C. He was asked to take anger management classes

    D. He was suspended indefinitely

    E. He was fined $30,000 and suspended for three games in the upcoming season

16. Who was the IU athletic director when Bob Knight was dismissed in September of 2000?

    A. Rick Greenspan

    B. Michael McNeely

    C. Terry Clapacs

    D. Clarence Doninger

    E. Bill Orwig

17. Who is the ESPN broadcaster who has continually lobbied over the years for Indiana to rename Assembly Hall after Robert Montgomery Knight?

A. Digger Phelps

B. Dan Shulman

C. Dick Vitale

D. Brent Musburger

E. Dave O'Brien

18. What was the name of the store on the south side of Indianapolis that sold Bob Knight merchandise and was operated by Knight's ex-wife Nancy and owned by his son, Tim?

A. Knight Life

B. RMK Enterprises

C. The General's Store

D. Hoosiers

E. Bob's Place

19. **What Indianapolis television station did Bob Knight once tell he would ban them from Bloomington if they showed footage of Knight at a golf outing attempting to hit a shot out of a ditch?**

A. WISH

B. WTHR

C. WRTV

D. WXIN

20. **What was the name of the eating establishment in Ellettsville, Ind. where Bob Knight had an altercation with Bloomington guitar maker Chris Foster in 1999?**

A. Waffle House

B. Los Chachos Mexican restaurant

C. The 3 Amigos

D. Nuestro Mexico

E. China Star

21. Who was the broadcaster who asked Bob Knight in a national television interview in 1988 the question, "There are times Bobby Knight can't do it his way—and what does he do then?", to which Knight replied "If rape is inevitable, relax and enjoy it."?

A. Dan Rather

B. Tom Brokaw

C. Connie Chung

D. Barbara Walters

E. Larry King

22. What did Bob Knight do on a grouse-hunting trip in Wisconsin in 1999 that drew a great deal of notoriety?

A. He shot himself in the foot.

B. He shot a friend in the back with shotgun pellets.

C. He broke his leg in three places.

D. He tore his ACL.

E. None of the above.

23. **Who was the ESPN broadcaster that Bob Knight had a tense exchange with shortly after Knight was dismissed where Knight was quoted as saying, "You've got a long way to go to be as good as your dad. You better keep that in mind."?**

A. Dan Patrick

B. Jeremy Schaap

C. Bob Ley

D. Mike Tirico

E. Scott Van Pelt

24. **Two days after Knight was dismissed at Indiana, he spoke to Indiana students at a large rally. Where did the rally take place?**

A. Dunn Meadow next to the Student Union

B. Assembly Hall

C. Memorial Stadium

D. Mellencamp Pavilion

E. Armstrong Stadium

25. According to the *Indiana Daily Student,* how many students turned out for Knight's rally?

A. 1,000

B. 3,000

C. 6,000

D. 10,000

E. More than 20,000

26. What player did Knight allegedly head butt in a game against Michigan State in 1994 that drew a national response?

A. Pat Knight

B. Brian Evans

C. Todd Lindeman

D. Sherron Wilkerson

E. Todd Leary

27. **Where did that player complete his eligibility?**

A. Transylvania University

B. The University of Rio Grande

C. The University of Southern Indiana

D. Georgia State University

E. Indiana University

28. **Who was the player that Knight kicked at in a 101-82 victory over Notre Dame in 1993? When the crowd behind the bench booed him, Knight turned and responded with an obscenity.**

A. Todd Leary

B. Pat Knight

C. Matt Nover

D. Chris Reynolds

E. Brian Evans

29. On Senior Night in 1998 at Assembly Hall, Knight was involved in a verbal altercation with a veteran official that ultimately resulted in him receiving three technical fouls. It would also be more than 10 years before that official was ever assigned another IU game because of the anger from Indiana fans. Who was the official?

A. Ed Hightower

B. Jim Burr

C. Ted Valentine

D. Tom O'Neill

E. Steve Welmer

30. The following day Knight was quoted as saying, "I've been coaching 33 years, and that's the greatest travesty I've ever seen in basketball." What was the Big Ten's reaction to that comment?

A. Knight was fined $10,000

B. Knight was suspended for one game

C. Knight was ordered to apologize to the officials

D. The Big Ten took no action

E. None of the above

31. **Early in his career at IU, Knight was known for wearing a red plaid sports coat. Later at IU, this became his most recognizable piece of clothing?**

A. A crimson tie

B. A Indiana polo shirt

C. A red sweater

D. Red Pants

E. None of the above

32. **Upset about two turnovers in a Big Ten game in 1976, Bob Knight grabbed a player by his jersey and yanked him down to his seat. Who was that player?**

A. Scott May

B. Tom Abernethy

C. Jim Crews

D. Wayne Radford

E. Jim Wisman

33. The next day the *Indianapolis Star* ran a large picture of the grab. Knight was upset about it and on his television show the next day he put the phone number of *Star* sports editor Bob Collins on the screen. What did Collins do the next day?

A. He called Knight and apologized

B. He laughed the whole thing off

C. He called Knight and the two had a loud argument on the phone

D. He wrote a column and published Knight's private home phone number in it

E. He called the IU athletic director and complained

F. None of the above

34. Who was the veteran Indiana broadcaster who co-hosted a television show with Bob Knight for all 29 of his years at Indiana?

A. Chuck Marlowe

B. Don Fischer

C. Don Hein

D. Tom Carnegie

E. Jerry Baker

35. **Bob Knight also had a weekly television show that dealt with an activity other than basketball. What was the activity?**

A. Bowling

B. Golf

C. Tennis

D. Ballroom dancing

E. Bridge

36. **When Knight arrived at Indiana in 1971, what big time Indiana player had just opted to leave for the NBA despite having two years of eligibility remaining because he needed to take care of his family?**

A. Ed Daniels

B. Bubbles Harris

C. George McGinnis

D. Steve Downing

E. Joby Wright

37. **What other big event in Indiana basketball history coincided with Knight's arrival in Bloomington in the fall of 1971?**

A. Gladstein Fieldhouse had been renovated

B. IU had a new athletic director

C. All of IU's games would be televised

D. It was the first year of Assembly Hall

E. IU was unveiling a new mascot

38. **Indiana opened the 1971-72 season with victories over Ball State, Miami and Kansas at home and then beat Kentucky on a neutral site. The next game IU would go on the road and lose its first game in the Knight era. Who did the Hoosiers lose to after beating Kansas and Kentucky in back-to-back games?**

A. Bowling Green

B. Toledo

C. Akron

D. Ohio

E. Ball State

39. On Senior Night in 1995, Knight referred to one of his graduating seniors as his all-time favorite Indiana University basketball player. Who was that player?

A. Alan Henderson

B. Andrae Patterson

C. Pat Knight

D. Brian Evans

E. Steve Hart

40. In a public feud with Knight in 1991, what did Illinois coach Lou Henson refer to Knight as?

A. A classic bully

B. A cry baby

C. A whiner

D. A disgrace

E. Mean-spirited person

41. True or False, Bob Knight is a member of the Indiana University Athletic Hall of Fame?

A. True

B. False

42. True or False, Bob Knight is a member of the National Basketball Hall of Fame?

A. True

B. False

43. What incident happened on a live radio talk show with IU play-by-play announcer Don Fischer while Knight was doing the show remotely from his home?

A. A gun fired while Knight was cleaning it in his garage

B. Knight was doing the show in his office and stepped away to take a shower

C. Knight was eating dinner at home and talking with his mouth full

D. Knight was eating dinner at home and began choking on a chicken bone

E. In the middle of an answer, a toilet flushing is heard loudly

F. All of the above

44. Who was the author that Bob Knight granted access to in order to follow Knight around in the 1985-86 season and get a year in the life story that would be ultimately be published in a best-selling book?

A. John Feinstein

B. Bob Hammel

C. John Laskowski

D. James Patterson

E. Tom Clancy

45. What was the name of the book?

A. *Knight Tales*

B. *Knight Life*

C. *A Season on the Brink*

D. *The Lost Season*

E. *The Night I Threw a Chair*

46. What school did Bob Knight consider leaving Indiana for in 1988 after a rift with the new college president?

A. Utah

B. New Mexico

C. New Mexico State

D. Arizona

E. Colorado

47. When Bob Knight arrived at IU, which of the following coaches was not one of his three assistants?

A. Dave Bliss

B. Bob Donewald

C. John Hulls

D. Bob Weitlich

E. All four were on his staff

48. **Dan Dakich and Joby Wright were both former players who later went on to be long time assistant coaches under Knight. Dakich was Knight's assistant for 10 years and Wright for nine years. A third former player spent eight seasons on Knight's staff. Who was that player?**

A. Tom Abernethy

B. Calbert Cheaney

C. Tom Bolyard

D. Kent Benson

E. Jim Crews

49. **What object did Bob Knight bring out at a press conference at the NCAA West Regional in Albuquerque, New Mexico in 1992 that caused a stir with the national media?**

A. Ruler

B. Hammer

C. Bull Whip

D. Gun

E. Bow and Arrow

50. When longtime *Bloomington Herald-Times* sports editor Bob Hammel retired following the 1996 season, Bob Knight presented him with a gift. What was Hammel's parting gift?

A. A $500 gift card

B. A gold watch

C. A Rolex

D. A new Ford Taurus

E. A fishing boat

Answers on page 232

Branch McCracken is pictured with Bill Garrett, who was the first African-American to play basketball at IU and the first one to start regularly in the Big Ten. (Indiana University Archives, P0038009)

8

WHO WORE THAT NUMBER?

1. In IU history, what number has been worn more times than any other number? Hint: It has been worn 29 times.

   A. 20

   B. 21

   C. 22

   D. 23

   E. 24

2. What number has been worn the second most times in IU history? Hint: It has been worn 28 times.

   A. 20

   B. 21

   C. 22

   D. 23

   E. 24

3. Only one number was on the roster of all five IU basketball national championship teams. What number was represented on all five teams?

A. 20

B. 23

C. 24

D. 30

E. 42

4. How many IU basketball numbers have been retired?

A. 6

B. 5

C. 4

D. 3

E. 2

F. 1

G. 0

5. **What was the first year IU players started having numbers on their jerseys?**

   A. 1901

   B. 1910

   C. 1915

   D. 1920

   E. 1924

6. **What is the highest number ever worn by an Indiana University basketball player?**

   A. 99

   B. 70

   C. 58

   D. 56

   E. 55

7. **What is the lowest number ever won by an Indiana University basketball player?**

   A. 0

   B. 1

   C. None of the above

8. **Only one player in IU history has ever worn No. 52. His last season at IU was 1986. Can you name him?**

   A. Winston Morgan

   B. Courtney Witte

   C. Steve Eyl

   D. Todd Jadlow

   E. Jim Thomas

9. **Only one player in IU history has ever worn No. 51. His last season was 2007. Can you name him?**

   A. Earl Calloway

   B. Lance Stemler

   C. Joey Shaw

   D. Xavier Keeling

   E. Kyle Taber

10. Two IU players in history have worn No. 53. The last one played on Bob Knight's final team at Indiana. Can you name him?

A. Lynn Washington

B. Jarrad Odle

C. Jeff Newton

D. Tom Geyer

E. Larry Richardson

11. Tim Priller wore No. 35 in the 2014-15 IU basketball season. Who was the last player to wear No. 35 before Priller?

A. Bobby Capobianco

B. Kirk Haston

C. Jeff Oliphant

D. Brandon McGhee

E. George McGinnis

12. **What single digit numbers can no longer be worn in college basketball per NCAA rules?**

    A. 0-2

    B. 3-5

    C. 6 and 7

    D. 6 and 8

    E. 6-9

13. **Who was the last IU basketball player to wear No. 55?**

    A. Jeff Newton

    B. Richard Mandeville

    C. Robbie Eggers

    D. Haris Mujezinovic

    E. Tom Abernethy

14. **Mike Giomi, in the 1983-84 season, was the last IU player to wear this number. What number is it?**

    A. 46

    B. 45

    C. 42

    D. 41

    E. 38

15. Name the two Indiana Mr. Basketball players who wore No. 23 at Indiana?

A. A.J. Ratliff

B. Dave Shepherd

C. Eric Gordon

D. Hallie Bryant

E. Delray Brooks

16. Name the two Indiana Mr. Basketball players who wore No. 54 at Indiana?

A. Kent Benson

B. Steve Bouchie

C. Cody Zeller

D. Dick Van Arsdale

E. George McGinnis

17. Name the two Indiana Mr. Basketball players who wore the No. 22 at Indiana?

A. Tom Van Arsdale

B. Damon Bailey

C. Lyndon Jones

D. Ed Scheinbein

E. Jimmy Rayl

18. The last player to wear No. 28 played on one of IU's five national championship teams. Which national title year had a No. 28 on its roster?

A. 1940

B. 1953

C. 1976

D. 1981

E. 1987

19. True or False, Jay Edwards was the first player to wear No. 3 at Indiana?

A. True

B. False

20. True or False, Kory Barnett was the first player in IU history to wear No. 0?

A. True

B. False

21. **Which of the following Indiana players DID NOT wear the No. 1 at IU?**

A. Armon Bassett

B. Jordon Hulls

C. Jared Jeffries

D. Luke Recker

E. Evan White

F. They all wore No. 1

22. **True or False, Jared Jeffries was the first player in IU history to wear No. 1?**

A. True

B. False

23. **What member of the IU team that made it to the national championship game in 2002 wore the No. 2?**

A. Jared Jeffries

B. Tom Coverdale

C. A.J. Moye

D. Donald Perry

E. Dane Fife

24. **Which of the following Indiana players DID NOT wear the No. 3 at IU?**

A. D.J. White

B. Charlie Miller

C. Maurice Creek

D. Tom Coverdale

E. Jay Edwards

F. They all wore No. 3

25. **Two Indiana Mr. Basketball players wore No. 4 at Indiana. The most recent one was Luke Recker. Who was the other No. 4?**

A. Jay Edwards

B. Lyndon Jones

C. Delray Brooks

D. Jordan Hulls

E. Tom Coverdale

26. **Two Indiana Mr. Basketball players wore No. 1 at Indiana. They both hail from the same town in the state. What town is that?**

A. Kokomo

B. Bloomington

C. Indianapolis

D. Fort Wayne

E. Evansville

27. **Which of the following Indiana players DID NOT wear the No. 5 at IU?**

A. Jordan Crawford

B. Marco Killingsworth

C. Jeremiah Rivers

D. George Leach

E. Neil Reed

F. Troy Williams

G. They all wore No. 5

28. **True or False, Bob Knight never had a player who wore the numbers 0, 1 or 2?**

A. True

B. False

29. **The last player in IU history to wear No. 19 played on the 1953 national championship team. Can you name him?**

A. Burke Scott

B. Jim Schooley

C. Don Schlundt

D. Dick Farley

E. Charlie Kraak

30. **Which of the following Indiana players DID NOT wear the No. 10 at IU?**

A. Antwaan Randle El

B. Will Sheehey

C. Rod Wilmont

D. Tony Freeman

E. Andre Owens

F. They all wore No. 10

G. None of have ever worn No. 10

31. True or False, Antwaan Randle El wore the same number with IU football and basketball?

A. True

B. False

32. True or False, James Hardy wore the same number with IU football and basketball?

A. True

B. False

33. True or False, Cam Cameron wore the same number with IU football and basketball?

A. True

B. False

34. A total of 15 players have worn the No. 8 at IU. Who was the last player to wear No. 8?

A. Mark Robinson

B. Noah Vonleh

C. Bill Garrett

D. Tom Pritchard

E. Hanner Mosquera-Perea

35. **Which of the following Indiana players have ever worn No. 9? (pick as many as you'd like)**

A. Marty Simmons

B. Gary Grieger

C. Randy Wittman

D. Ken Johnson

E. Chuckie White

F. They all wore No. 9

G. None have worn No. 9

36. **Which of the following Indiana players DID NOT wear the No. 11 at IU?**

A. Todd Jadlow

B. Yogi Ferrell

C. Dane Fife

D. Isiah Thomas

E. Dan Dakich

F. They all wore No. 11

37. **True or False, Steve Alford is the only All-American in IU history to wear No. 12?**

A. True

B. False

38. Which of the following Indiana players DID NOT wear No. 20 at IU?

A. Bobby Wilkerson

B. Richard Mandeville

C. Frank Wilson

D. Sherron Wilkerson

E. Greg Graham

F. They all wore No. 20

39. True or False, Quinn Buckner was the only All-American in IU history to wear No. 21?

A. True

B. False

40. Which number was worn by IU players such as Steve Downing, Kyle Hornsby and Landon Turner?

A. 32

B. 33

C. 34

D. 35

E. 24

41. **Which of the following IU players wore No. 24 at IU? (pick as many as you'd like)**

A. Michael Lewis

B. Matt Nover

C. Ray Pavy

D. Daryl Thomas

E. Randy Wittman

F. They all wore No. 24

G. None of them wore No. 24

42. **Which of the following IU players wore No. 25 at IU? (pick as many as you'd like)**

A. Damon Bailey

B. Robert Vaden

C. Dean Garrett

D. A.J. Guyton

E. Pat Knight

43. Two IU All-Americans wore No. 30 at Indiana. Can you name them?

A. Archie Dees

B. Lou Watson

C. Dick Van Arsdale

D. Tom Van Arsdale

E. Ted Kitchel

44. A total of 25 players in IU history have worn No. 32. Two earned All-American status. Name the two All-Americans who wore No. 32?

A. Landon Turner

B. Steve Downing

C. Randy Wittman

D. Steve Green

E. Bobby Leonard

45. True or False, all of the following players wore No. 35 at IU: Walt Bellamy, Kirk Haston, George McGinnis, Dick Neal, Jeff Oliphant and Lou Scott.

A. True

B. False

46. True or False, all of the following players wore No. 40 at IU: Calbert Cheaney, Butch Carter, Jason Collier, Glen Grunwald, Tijan Jobe and Cody Zeller.

   A. True

   B. False

47. True or False, all of the following players wore No. 44 at IU: Wally Choice, Alan Henderson, Joe Hillman, Phil Isenbarger, Kyle Taber, Lynn Washington and Joby Wright.

   A. True

   B. False

48. Jarrad Odle was the last player at IU to wear what number?

   A. 33

   B. 42

   C. 43

   D. 44

   E. 50

49. **What number did Branch McCracken wear at Indiana?**

   A. 6

   B. 7

   C. 8

   D. 9

   E. 10

50. **The last time the numbers 16, 17, 18 or 19 were worn at Indiana was what season?**

   A. 1980

   B. 1972

   C. 1960

   D. 1953

   E. 1944

Answers on page 235

Here is one of IU's all-time greats, 1976 national champion Quinn Buckner. (Indiana University Archives, P0020734)

9

WHO AM I?

You will have five hints to guess the name of each player. Points are awarded based on how quickly you can identify the person described. For example, you get 4 points if you guess the player on the first hint, 3 on the second hint and 2 on the third. You get 1 for either of the final two hints.

Player 1

1. I was a front court player on Big Ten championship teams in 1980 and 1981.

2. I'm in both the Indiana High School and IU Athletics Hall of Fames.

3. I was the Big Ten MVP in 1981, the year we won the national championship.

4. I was a first round draft pick of the New Jersey Nets.

5. I was named Mr. Basketball in Indiana in 1977 out of Anderson Madison Heights.

Player 2

1. I rarely started in my IU playing career which spanned the early to mid-1970's but I was a fan favorite.

2. My high school coach was future Bob Knight assistant coach Bob Donewald.

3. My nickname at IU was Super Sub.

4. I've done work as both a color and play-by-play analyst on the Big Ten Network.

5. Most people know me by a three-letter nickname ending in 'z'.

Player 3

1. I played high school basketball in the state of Indiana in the mid 1990's and scored more points than players such as Calbert Cheaney and Steve Alford while in high school.

2. I hold the IU record for assists with 545.

3. I was an assistant coach on Bob Knight's staff at Texas Tech.

4. I'm currently an assistant coach for a Division I men's basketball team.

5. I played high school basketball at Jasper.

Player 4

1. I had a decent outside shot but I was known as a defensive player first.

2. I played on the only IU team in history to make it to the national championship game but not win it.

3. When people think of the best floppers in IU history, many think of me.

4. I was on coach Knight's final IU basketball team.

5. I am currently a Division I men's basketball assistant coach in the Big Ten.

Player 5

1. In my Indiana basketball career we went 90-33 with an NCAA title and three Big Ten championships.

2. I started 27 games as a sophomore on an IU national championship team.

3. I was a two-time Indiana All-American and finished my career with more than 1,300 points.

4. I played at Lewis-Cass High School in Walton, Ind.

5. My roommate at IU was Randy Wittman.

Player 6

1. I only played two seasons at Indiana but scored more than 1,000 points in my career.

2. As a freshman I was Big Ten Freshman of the Year and hit 53.6 percent of my shots from beyond the arc.

3. I had three last second shots my sophomore year. Two of them won games and the other should have except Nick Anderson of Illinois threw in a 35-footer at the buzzer to win.

4. I played high school basketball at Marion.

5. I gave up my final two years of college basketball and was drafted in the second round of the NBA Draft by the L.A. Clippers.

Player 7

1. Most people consider me the heart and soul of the 2002 IU team that played Maryland for the national championship.

2. A lot of people remember me from my ankle injury that season.

3. I was Mr. Basketball in Indiana in 1998.

4. After two years of professional basketball, I worked on the basketball staff at Louisiana-Monroe.

5. I played my high school basketball at Noblesville.

Player 8

1. I was Indiana's Mr. Basketball in 1953 at Crispus Attucks High School in Indianapolis.

2. I was a member of IU's 1957 Big Ten co-championship team coached by Branch McCracken.

3. I am a lifelong resident of the state of Indiana.

4. I played 13 seasons for the Harlem Globetrotters.

5. Prior to that, I was a commissioned officer in the United States Army for two years.

Player 9

1. I was IU's most valuable player in 1949 and 1950 for Branch McCracken.

2. When I left IU, I held the school scoring record with 757 career points.

3. I later was an assistant for coach McCracken and when he left IU, I became the head coach.

4. I was the IU coach that was let go that made way for a young coach from Army in the 1971-72 season.

5. I was a four-year starter at Jeffersonville High School.

Player 10

1. I grew up in Bloomington, Indiana and dreamed about one day playing for the Hoosiers.

2. My high school team had a 66-7 record my final three seasons including an unbeaten state championship my senior year.

3. My grandfather came to IU from Army in 1971 with Bob Knight and served as IU's shooting coach.

4. I scored more than 1,300 points in my IU career and was known as a deadly 3-point shooter.

5. I was the Indiana Mr. Basketball in 2009 from Bloomington South.

Player 11

1. I'm the only player in IU history to be named to major All-American teams in both football and basketball.

2. My high school basketball team at New Castle won the 1932 Indiana state championship.

3. I'm a member of both the Indiana High School and IU Athletics Hall of Fames.

4. My brother played on IU's 1940 national championship team and was considered one of the integral players on that team.

5. I didn't play professional basketball but rather played two seasons of professional football with the Detroit Lions.

Player 12

1. I was part of a dream team recruiting class to IU that also included Calbert Cheaney, Greg Graham and Lawrence Funderburke.

2. I was Indiana's Mr. Basketball in 1989 and a McDonald's All-American.

3. I played high school basketball at Floyd Central in Floyds Knobs, Indiana.

4. I was one of two players in my recruiting class with the same last name but we're not related.

5. I played in 102 career games at IU and averaged 8.7 points per game.

Player 13

1. I will forever hold the distinction of being IU's first basketball All-American.

2. I did so in 1921 when I led my team to a 15-6 record and averaged 10.7 points per game.

3. Seven times in my career, I scored more points than the opposing team combined.

4. After my playing days were over, I spent 14 years as IU's head basketball coach.

5. One of my players was Branch McCracken, who later took my place when I left IU.

Player 14

1. I played two seasons at IU and was an All-American in both.

2. I was an Indiana Mr. Basketball and one of three boys in my family to win that award.

3. I scored nearly 1,200 points in my two seasons at IU and hold IU's record for career field goal percentage at 59.1 percent.

4. My high school team at Washington High School won three consecutive Indiana state titles.

5. My sophomore season we won the Big Ten title outright on the final game of the year at Michigan and were a No. 1 seed in the NCAA Tournament.

Player 15

1. I was the first African-American player to play basketball at Indiana University.

2. I led IU in scoring all three years of college and when I graduated I held the school record for scoring with 792 career points.

3. I was Indiana's Mr. Basketball in 1947 at Shelbyville and led my team to a state championship.

4. I was a second round pick of the Boston Celtics and also played with the Harlem Globetrotters.

5. I died at the age of 45 of a heart attack.

Player 16

1. I was the first All-American to play at Indiana under Bob Knight.

2. Later when coach Knight left Indiana and went to Texas Tech, I went as well as an associate athletic director.

3. In a game against Kentucky in 1971, I scored 47 points and pulled down 25 rebounds.

4. I was a first round draft pick of the Boston Celtics and later won an NBA championship with them in 1974.

5. I was a high school teammate of IU legend George McGinnis.

Player 17

1. I was a three-time All-American at IU and won a national championship.

2. When I left IU my 1,740 points ranked second all-time in school history.

3. I had a healthy head of red hair.

4. I was Indiana's Mr. Basketball in 1973 at New Castle.

5. I was the first player selected in the 1977 NBA Draft by Milwaukee.

Player 18

1. I may have been the most celebrated high school player all-time in the state of Indiana. Bob Knight recruited me beginning in the eighth grade.

2. My senior year, a national record crowd of 41,046 filled the Hoosier Dome in Indianapolis to watch my team win the state championship.

3. I started 95 games at IU and had double digit scoring averages in all four seasons. I finished with 1,741 points, one more than Kent Benson.

4. I was named USA Today's High School Player of the Decade.

5. I was a second round pick of the Indiana Pacers in the 1994 NBA Draft.

Player 19

1. I was an All-American and Big Ten MVP my senior season in the mid-1990's.

2. I was the first player under coach Knight to win the Big Ten's scoring title and averaged 22.2 points in Big Ten play that year.

3. I averaged 17.4 points as a junior and 21.2 points as a senior.

4. I played high school basketball at Terre Haute South. My team made the Final Four in 1991.

5. I was a first round draft pick by Orlando in the 1996 NBA Draft.

Player 20

1. I should have played on an unbeaten national championship team but we fell just short my senior year.

2. I was an All-American at Indiana in both 1974 and 1975.

3. I was the leading scorer at IU my junior year on a team that also featured Scott May, Kent Benson, Quinn Buckner and Bobby Wilkerson.

4. I attended Silver Creek High School in Sellersburg, Indiana where I played for my father.

5. I have been practicing dentistry in Central Indiana since 1984.

Player 21

1. I only played one season of college basketball at Indiana but scored 669 points and averaged 20.9 points per game.

2. As a high school senior at North Central in Indianapolis I was Indiana's Mr. Basketball and led my team to the state championship.

3. I led the Big Ten in scoring and was named an All-American.

4. I originally committed to another Big Ten school before changing my mind.

5. I was the seventh player selected overall in the NBA Draft by the Los Angeles Clippers.

Player 22

1. I was an All-American at Indiana but most people know me for something else.

2. When I left IU, I was the all-time leading scorer in IU and Big Ten history.

3. What I'm most known for is the 24 years I spent as IU's men's basketball coach.

4. I was the coach of two national championship teams at IU.

5. I went to Monrovia High School in Indiana.

Player 23

1. Most people consider me the best player in Indiana history that didn't win a national championship.

2. I am the leading scorer in Indiana history and Big Ten history, a mark that still stands and has stood for more than 20 years.

3. I was a three-time All-American at IU.

4. My career scoring average is 19.8 points per game and my teams were 87-16 in my four years at IU.

5. I'm currently a Division I assistant men's basketball coach.

Player 24

1. I won Big Ten MVP as a junior and opted to forego my senior season at IU.

2. Most people remember me for a shot I hit my junior season that knocked off No. 1 Michigan State at Assembly Hall. Tom Coverdale lifted me off the ground after I hit it.

3. I'm from Lobelville, Tenn. and still live there today where I coach high school basketball.

4. I scored more than 1,400 points my three seasons at IU and I'm currently ninth overall in career rebounds with 748.

5. My final year at IU was Mike Davis's first season with the Hoosiers.

Player 25

1. My senior year I averaged a double-double for the season and was the Big Ten player of the year.

2. I battled through a lot of injuries in my IU career but still managed to start 97 of 99 games and score nearly 1,500 points.

3. I played high school basketball in Alabama.

4. I was a first round pick of the Detroit Pistons in the 2008 NBA Draft.

5. My best game of my senior year was a 21-point, 22-rebound game at Michigan.

Player 26

1. I'm one of two players in IU basketball history to win Big Ten MVP in back-to-back seasons. I did it in 1957 and 1958.

2. I played three seasons at IU and still scored 1,546 points. My career average was 22.7 points.

3. I played high school basketball in Illinois.

4. I played at a time when IU had some great big men. Don Schlundt was the center before me, Walt Bellamy after me and I was in between.

5. I later was in the insurance business with Schlundt in Bloomington.

Player 27

1. Some call me the greatest pure shooter in Indiana basketball history.

2. I hold the school record for most points scored in a game and I did it twice.

3. In two games against Michigan State my senior year, I scored a total of 100 points.

4. I was Indiana's Mr. Basketball in 1959 at Kokomo.

5. I scored 1,322 points over my final two seasons at Indiana.

Player 28

1. I only played one season at Indiana but no one has ever averaged more points in one year than I did.

2. I led the Big Ten in scoring with a 29.9 per game average and a 14.9 rebounding average.

3. I scored 20 or more points in 21 of my first 24 games including an IU record 14 times in a row.

4. I played high school basketball in Indianapolis with another IU great, Steve Downing.

5. Danny Bridges believes I'm the greatest player in IU history.

Player 29

1. In my four year career at Indiana, we won the Big Ten all four seasons, had two undefeated conference seasons and an unbeaten national championship season.

2. I was the team captain my junior and senior season.

3. I have a gold medal from the 1976 Olympic team as we went 8-0 to win it all.

4. I'm one of only a few players who ever won a title in high school, college, the Olympics and the NBA.

5. I played 10 seasons with the Boston Celtics.

Player 30

1. I led my team to the NIT championship my junior year.

2. As a senior, I was injured and only played the final six Big Ten games but was still voted the conference's MVP.

3. I was a two-time All-American at IU and one of only five players to score more than 2,000 points in my IU career.

4. I played 11 years in the NBA and scored nearly 11,000 points.

5. I am currently an NBA assistant coach but I had a long stint as an NBA head coach, too.

Player 31

1. I was an All-American and a Big Ten MVP my senior year in the early 1980's.

2. I averaged double figures on the 1981 national championship team.

3. My roommate for five years at IU was Ted Kitchel.

4. I played high school basketball at Ben Davis in Indianapolis.

5. I'm currently a head coach in the NBA.

Player 32

1. I only played two seasons at IU but my second year I helped lead my team to the national championship.

2. Before I ever played a game at IU, I played on Bob Knight's gold medal winning U.S. team in the Pan American Games.

3. I was known as a big time scorer but I also had 356 assists in two years, a 5.7 career average.

4. I played professionally for the Detroit Pistons, led my team to two NBA titles, and my No. 11 was retired by the Pistons.

5. I was later an NBA head coach in Indiana.

Player 33

1. I was a three-time IU All-American and won a national championship.

2. Before I came to IU the school scoring record was less than 800 points. When I left I had scored 2,192 points.

3. I shot 1,076 free throws in my IU career and made 826. Both are school and Big Ten records by hundreds of shots.

4. I won three consecutive Big Ten scoring titles. My career scoring average was 23.3 points.

5. I was able to play four years at IU because of the Korean War exemption.

Player 34

1. My senior year in college was the first year for the 3-point shot and I hit 107 of them.

2. I was an Indiana Mr. Basketball and averaged 37 points per game as a senior in high school. In my last two years of high school I never scored less than 20 points in a game.

3. I was the Big Ten MVP my senior year and led IU to the national championship.

4. I'm the second all-time leading scorer in IU history with 2,438 points.

5. I'm a Division 1 college basketball head coach on the West Coast.

Player 35

1. I hold IU's career rebounding record with 1,091 rebounds.

2. Most people feel my team could have won a national championship my sophomore year before I tore a ligament in my knee in February.

3. I played high school basketball in Indianapolis at Brebeuf.

4. As a college senior, I scored 20 points or more in 24 games and I had 50 double-doubles in my career.

5. I was a first round draft pick of the Atlanta Hawks.

Player 36

1. I'm one of just five players to have scored more than 2,000 points in my IU career.

2. I played my high school basketball in the western end of the state of Illinois.

3. I was Big Ten Freshman of the Year and then later I was Big Ten player of the year as a senior.

4. I was a member of IU's All-Century team.

5. I was the leading scorer on coach Knight's final team at Indiana.

Player 37

1. I only played two seasons at Indiana and I just missed out on winning a national championship.

2. I was Big Ten Freshman of the Year my first year and Big Ten MVP by second year.

3. I was Indiana's Mr. Basketball in high school at Bloomington North.

4. Despite only playing two seasons, I eclipsed the 1,000 point scoring mark at IU.

5. I was the 11th pick overall of the 2002 NBA Draft by Washington.

Player 38

1. I came to IU with very little fanfare but left as one of the most beloved Hoosiers of all time.

2. I left after my junior season but was the co-national defensive player of the year and the Big Ten defensive player of the year.

3. I played my high school basketball in Washington D.C. and hail from Upper Marlboro, Md.

4. I helped lead IU to back-to-back Sweet Sixteen performances for the first time in 20 years.

5. I was the second player selected overall in the 2013 NBA Draft by Orlando.

Player 39

1. I was a two-time All-American at IU in the 1950's and helped lead my team to IU's second national championship.

2. I scored more than 1,000 points in my three-year career and had a career 15.5 point scoring average.

3. I'm best known as an ABA coach in the state of Indiana.

4. I'm also known for my 'Boom Baby' declaration whenever Reggie Miller made a 3-pointer for the Pacers.

5. I played high school basketball in Terre Haute.

Player 40

1. I had a career average of more than 20 points per game in three years at IU.

2. I was an All-American big man in both 1960 and 1961.

3. In my final collegiate game I had 28 points and 33 rebounds against Michigan.

4. I won a gold medal for the U.S. in the 1960 Olympics.

5. I was the first IU player ever to be selected as the No. 1 player overall in the NBA Draft and I was also IU's first NBA Rookie of the Year.

Player 41

1. I was an integral part of IU winning the national championship in 1981.

2. I'm remembered most for a tragic accident I was involved in the summer after my junior season.

3. I played high school basketball at Indianapolis Tech.

4. I was honored with the Sagamore of the Wabash in 1989, the highest individual honor that can be bestowed by the governor of Indiana.

5. I graduated from IU in 1984 and went on to play wheelchair basketball and also serve as an inspirational speaker.

Player 42

1. My senior season was Branch McCracken's final year at Indiana.

2. My brother Tom and I were both All-Americans in 1965 at IU.

3. I finished my career with 1,240 points and 719 rebounds.

4. I played high school basketball at Manual High School in Indianapolis.

5. I played 12 seasons in the NBA for both New York and Phoenix.

Player 43

1. I was a junior college transfer that made my mark at Indiana.

2. I hit what Indiana fans think of as 'The Shot' that won a national title.

3. I played high school basketball in Baton Rouge, La.

4. I had a cup of coffee in the NBA with the San Antonio Spurs as a player.

5. I'm better known as both an NBA head and assistant coach.

Player 44

1. A later generation of IU fans think of me when they think of 'The Shot'.

2. As a junior and senior my teams made back-to-back Sweet Sixteen appearances.

3. I played high school basketball in Birmingham, Ala.

4. I rank in the top 10 all-time in Indiana scoring history with 1,730 points.

5. I have a three letter nickname that rhymes with 'hot'.

Player 45

1. I came to IU as a basketball manager.

2. As a sophomore in 2009, Tom Crean elevated me to the roster and I suited up.

3. I wore No. 1.

4. I went to high school in Huntington, Ind.

5. I'm currently working as a General Manager at IU Event Services.

Player 46

1. I'm remembered more for transferring than playing at IU.

2. I was an Indiana Mr. Basketball.

3. I'm from Auburn, Ind. and played at DeKalb.

4. I left IU after my sophomore year.

5. I finished my career at Iowa.

Player 47

1. I was an All-American as a senior at IU in 1965.

2. My brother Dick and I were co-Indiana Mr. Basketball recipients at Manual High School in Indianapolis.

3. My junior year at IU I averaged 21.3 points and 12.3 rebounds per game.

4. I was a member of the gold medal World University Games team.

5. I played 12 seasons in the NBA and retired following the 1976-77 season with the Phoenix Suns.

Player 48

1. I never led an IU team in scoring but finished my career with 1,299 points.

2. I'm the 10th fastest player in IU history to score 1,000 points. I did it in 60 games.

3. I played high school basketball at Fort Wayne South and led my team to the state championship.

4. I was drafted and signed professionally by the Washington Bullets.

5. I was on Lou Watson's staff as an assistant coach from 1965-71.

Player 49

1. I was a two-time All-American at Indiana and played on a national championship team.

2. I was the college player of the year for the unbeaten 1976 Hoosiers.

3. Many people believe if I hadn't have broken my arm the year before we would have won the title twice.

4. I scored 1,593 points in my IU career.

5. One of my sons played at North Carolina and another one at IU.

Player 50

1. I was a part of one of the most celebrated recruiting classes in IU history.

2. I played high school basketball in Indianapolis and later returned there as the head varsity coach.

3. I was the second leading scorer in both my junior and senior years at IU behind Calbert Cheaney.

4. I scored nearly 1,600 points in my IU career and rank as one of the top 15 scorers of all time.

5. I was a first round draft pick in the NBA by Charlotte, the 17th player selected overall.

Answers on page 237

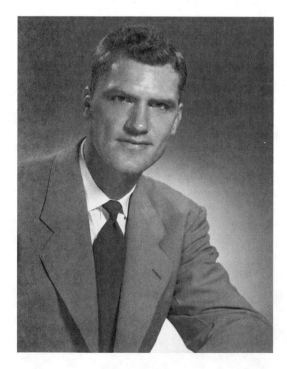

Lou Watson was an IU All-American in 1950 and has the distinction of being the IU head coach sandwiched in between Branch McCracken and Bob Knight at Indiana. (Indiana University Archives, P0055482)

10

THE ANSWERS

Chapter 1 (Warm Up Trivia)

1. D. Calbert Cheaney

2. B. Keith Smart

3. A. Rupp Arena (A sea of red was a beautiful thing at Kentucky)

4. D. Alan Henderson. He had four more than Walt Bellamy.

5. B. Jimmy Rayl. He did it against Minnesota in 1962 and Michigan State in 1963.

6. D. 65. The final was 94-29.

7. C. Steve Alford. He was 107-for-202 in the first year of the 3-point shot in college basketball.

8. A. Jordan Hulls. He hit 41 in a row in the 2010-11 season.

9. C. Greg Graham. He did it against Purdue in 1993.

10. B. Eric Gordon. He had 669 points in the 2007-08 season.

11. E. Steve Downing. He had 28 points, 17 rebounds and 10 blocks against Michigan on Feb. 23, 1971.

12. C. Points/Rebounds/Blocks.

13. D. 56. The streak was from 1991-95.

14. D. Maryland in Assembly Hall.

15. D. 3. 1987, 1993, 2013. The NCAA started seeding teams in 1979.

16. C. 2013.

17. D. IU has never won it

18. C. 2. Walt Bellamy in 1961 and Kent Benson in 1977

19. B. Calbert Cheaney was the 6th pick overall.

20. D. 6. Tom Abernethy, Kent Benson, Quinn Buckner, Scott May, Wayne Radford, Bobby Wilkerson.

21. B. Scott May

22. A. Alan Henderson

23. C. Wasbash. IU won the game, 26-17.

24. B. Dan Dakich. He went 3-4 including a 3-2 regular season record.

25. C. Verdell Jones III.

26. B. Jimmy Rayl

27. B. 37 from 1974-77.

28. E. 50 in a 106-56 loss at Minnesota.

29. D. 122

30. B. 34 over the 1974 and 1975 seasons

31. C. Calbert Cheaney had 734 points in the 1990-91 season

32. A & B. Jay Edwards and Jimmy Rayl.

33. D. Noah Vonleh had 269 in the 2013-14 season

34. C. Cody Zeller signed with Indiana

35. A. 1993 and 1994

36. D. 18 years

37. B. Vanderbilt

38. B. Kentucky

39. D. 31-0

40. A. Chicago Bulls

41. False. Kind of a trick question though. Yes, IU had the Big Ten MVP in each of the last four national championship seasons. In 1940 though there was no official Big Ten MVP award. That award started in 1946.

42. D. Once. It was 2001.

43. B. Steve Alford in 1987.

44. C. Will Sheehey in 2013.

45. D. Stew Robinson

46. E. All of the above

47. E. Damon Bailey

48. B. 11

49. D. Jay Edwards announced he was declaring for the NBA Draft. Leary had just returned from a recruiting visit along with Matt Painter to Minnesota.

50. D. 12

Chapter 2 (Player Trivia)

1. B. Everett Dean in 1921

2. B. Calbert Cheaney

3. A. Calbert Cheaney

4. B & C. Archie Dees and Scott May

5. B & E. Michael Lewis and Keith Smart

6. B. Walt Bellamy in 1960-61.

7. A. Calbert Cheaney with 1,556 in Big Ten games only.

8. A. George McGinnis

9. E. Calbert Cheaney. His career high was 36 vs. Seton Hall in 1992.

10. C. A.J. Guyton. His career high was 34 vs. Michigan State in 2000.

11. C. Noah Vonleh's career high was 19 at Penn State in 2014.

12. B. Walt Bellamy. He had 33 against Michigan in the final game of 1961. In the previous game he had 28, which is tied with Alan Henderson for the second most in IU history in one game.

13. E. George McGinnis. His career high was 23.

14. B. Scott May. He had nine vs. Michigan in 1976.

15. C. Steve Downing. He had 10 blocks against Michigan in 1971.

16. D. Dean Garrett. He had 99 in 1988 and 93 in 1987.

17. B & C. Matt Roth and Rod Wilmont. Roth was against Ohio State and Wilmont against Northwestern.

18. B. Don Schlundt versus Ohio State in 1955.

19. B. Don Schlundt

20. F. Archie Dees

21. A. Walt Bellamy

22. D. Archie Dees with 42

23. C & D. Archie Dees and George McGinnis

24. B. Jordan Hulls. Two more than Randy Wittman and Jeff Newton

25. D. Dane Fife with 37 starts in 2002

26. B. Andrae Patterson

27. A. George McGinnis

28. C. Jimmy Rayl

29. B. Don Schlundt

30. D. Archie Dees

31. True

32. False

33. True

34. D. Matt Nover

35. D. Bracey Wright

36. C. Calbert Cheaney

37. B. Steve Alford

38. D. Lewis Monroe

39. C. Shutting down Michael Jordan in the 1984 Sweet Sixteen

40. A. Kentucky

41. True. It was called the Korean War Exemption.

42. D. 26

43. A. Ed Scheinbein

44. C. Crispus Attucks

45. E. He took 48 shots

46. E. 17. He could have had 73 points.

47. A & D. Van Arsdale's and Huffman's.

48. B. Baseball

49. C. Eric Gordon

50. E. A.J. Moye

Chapter 3 (Coach Trivia)

1. C. Everett Dean with 162 victories
2. A. Lou Watson
3. B. 28
4. C. 98
5. C. 12
6. A. Army
7. E. None of the above. Knight was 138-82 in seven seasons at Texas Tech.
8. E. 0
9. B. 17
10. B. Indiana
11. C. Oklahoma
12. A. Marquette
13. C. 2. His first year was 1938-39 and he won the title his second year.
14. E. None of the above. His first year was 1971-72, and he won it in his fifth year.
15. C. 2. His first year was 2000-01 and he reached the title game his second year.
16. B. 7. Lou Watson, Jerry Oliver, Bob Knight, Mike Davis, Kelvin Sampson, Dan Dakich and Tom Crean.
17. C. Ernie Andres was an IU All-American in 1938.
18. C. 1987. Iowa's Tom Davis took home the honor in his rookie year with the Hawks in '87.
19. D. Taking a job in a furniture factory.
20. C. Everett Dean
21. C. Harry Good

22. B. Jordan Hulls. John Hulls was on Knight's staff his first two years at Indiana.

23. B. Ron Felling

24. C. Tom Bolyard

25. C. He played professional baseball. In '23, he was a 30-year-old outfielder with the St. Louis Cardinals. But he also played on the Chicago Cubs World Series team in 1918.

26. C. 11

27. B. 45

28. E. Zero

29. False

30. C. 2. Tom Crean at Marquette and Kelvin Sampson at Oklahoma

31. C. 1. Bob Knight

32. B, C & D. Everyone but Tom Izzo who he didn't face in the tournament

33. B. J.H. Horne

34. E. 2

35. C. Had surgery to remove cancer from his back

36. B. Jerry Oliver

37. C. 4. 1975, 1976, 1987, 1989.

38. True

39. C. 22-4.

40. D. 2. Kyle Taber and Brett Finkelmeier

41. F. Zero

42. False. It was Ellis and Armon Bassett who were the first two dismissed by Dakich.

43. C. Loyola (Md.)

44. B. Ball State

45. B. He coached freshman football at IU

46. A. Branch McCracken (for Everett Dean), Lou Watson (for Branch McCracken) and Phelps Darby (for J.H. Horne)

47. B. UCLA

48. False. There was no love lost there from the start.

49. D. Mike Davis

50. True. The last one had been Leslie Mann in 1923.

Chapter 4 (Venue Trivia)

1. E. 1971-72

2. C. A Homecoming variety review featuring Bob Hope and Petula Clark on Oct. 23, 1971.

3. D. Led Zeppelin

4. C. Bear. A Kodiak bear from the circus that was using the venue got loose in the halls before it was recaptured. There was havoc for a while though. Happened in the mid-1970's.

5. A. Ball State

6. B. Most rebounds by an IU player. Steve Downing had 26.

7. C. Branch McCracken Court

8. C. Gladstein Fieldhouse.

9. B. Paneling the wall of a horse barn. Not sure it was ever done but it was being used as scrap wood and this was one of the possibilities.

10. D. The Bleachers. Bleachers on the south wall of Gladstein Fieldhouse were used at both Assembly Hall and Memorial Stadium. They were unscrewed, flipped over, renumbered and reused.

11. C. Cincinnati Reds

12. E. $5.50

13. A. Cattle Auction House (Inspired by Dorton Arena in Raleigh, N.C.)

14. C. A Carpenter's Shop. The gymnasium was booked.

15. C. $12,000

16. E. 600

17. B. Swimming pool

18. C. Glass backboards

19. D. 12

20. B. Branch McCracken

21. D. Netting to keep players from sliding off the floor

22. A. $12.2 million

23. E. 25,000. According to Chuck Crabb, the seats would have been all in one level.

24. A. True. The Pacers played a playoff game in Assembly Hall in 1972 and an exhibition game there in 2009.

25. A. Farm. The Faris family farm was on the site until the athletic plant began construction in the 1950's.

26. D. A metal beam fell on an area of seating

27. D. All of the above

28. True

29. B. Apples

30. B. Falling behind in recruiting

31. D. Indiana High School state tournament

32. C. Jim Thorpe

33. A. Banking for joggers

34. C. They're secured to the floor. Somebody threw one one time.

35. B. Railroad speed record in delivery of a key item from Seattle to Bloomington

36. C. Two feet

37. B. Dangerously slick

38. B. U.S. Cellular Field in Chicago

39. B. An unnamed person was found to be residing in the halls

40. True

41. B. Bob Knight played for Ohio State

42. C. A hospital

43. D. 25 cents

44. D. 50 cents

45. E. 1957

46. D. All of the above

47. True

48. A. Fall of 1967

49. False. McCracken died June 4, 1970, a full year before Knight arrived.

50. True

Chapter 5 (National Championship Trivia)

1. B. Daryl Thomas
2. A. Ray Tolbert
3. B. Kent Benson
4. E. None of the Above (Bobby Leonard)
5. A. Herm Schaefer
6. B. Keith Smart
7. B. Scott Dolson
8. D. Todd Meier
9. C. UNLV
10. A. New Orleans
11. E. Assembly Hall
12. C. LSU
13. A. Isiah Thomas
14. B. Philadelphia
15. B. 32
16. E. 10
17. B. Philadelphia
18. B. Kent Benson
19. C. Don Schlundt
20. D. Kansas City
21. B. Bobby Leonard
22. C. LSU
23. E. Kansas
24. D. 3
25. C. Kansas City
26. C. 3. They shared in '87 and finished in second place in 1940.

27. D. 3 times

28. B & D. The Crimsons and The MacMen

29. B. Second

30. C. 6-foot-4

31. B. Bobby Wilkerson

32. C. North Carolina

33. C. 1-2

34. A. Minnesota

35. B. Dean Garrett

36. D. Purdue

37. B. Ricky Calloway

38. True

39. C. Ronald Reagan

40. D. Butch Carter

41. False. It was the first time

42. True

43. B. 64,959

44. True

45. C. 3. In 1976, they trailed by six at half. In 1953, they were tied

46. D. All of the above

47. C. 5. He had 5 points on 1-of-4 shooting

48. C. No. 3

49. D. 4. January 6-27

50. C. No. 9

Chapter 6 (Fun Facts)

1. D. Blab
2. E. 7-2
3. C. Plane headed toward Cuba
4. B. 3
5. C. 6
6. B. Michael Lewis
7. C. Dane Fife
8. A. Indiana Avenue
9. C. Calbert Cheaney and E. Kent Benson
10. D. 1971-72
11. C. Bracey Wright
12. B. Jack (his last name was Ass)
13. E. Michael Santa
14. B. Tom Geyer
15. B Maine
16. E. 6
17. C. Illinois with 56
18. B. Bloomington
19. B. Names on back of jerseys
20. E. 144
21. C. Players had smoked marijuana on trip
22. B. 53-1
23. C. Lawrence Frank
24. A. 1951-52
25. D. 8
26. D. Todd Leary

27. C. Jamal Meeks

28. E. 44. He scored an even 100 versus Michigan State for the season

29. E. Purdue

30. C. Uwe Blab played for West Germany. He actually also played in the 1992 Olympics and represented West Germany again.

31. A. Zeller, Hulls, Oladipo, Watford, Sheehey and Ferrell.

32. B. Mike Woodson

33. C. 17

34. D. Martha the Mop Lady. Her real name is Martha Webster.

35. D. George Leach injured his ankle on the opening tip

36. C. He took off his shirt to rile up the crowd

37. C. 2. Bob Knight and Mike Davis

38. False. But his brothers were making bet that he just might do it.

39. B. Blue Chips

40. False. It wasn't filmed in Bloomington

41. C. Appeared in a sorority calendar to raise money for handicapped kids

42. E. Kentucky

43. B. Ivan Renko

44. C. Yugoslavia

45. B. Todd Leary

46. B. Dane Fife

47. C. The story broke on SI.com

48. True

49. D. Dane Fife

50. False. He started broadcasting IU games in 1973. But I love to joke with him that he has indeed been around that long.

Chapter 7 (Bob Knight Trivia)

1. B. Orrville

2. C. Ohio State

3. A, D & E. Dean Smith, Bob Knight and Joe B. Hall

4. True

5. D. He coached junior varsity basketball at Cuyahoga Falls High School in Ohio

6. A. He was ranked first. He now ranks second behind former player and assistant coach Mike Krzyzewski.

7. D. All of the above

8. D. Bill Self

9. B. 40. He had 29 winning seasons in as many years at IU.

10. True

11. D. 4

12. B. He said Knight grabbed him and admonished him after he yelled 'Hey Knight' at the IU coach.

13. C. Knight was fired by IU president Myles Brand for "a pattern of unacceptable behavior."

14. C. Zero

15. E. He was fined $30,000 and suspended for three games in the upcoming season.

16. D. Clarence Doninger

17. C. Dick Vitale

18. C. The General's Store

19. C. WRTV

20. D. Nuestro Mexico

21. C. Connie Chung

22. B. He shot a friend in the back with shotgun pellets

23. B. Jeremy Schaap

24. A. Dunn Meadow next to the Student Union

25. C. 6,000

26. D. Sherron Wilkerson

27. B. The University of Rio Grande, Ohio. He later was an assistant coach for Pat Knight at Lamar.

28. B. Pat Knight

29. C. Ted Valentine

30. A. Knight was fined $10,000

31. C. Red Sweater

32. E. Jim Wisman

33. D. He wrote a column and published Knight's private home phone number. After that the two became great friends.

34. A. Chuck Marlowe

35. B. Golf

36. C. George McGinnis

37. D. It was the first year of Assembly Hall

38. D. Ohio

39. C. Pat Knight

40. A. A classic bully

41. True

42. True

43. F. All of the above

44. A. John Feinstein

45. A. *A Season on the Brink*

46. B. New Mexico. The college president was Thomas Ehrlich.

47. B. Bob Donewald

48. E. Jim Crews

49. C. Bull Whip

50. D. A new Ford Taurus

Chapter 8 (Who wore that number?)

1. D. 23
2. E. 24
3. A. 20
4. G. 0
5. E. 1924
6. E. 55
7. A. 0
8. B. Courtney Witte
9. A. Earl Calloway
10. D. Tom Geyer
11. B. Kirk Haston
12. E. 6-9
13. D. Haris Mujezinovic
14. D. 41
15. C & E. Eric Gordon and Delray Brooks
16. A & B. Kent Benson and Steve Bouchie
17. B & E. Damon Bailey and Jimmy Rayl
18. A. 1940. It was William Torphy of Bedford, Ind.
19. False. Paul Parker 1923-24.
20. True
21. D. Luke Recker
22. False. Ken Alward 1923-24
23. C. A.J. Moye
24. F. They all wore No. 3
25. B. Lyndon Jones
26. B. Bloomington. Jared Jeffries and Jordan Hulls

27. G. They are all wore it.

28. True

29. B. Jim Schooley

30. E. Andre Owens

31. False. No. 10 in basketball and No. 11 in football.

32. False. No. 2 in basketball and No. 82 in football.

33. False. No. 25 in basketball and No. 12 in football.

34. C. Bill Garrett

35. G. None have worn it

36. F. They all wore it

37. True

38. B. Richard Mandeville. He wore No. 21

39. False. Bobby Leonard

40. A. 32

41. F. They all wore it

42. D & E. A.J. Guyton and Pat Knight

43. C & E. Dick Van Arsdale and Ted Kitchel

44. A & B. Landon Turner and Steve Downing

45. True

46. False. Butch Carter did not.

47. True

48. C. 43

49. B. 7

50. D. 1953. Jim Schooley wore No. 19

Chapter 9 (Who am I?)

1. Ray Tolbert
2. John Laskowski
3. Michael Lewis
4. Dane Fife
5. Ted Kitchel
6. Jay Edwards
7. Tom Coverdale
8. Hallie Bryant
9. Lou Watson
10. Jordan Hulls
11. Vern Huffman
12. Pat Graham
13. Everett Dean
14. Cody Zeller
15. Bill Garrett
16. Steve Downing
17. Kent Benson
18. Damon Bailey
19. Brian Evans
20. Steve Green
21. Eric Gordon
22. Branch McCracken
23. Calbert Cheaney
24. Kirk Haston
25. D.J. White
26. Archie Dees

27. Jimmy Rayl

28. George McGinnis

29. Quinn Buckner

30. Mike Woodson

31. Randy Wittman

32. Isiah Thomas

33. Don Schlundt

34. Steve Alford

35. Alan Henderson

36. A.J. Guyton

37. Jared Jeffries

38. Victor Oladipo

39. Bobby Leonard

40. Walt Bellamy

41. Landon Turner

42. Dick Van Arsdale

43. Keith Smart

44. Christian Watford

45. Michael Santa

46. Luke Recker

47. Tom Van Arsdale

48. Tom Bolyard

49. Scott May

50. Greg Graham